CARNEGIE ENDOWMENT FOR INTERNATIONAL PEACE
Division of Economics and History
JAMES T. SHOTWELL, LL.D., *Director*

•

COMMERCIAL AND TARIFF HISTORY
MICHAEL T. FLORINSKY, Ph.D., *Editor*

GREAT BRITAIN UNDER PROTECTION

THE MACMILLAN COMPANY
NEW YORK · BOSTON · CHICAGO
DALLAS · ATLANTA · SAN FRANCISCO

MACMILLAN AND CO., LIMITED
LONDON · BOMBAY · CALCUTTA
MADRAS · MELBOURNE

**THE MACMILLAN COMPANY
OF CANADA, LIMITED**
TORONTO

GREAT BRITAIN
UNDER PROTECTION

BY
FREDERIC BENHAM
SIR ERNEST CASSEL READER IN COMMERCE
IN THE UNIVERSITY OF LONDON

New York
THE MACMILLAN COMPANY
1941

EDITOR'S PREFACE

WHATEVER preconceived notions one may have of the influence of economic factors in shaping the destinies of mankind it seems difficult to escape the conclusion that the unwise economic policies pursued in the last two decades, and especially since the depression of 1929, by every country irrespective of its form of government and political ideology have been an important element in unleashing the storm that is devastating Europe and threatening to spread to other parts of the world. The gradual strangulation of international trade and the breakdown of the delicate and complex mechanism of monetary exchanges (in reality two aspects of the same problem) have infinite ramifications and repercussions which sooner or later affect, if only indirectly, the position of every man and woman, however remote from the apparent center of the disturbance.

It was in recognition of the vital importance of international trade in the modern world that the present Series was projected. There is no assurance, of course, that a more enlightened approach to international economic problems would have saved Europe from the ravages of the war that broke out in September 1939. Yet it seems clear that political sanity cannot be restored on anything like a solid foundation unless there is a far-reaching adjustment in the field of international commercial and monetary policies. It is hoped that the volumes of the Commercial and Tariff History of the Principal European Countries, prepared under the auspices of the Carnegie Endowment for International Peace, may not only fill an important gap in economic literature but, by pointing to the costly failures of the past, may also be of some service in charting the course to be followed in the future.

In the entire economic history of the restless, tormented and unhappy world that emerged from the war of 1914-18 there is probably no more dramatic and significant chapter than the abandonment of free trade by Great Britain, a development that provides one of the central themes of Dr. Benham's volume. Other countries have long followed protective policies and some of them, for instance the United States, have erected trade barriers compared with which the British tariff appears almost innocuous; nevertheless, the drastic action taken by the British National Government and by Parliament as a consequence of the banking and financial crisis of 1931 dealt a staggering blow to the very economic system of which Great Britain was both the pillar and the living symbol. The adoption of protection by Great Britain had incalculable effects not only because of the exceptional position the far-flung British Empire occupies as the chief trading nation in the world, but also, perhaps, because there seems to be a certain inner kinship between the idea of free trade and that of political democracy. Economic and political liberalism have come to be regarded by many as two manifestations of the same philosophy, just as economic regimentation and meticulous supervision of international trade are generally believed to be inherent in the nature of totalitarian states. Historically, of course, such notions are entirely unwarranted. Many political democracies—the United States, France, Canada—have consistently practised the most aggressive form of protectionism. On the other hand, as it has been frequently pointed out by competent authorities, at least some of the most objectionable restrictions on international trade have been imposed by the totalitarian states under the pressure of conditions largely outside their control. The volumes of the present Series, it is hoped, may be of some usefulness in elucidating the question why nations sharing the same political ideals have nevertheless followed widely divergent economic policies. The fact remains, however, that from the middle of the nineteenth century until the end of 1931 free trade in England was a kind of economic counterpart of parliamentary government and all it stands for, and every attempt to challenge the venerable doctrine of free trade invariably met with disaster at the polls. Little wonder therefore that the repudiation of free trade by its chief protagonist sounded like a death sentence to the hopes for the liberalization of international commerce so eloquently voiced by the Geneva World Economic Conference of 1927. The *coup de grâce* to all comprehensive attempts to reduce trade barriers was dealt during the ill-fated London Economic and Monetary Conference of 1933 by President Roosevelt's obstinate refusal to stabilize the value of the dollar. It is only fair to add that the London Conference's chances of success were never too bright and that Secretary Cordell Hull has been an untiring champion of the liberalization of commerce through a policy of reciprocal trade agreements based on the most-favored-nation clause. The recognition by the United States Government of the desirability of lowering trade barriers was in itself a revolutionary departure from the traditional policy of this country, a departure that gave new hope to all those who believe in freer trade. It is unfortunate that the Trade Agreements Act of 1934 has confined the action of the Administration within very narrow limits and that the devaluation of the dollar in 1933 had the inevitable result of raising still higher the tariff wall which surrounds one of the world's greatest markets.

By a tragic coincidence the Anglo-American trade agreement, undoubtedly the most important of the agreements negotiated so far, came into effect on January 1, 1939, only a few months before the outbreak of the war, which prevented its smooth operation.

Dr. Benham's study speaks for itself and little need be said here of his penetrating and comprehensive analysis of British commercial policy and its effects upon the country. It may be pertinent to observe, however, that the manuscript of the present volume reached the editor at the end of May 1940 when German armies were rolling over the plains of Holland, Belgium and Northern France and were establishing themselves on the shores of the English Channel. Dr. Benham, who lives in London, has written much of his book since the outbreak of the war in September 1939 and the strain under which he had to work was undoubtedly great. He has nevertheless maintained throughout his discussion a truly admirable objectivity and detachment, the very essence of any scientific investigation. The author has never permitted his emotions, however legitimate, to interfere with the logical flow of his argument which is based on an intimate knowledge of both the theory and the practice of international trade. This approach is a fine tribute to that great tradition of English liberalism which is perhaps Great Britain's most valuable contribution to the common heritage received from past generations, and described by the somewhat vague term of modern civilization. The impairment of this tradition would be calamitous; its complete abandonment a disaster which the author of these lines finds it impossible to envisage.

A few words must be added about the present Series. It has been prepared under the general supervision of the director of the Division of Economics and History of the Carnegie Endowment for International Peace, Dr. James T. Shotwell, who has entrusted to me the organization of the Series and the editorship of the several volumes. A study of the commercial policy of France by F. A. Haight is now in press and will be published by the Macmillan Company of New York in January 1941. It is hoped that a volume on Italy by Senator Luigi Einaudi, Professor of Economics in the University of Turin, and a volume on Germany by Dr. Andreas Predöhl, Director of the *Institut für Weltwirtschaft* in Kiel, will be made available in the near future.

The views expressed by the respective authors are, of course, in no way binding on the Carnegie Endowment for International Peace or on its officers, and for the opinions presented in this Preface I alone am responsible.

It is my pleasant duty to express my sincere gratitude to the Macmillan Company of New York whose interest and encouragement have been invaluable at every stage of our work.

MICHAEL T. FLORINSKY

November 1, 1940
Columbia University
New York City

ACKNOWLEDGMENTS

I HAVE drawn freely upon publications, such as the *Economist*. But I have also had the privilege of consulting unpublished memoranda, on the tariff and allied subjects, prepared by the National Institute of Economic Research, and a draft memorandum on *British External Economic Policy in Recent Years* prepared by a Study Group for the International Studies Conference of 1939.

The Economic Research Division of the London School of Economics kindly provided me with research assistance. Professor A. Plant and Mr. F. Paish have read the manuscript and made valuable suggestions. But I alone am to blame for any opinions or errors of fact in the following pages.

I am very grateful to the Carnegie Endowment for International Peace without whose assistance this book would not have been written.

F. B.

CONTENTS

CHAPTER IV: IMPERIAL PREFERENCE

CHAPTER V: TRADE AGREEMENTS

CHAPTER VI: MONETARY POLICY

CHAPTER VII: IRON AND STEEL

CHAPTER VIII: AGRICULTURE

CHAPTER IX: ECONOMIC RECOVERY

STATISTICAL APPENDIX

TABLE

Chapter I

GREAT BRITAIN UNDER FREE TRADE

1. Introduction

THIS BOOK deals mostly with events since 1931. It describes the main features of the British tariff and of British commercial policy during recent years and it makes some attempt to estimate what their effect has been both on Great Britain and on the rest of the world. It outlines the progress of economic recovery in Great Britain, paying particular attention to the protected industries of iron and steel and agriculture.

The present chapter is a kind of prologue. It describes very briefly how Great Britain came to adopt free trade about the middle of the nineteenth century, how she prospered under free trade until the war of 1914, and how the difficulties of the post-war years culminated in the crisis of 1931 and the return to protection.

Although our subject is commercial policy, we cannot possibly leave monetary policy out of the picture. What may be termed external monetary policy—the departure from gold, the use of the Exchange Equalization Fund, and the unofficial ban on foreign lending—is directly relevant to the question of the tariff. Imports can be discouraged just as effectively by reducing the exchange value of the national currency as by imposing a general tariff. Before September 1931 the two methods were discussed as alternatives; either devaluation or a tariff, it was said, was needed to reduce the adverse balance of trade. In the end both, or more accurately both exchange depreciation and restrictions on particular imports, were adopted.

The departure from gold was just as much a break with tradition as the departure from free trade, and its effects on the rest of the world were perhaps even more important. The gold standard prevents any considerable fluctuations in exchange rates between the countries on it, always provided that they stay on it. It is a great convenience for all districts in the same country to have a common currency. The gold standard in effect provides that same convenience for all the countries which adopt it. International trade is greatly hampered by fluctuating exchange rates. Transactions which would otherwise be profitable to both parties are ruled out because the exchange risk is too great. "A virtual elimination of this exchange uncertainty," said the Gold Delegation of the Financial Committee of the League of Nations, "was the main monetary achievement of the last decade." It was achieved through the gold standard. On September 21, 1931, Great Britain suspended gold payments and a new era of exchange uncertainty began. The present chapter must say something about this as well as about the tariff.

2. THE FREE TRADE MOVEMENT

Newmarch describes the tariff system of Great Britain in 1820 in the following words:[1]

At the time the system of prohibition, protection, and fiscal confusion was at its height. It was said by competent authorities that the number of Acts of Parliament relating to the entry, export and custody of goods as matters of Custom House supervision, was not less than fifteen hundred. All the special interests were in full possession of the vested rights to which they laid claim. There was the Corn Law of 1815; there were the differential duties in favour of the West India proprietors; the monopoly of the East India Company; the vigorous appli-

[1] Tooke and Newmarch, *History of Prices*, 1857, pp. 400-40.

cation of the navigation laws against competition on freights. There were heavy duties on raw materials of industry, and prohibitive or extravagant duties on foreign manufactures.

By 1860 all this had been swept away, leaving Great Britain a free-trade country with import duties for purely revenue purposes on only about a dozen articles, notably tobacco, tea, and wines and spirits.

The movement, headed by Cobden and Bright, for the repeal of the Corn Laws (the 1842 Act imposed a duty of 20 shillings a quarter on imported wheat when the price of wheat was at or below 50 shillings) succeeded in 1846, when Sir Robert Peel went to the country on a policy of abolishing the Corn Laws and was re-elected. He promptly repealed the 1842 Act, substituting much lower duties until February 1, 1849, and a flat rate of one shilling a quarter thereafter. The flat rate was abolished, leaving the import of corn entirely free, by Gladstone[2] in 1869.

The Navigation Acts, which had been passed from 1381 onwards and especially around 1660, were designed to reserve the carrying trade between Great Britain and the Colonies, between the Colonies themselves, and between the Colonies and other countries, to British and colonial ships. The coastal trade of Great Britain was reserved to British ships. Certain goods, such as timber, corn, and wine, coming from Europe to Great Britain, could come only in British ships, and certain other goods were subject to higher duties if they came in foreign ships. The protection thus afforded to British shipping was substantially reduced by a series of laws between 1822 and 1825 and by the reciprocity treaties concluded with various foreign countries during the next twenty years or so, and was completely abolished (except for the reservation of the coastal

[2] Gladstone was Prime Minister; Robert Lowe was Chancellor.

trade, which went in 1854) by the repeal of the Navigation Acts in 1849. Henceforward the Colonies, as well as British firms, could trade freely with whom they chose and could employ ships of any nationality.

Huskisson's tariff of 1825 made substantial reductions in the protective duties on many raw materials and manufactured goods, and most of these duties were abolished by Peel between 1842 and 1846, leaving only a few to be swept away by Gladstone in 1853 and 1860. The export of machinery was permitted to a large extent in 1825 and was freed from all restrictions in 1843.

It may be noted that customs revenue was actually greater under free trade than before. Its yield averaged less than £10 million a year in the decade 1800-09; less than £14 million in 1810-19; and less than £16 million in 1820-29. Thereafter, until the close of the century, it averaged rather more than £20 million a year, mainly from tobacco and tea. This was due to the growth of population and to the rise of the standard of living, resulting in an increased consumption of tobacco, tea, and alcohol.[3] In 1860 Cobden negotiated his famous commercial treaty with France. France had prohibited many British goods and imposed high duties on others. She removed all prohibitions and agreed to reduce her duties on a number of goods. In return, Great Britain reduced her duties on imported wines and spirits (other than rum), abolished duties on certain articles produced in France, and promised not to prohibit the export of coal. This treaty contained a

[3] Rates of duty were reduced, on the whole. The duty on tea was reduced from 2/1d. per lb. in the 40's to 1.8¾d. in the 50's, 10½d. in the 60's, 6d. in the 70's and 80's, and 4d. in the 90's. The duty on sugar was abolished in 1874. The duties on wine, and on brandy and gin, were lower in the latter half of the century; those on tobacco were somewhat higher.

most-favored-nation clause: "Each of the two high contracting powers engages to confer on the other any favour,
privilege, or reduction in the tariff of duties of importation
on the articles mentioned in the present treaty which the
said power may concede to any third power." In the trade
treaty of 1862 between Great Britain and Belgium, the
most-favored-nation clause appears in its widest form. All
concessions on all goods, whether or not mentioned in the
treaty, were to be extended to each other if granted to a
third power, and there were to be no restrictions or prohibitions except those applying to all countries equally.

From 1860 onwards Great Britain concluded a whole
series of trade agreements with foreign countries, nearly all
containing the unconditional most-favored-nation clause.
This was done partly in order to remove the disadvantage
which British exports suffered in a number of markets,
many countries granting concessions to one another which
did not apply to British goods. But also it was done in the
belief that greater freedom of trade all round would benefit the world as a whole and Great Britain in particular.
Before the war of 1914, eighty British trade treaties containing the unconditional most-favored-nation clause were
in force.

The triumph of free trade was due to several factors.
The arguments of Adam Smith, whose *Wealth of Nations*
contained a trenchant attack on the Mercantile System,
had exercised a considerable influence on students of economic policy, and had been reproduced and reinforced
by later economists such as Ricardo. William Pitt the
younger was disposed to agree with Adam Smith, but he
had to cope with the French wars, and, as he said, you do
not put your house in order during a hurricane. Huskisson
too was a follower of Bentham and inclined to free trade,

but his reforms[4] were checked in 1827 by the break-up of his ministry owing to the death of the Prime Minister, Lord Liverpool. Cobden and his group doubtless appreciated the academic arguments for free trade, but they did not make much use of them in addressing either public meetings or Parliament. Abstract reasoning did not play a very important part in sweeping away protection, and seventy years elapsed between the publication of the *Wealth of Nations* and the repeal of the Corn Laws.

The latter event was due mainly to the campaign of Cobden and Bright, and immediately to the distress caused by the Irish famine of 1845, which probably caused the repeal to come several years sooner than it would otherwise have done. The campaign was won on the slogan of "cheap bread." It was supported by the mass of the people, by a number of manufacturers, who thought that cheap food meant lower wages, and by idealists who believed that free trade made for international good will and peace among nations. This last belief was held with great conviction by Cobden himself and most of his friends—a group whose equal for sincerity and public spirit has seldom been matched in any age or country.

Another factor in favor of the free trade movement was the change in the relative importance of different interests in the nation. The majority of the people still had no vote, but the power of the landlords was diminishing and that of the manufacturers and export merchants was increasing. The latter were by no means all free traders but they were anxious to expand their markets overseas.

Last, but certainly not least, the civil servants were in favor of fewer duties. They realized that the abolition of a

---

[4] He reduced the 1500 Acts mentioned at the beginning of this section to eleven.

mass of complicated tariffs would simplify administration without substantially reducing revenue.

3. Free Trade and Prosperity

The period from the middle of the nineteenth century until the war of 1914 was for Great Britain an era of increasing prosperity, rapid industrial progress, and expanding trade. Her annual output of coal increased steadily from an average of 66 million tons in 1855-59 to 270 million tons in 1910-14; over the same period her annual output of pig iron increased from 3.5 to 9.5 million tons and of steel from less than 200,000 tons to 7 million, and her annual consumption of raw cotton from 7.9 to 17.6 million cwt.[5] The annual value of British exports increased decade by decade from an average of £55 million in 1840-49 to £121 million in 1850-59, £237 million in 1890-99, and £474 million in 1910-13. Deposits in British joint-stock banks increased from £271 million in 1877-79 to an average of £992 million in 1910-14, although the price level was lower in the latter period.

To some extent, these figures reflect the growth of population. The total population of the United Kingdom increased from less than 27 million in 1841 to nearly 35 million in 1881 and over 45 million in 1911. This was not due to an increase in the birth rate. On the contrary, from about 1870 onwards the birth rate steadily declined. The crude birth rate—births per 1,000 population in the United Kingdom—fell from 34.1 in 1870-72 to 24.5 in 1910-12, and over the same period the birth rate per 1,000 women aged 15-45 fell from 148.7 to 99.7. The growth of

[5] These figures are all from *An Introduction to the Study of Prices* by W. T. Layton. Most of the figures quoted in this section are either from this source or from the *Statistical Abstracts for the United Kingdom.*

population took place in spite of the fall in the birth rate, because less inadequate nutrition and improvements in medical science made the death rate fall even faster. The crude death rate—deaths per 1,000 persons in the United Kingdom—fell from over 21 in 1870-72 to less than 15 in 1910-12. Infantile mortality—deaths of infants under one year per thousand births—fell during this period from 144 to 108. This great reduction in death rates is one of the surest indications of the progress made in knowledge and in standards of living during this era.

About a hundred years ago, many workers were living under conditions of what would now be considered great poverty. They worked very long hours for low pay; they enjoyed little travel or recreation; and most of them could neither read nor write. Since about the middle of the last century there has been a marked upward trend in the economic welfare of the average worker. It has been calculated that average money wages in 1910-14 were 85 per cent higher than in 1850. Retail prices were at about the same level; hours of work in most trades were shorter; working conditions had been improved by a series of Factory Acts; free education, free libraries, and cheap transport made life more interesting. The consumption per head of tea and sugar had considerably more than doubled and that of tobacco had increased by well over 50 per cent.

We do not claim for one moment that all this was due to free trade. The main factors were the continuous progress of technical knowledge and the growth of investment, together with the absence of serious wars. Hundreds or thousands of inventions were made every year; methods of production were constantly improved; new industries and new occupations came into being. The rapidly increasing control of man over nature made possible a larger margin for saving; and savings were invested in plant and equipment, in means of transport, and in buildings, or were lent overseas, where they helped to develop the countries of the New World. The rapid growth of population assisted economic progress. New entrants to the labor market could go into the expanding trades, such as engineering and transport, instead of entering the declining ones, such as agriculture. There was therefore little need to attempt the much more difficult task of actually transferring large numbers of persons from one industry to another. Moreover, the risks of investment were small, for the total consumption of most products and services was expanding. If some particular factory or railway line, for example, was not immediately as profitable as had been expected, the investors had only to wait a little and the demand would "catch up."

Nevertheless free trade was, in my view, quite an important factor. It is generally agreed that one of the chief elements in the growth of prosperity was the constant improvement of transport facilities, both in Great Britain and in other countries. The railways opened up whole continents and, together with improved and cheaper shipping, enabled the agricultural produce and raw materials of the New World to exchange on a large scale against the manufactures of Europe, and especially of Great Britain. A protective tariff would have impeded this tendency. As it was, British manufacturers were able to produce on a large scale for a world market. British consumers, particularly after about 1870, when it became profitable to send grain from the New World, obtained the benefits of cheap food produced where land was plentiful; and in the eighties this benefit was increased by the improvements in refrigeration, which enabled meat and, later, fruit to travel halfway across the world—a phenomenon deemed impossible a generation before. This meant a depression in British agriculture. Agricultural land values declined considerably; agricultural wages remained low; and Great Britain became increasingly an urban and a food-importing country. But against the relative poverty of the million-odd persons in agriculture had to be set the benefits of cheap food and the increasing wages and profits in the export trades. Great Britain was concentrating on the more profitable industries and occupations. She was taking full advantage of her resources of coal and iron, her geographical position, the skill of her workers, and the enterprize of her leaders of commerce and industry, to become the workshop of the world. Her investments abroad helped the newer countries to produce cheaply the foodstuffs and raw materials which she required, and they in turn provided markets for her goods. Her vast and growing international trade, together with the firm link between sterling and gold, made London the financial center of the world, drawing banking, insurance, and similar commissions from other countries. British ships carried over half the trade of the world. It was no wonder that liberal doctrines flourished on British soil. To what extent this prosperity was really due to free trade is perhaps a matter for debate. But it was obvious and beyond dispute that material progress under free trade had happened to be great and indeed unprecedented, particularly if contrasted with the poverty—doubtless due largely to the waste and destruction of the Napoleonic Wars—prevailing in the early part of the nineteenth century. Thus protection, when proposed by Mr. Joseph Chamberlain and others in

1903-06, really had not a hope of success. This probably had little to do with abstract theory. It was rather a case of *post hoc ergo propter hoc*. Free trade and prosperity had marched together. Maybe one was the cause of the other, maybe not. In any event, the British public was not going to risk a change.

4. THE POST-WAR YEARS

If we ask why Great Britain gave up free trade, one possible answer is that there is no need to look back further than the close of 1929: that it was entirely due to the great depression. The number of insured workers unemployed increased steadily from 1.2 million in September 1929 to a peak of nearly 2.9 million in September 1931. The volume of British exports fell until, for the first three quarters of 1931, it was more than 30 per cent below the 1929 level. The balance of trade was becoming increasingly adverse. The Budget was believed, in the summer of 1931, to be seriously unbalanced. Many important industries, including agriculture and iron and steel, were in considerable distress. "Diseases desperate grown by desperate remedies are alliev'd or not at all"—let us try a tariff!

In much the same way, it can be argued that it was simply the "economic blizzard" of this period which drove Great Britain off gold. The *Kredit Anstalt* closed its doors on May 14, 1931; the Danat Bank on July 13th. There was a general scramble for liquidity. It was known that the gold reserve of the Bank of England was only about £150 million and that Great Britain owed much more[6] than this

[6] The Report of the MacMillan Committee, published on July 13th, estimated the net short-term liabilities of London on foreign account in March 1931 at £254 million, and in fact this estimate was probably well below the mark.

on short-term abroad, whereas her short-term claims on foreign countries were much smaller and a large part of them was practically immobilized in Germany. A flight from sterling developed. During the last week or so of July the Bank of England lost over £25 million of gold. £130 million was borrowed in August from France and the United States, but on September 19th the Bank of England had to tell the Government that these credits were "practically exhausted," and that the drain of gold was continuing. The Gold Standard Suspension Act was passed on September 21st. Once the traditional policy of maintaining the gold standard had gone, the public was more willing—however illogically—to let free trade go also.

This line of reasoning is plausible but rather superficial. The facts cited are correct, and no doubt the great depression did hasten the abandonment of both the gold standard and free trade, just as the Irish famine hastened the repeal of the Corn Laws. But if Great Britain had followed a rather different economic policy during the post-war years, if she had adapted herself more fully to the changed conditions of the post-war world, there might even have been a flight towards sterling instead of away from it during those months of crisis, and the protectionists would not have gained such an easy victory, if indeed they had won at all.

We must therefore consider the years before 1930. We shall discuss mainly the period from 1925 to 1929. It seems generally agreed that the immediate post-war years were an unsettled period of reconstruction and of changing-over from war to peace conditions. Armament and other wartime industries had greatly expanded and were compelled to contract; the men demobilized from the Forces had to be reabsorbed in industry; the devastated areas of France had to be restored and the Reparations question to be settled; there was the occupation of the Ruhr in 1923; there was inflation in leading European countries; and there were great fluctuations in exchange rates.

The *World Economic Survey* for 1931-32 remarks that 1925 "is now generally recognized as a turning point in post-war development." The Dawes Plan had been accepted in August 1924; the German mark had been stabilized at 4,200 milliard of the old paper marks to the dollar; and Germany seemed well on the road to economic recovery. Great Britain returned to gold, at the old parity, on May 1, 1925. Belgium, it is true, did not return to gold until October 1926, nor Italy until December 1927, nor France until June 1928; nevertheless there was much less instability and uncertainty from 1925 onwards. International post-war adjustments had been largely, although not completely, accomplished and the stage was set for recovery and expansion.

There is no doubt that in the world as a whole the next five years were marked by rapid technical progress and a considerable expansion of output, employment, and trade. There was some economic progress in Great Britain. Death rates continued to fall. The average worker was better off than before the war. In 1913 most workers had a working week of fifty-four hours; by 1929 they were working only forty-eight hours or less, and some 12 million were insured against unemployment. In 1924 the standard of living of the average worker was somewhat higher than before the war, and from 1924 to 1929 money wages remained fairly stable while the cost of living fell by 6 or 7 per cent. Over the same period, production increased by 12 per cent and there was some rise in profits.

Nevertheless Great Britain was not happy in the economic saddle. She was falling behind her rivals. Output in other leading countries increased considerably more than in Great Britain, and her share of the total exports of manufactures of leading manufacturing countries fell from 26 to 22 per cent.[7] The chief symptom of her economic *malaise* was unemployment. The number of insured workers unemployed in 1924 was 1,200,000 and it remained near this level until the end of 1929, when it began to rise rapidly. This meant about 10 per cent unemployed, as compared with an average of 4½ per cent over a long period before the war.

One school of thought maintained that depression in the export industries and the high level of unemployment were both due to the same cause, namely, the return to gold at the old parity of 84s. 11½d. per ounce of fine gold. Six members of the MacMillan Committee on Finance and Industry, which presented its Report in June 1931, advocated[8] as a remedy a general revenue tariff of, say, 10 per cent on all imports together with an equal subsidy on all exports. This would have reduced the adverse balance of trade by discouraging imports and encouraging exports, whilst leaving the gold value of the pound sterling unchanged. The alternative was either devaluation or a general reduction of money incomes. Devaluation was not favored, because it would reduce the gold value of interest payments due to Great Britain and fixed in sterling,

---

[7] Calculated by Mr. Colin Clark. See the *Economic Journal*, September 1931, p. 344.

[8] See the MacMillan Report, Cmd. 3897 of 1931, Addendum I.

amounting to more than £100 million a year, and because it might begin a new period of uncertainty as to exchange rates, besides possibly weakening the financial prestige of London. A general reduction of money incomes, however, seemed impracticable. Hence the tariff-plus-bounty was proposed. But as a bounty on exports was contrary to some existing trade treaties, and in any event would have been resented by competing countries, the proposal in practice boiled down to a plea for a general revenue tariff on all imports.

Certainly there was a good deal of connection between depression in the export industries and unemployment. Unemployment was particularly heavy in the "staple" export industries of coal, cotton, woolen and worsted, iron and steel, and shipbuilding. As these export industries were largely localized, notably on the Clyde, the Tyne, the Tee, and in Lancashire and South Wales, unemployment in these "depressed areas" was about twice as high, relatively to population, as in the rest of the country. Unemployment in occupations (such as the distributive trades) working for the home market was much higher in these depressed areas than elsewhere.

It is also true that Great Britain was having difficulty in maintaining the gold standard at the old pre-war parity. Over most of the period from May 1, 1925, to September 21, 1931, the pound sterling tended to be below gold parity with the dollar—although, of course, it could not fall more than a fraction below so long as both countries remained on gold—and the Bank of England was tending to lose gold.[9] The balance of payments on income account was as follows:

[9] For figures see my *British Monetary Policy*, P. S. King, London, 1932. where the whole subject is treated in more detail.

UNITED KINGDOM BALANCE OF PAYMENTS ON INCOME ACCOUNT, 1924–1931

	1924	1925	1926	1927	1928	1929	1930	1931
	Credits £ Millions							
Exports of British produce	801	773	653	709	724	729	571	389
Exports of silver coin and bullion	12	12	11	7	9	9	8	7
Exports of gold coin and bullion	49	50	27	29	61	78	82	133
Estimated net national shipping income	140	124	120	140	130	130	105	80
Estimated net income from overseas investment	220	250	250	250	250	250	220	165
Estimated net income from short interest and commissions	60	60	60	63	65	65	55	30
Estimated net receipts from other sources	15	15	15	15	15	15	15	10
Net excess of government receipts	—	—	4	1	15	24	19	16
TOTAL	1,297	1,284	1,140	1,214	1,269	1,300	1,075	830
	Debits £ Millions							
Retained imports of merchandise	1,137	1,167	1,116	1,095	1,075	1,111	957	798
Imports of silver coin and bullion	14	11	11	7	10	8	9	8
Imports of gold coin and bullion	36	41	39	32	48	62	87	98
Net excess of government payments	25	11	—	—	—	—	—	—
TOTAL	1,212	1,230	1,166	1,134	1,133	1,181	1,053	904
CREDIT (+) or DEBIT (−) on above items[1]	+86	+54	−26	+79	+137	+118	+23	−75

[1] Most of these amounts differ by £1 million from the arithmetical difference between total credits and total debits as shown, e.g., 1924 is £86 million and not £85 million. This is because decimal points have been omitted. The net credits and debits as shown are correct.

Estimates of the various capital items are not available. The only figure known is that of new issues floated for overseas on the London market. If we subtract this from the "net credit" (or "net debit") given above, we get the following result:

	Net credit (+) or debit (−) £million	New issues £million	Difference £million
1924.................	+ 86	134	− 48
1925.................	+ 54	88	− 34
1926.................	− 26	1112	−138
1927.................	+ 79	139	− 60
1928.................	+137	143	− 6
1929.................	+118	94	+ 24
1930.................	+ 23	109	− 86
1931.................	− 75	46	−121

This suggests that the alarm at the size of the adverse (merchandise) balance of trade was well founded. We know now what was happening. Balances held in London by central banks and other foreign creditors were piling up. Great Britain was becoming increasingly vulnerable to a foreign drain of gold.

Nevertheless the "over-valuation" of the pound sterling does not explain everything. The volume of British exports in 1924 was only about 75 per cent of its pre-war level. During the war, the expense and difficulty of obtaining British goods had stimulated a number of countries, including most British Dominions, to establish or expand their own industries, and after the war they protected them with tariffs. This applied especially to textiles. To take a leading example, in 1913 British India imported 3,057 million yards of cotton piece goods from the United Kingdom; by 1924 this had fallen to 1,705 million yards; and after that it continued to decline, owing mainly to the growth of Indian production, under the stimulus of import duties which increased from 3½ per cent ad valorem in 1914 to 25 per cent in 1933.[10] The total export of British cotton piece goods fell from 4,436 million square yards in 1925 to 3,672 million in 1929 and 1,716 million in 1931. Moreover, a number of the British coal mines were becoming "worked out" in the sense that the easiest coal to win had already been taken, so that average output per worker was considerably below what it had been forty or fifty years before, while increased use was being made of substitutes for coal, such as fuel oil and hydro-electric power; and other countries were subsidizing their ship-building and shipping, and their exports of iron and steel.

On any realistic view, therefore, the "staple" British export industries could not hope to regain their pre-war position. Neither a 10 per cent nor a 20 per cent devalua-tion of the pound could turn back the clock in this way. Great Britain needed to look to the future and not to the past. She needed to adjust her economy to the changed conditions of the post-war world.

Between 1924 and 1929 the values of most classes of British exports, other than textiles and apparel, coal, iron and steel, and ships showed an increase. What was needed was a transference of workers from the old staple industries and occupations, to the newer export industries in the more prosperous South. Some such transference did take place. For example, between July 1923, and July 1930, the

[10]	Cotton cloth	1924	1933
		(Million yards)	
	Indian mill production	1840	3550
	Total imports	1705	870
	Imports from the United Kingdom	1508	456
	Imports from Japan	146	379

following changes, among others, took place in the numbers atached to different industries.[11]

Expansion

	Thousands		
Distributive trades...............	1,254	to	1,764
Motor vehicles (manufacture).....	192	to	247
Hotels and boarding houses.......	259	to	351
Electrical engineering............	61	to	90
Silk and artificial silk.............	37	to	78

Contraction

Coal mining....................	1,244	to	1,070
Shipbuilding....................	270	to	205
General engineering..............	667	to	592
Wool and worsted..............	269	to	240

Accompanying this was a movement away from the North and South Wales towards the South. The *Census Preliminary Report,* 1931 (p. XIV), remarks:

It will be observed that the counties north of Cheshire and Yorkshire inclusive have on balance lost as many as 443,000 of their population by migration during the past decennium and that from the central belt Wales has lost 259,000, the Midlands 81,000, and the Eastern region 41,000. . . . In the South-Eastern Section the net immigration numbers 615,000.

But this was not enough. Movement into expanding industries was checked by the relatively high wages there and by trade-union regulations. The general rigidity of wages was largely due to the Unemployment Insurance Scheme—the so-called "dole." If the writer may express his own opinion, a minimum national income for all—irrespective of earnings and paid for out of taxation—would achieve more logically and completely the humanitarian aims of the "dole" without resulting in the unemployment, the hindrances to mobility, the introduction of labor-saving devices adopted in certain industries only be-

[11] *Ministry of Labour Gazette,* November 1930, p. 423.

cause wages there are maintained above the equilibrium level, and the tendency to export capital instead of investing it at home because a higher return can be obtained from abroad, all of which were consequences of the Unemployment Insurance Scheme.

Be that as it may, the great depression aggravated the troubles of the preceding years. The volume of exports fell, unemployment increased, agriculture was depressed, the balance-of-payments situation grew worse, and towards the close of 1931 Great Britain was driven off gold and turned to protection.

5. Why Great Britain Adopted Protection

A Committee on National Expenditure, under the chairmanship of Sir George May, was appointed at the end of March 1931. Its Report, published on July 31, created consternation. It forecast a deficit of £120 million, unless new taxation was imposed or new economies were made, in the following financial year. This estimate included under normal expenditure over £50 million towards debt redemption and in general took rather a gloomy view of the situation, but it made most people feel that something drastic should be done, for at that time the view that a budget deficit might be a good weapon for fighting a trade slump had very few adherents. Incidentally, the Report increased the flight from sterling.

The Labor Cabinet, however, could not agree as to how far the recommendations of the Report, notably those advocating cuts in unemployment benefit and in the pay of teachers and other government employees, should be adopted, and on August 24 it resigned and was replaced by a National Government under the same Prime Minister, Mr. Ramsay MacDonald. The general election held shortly afterwards resulted in an overwhelming victory for the coalition, or National Government, candidates. Most of these were in fact Conservatives, although under the banner of the National Government. The Conservative Party was known to favor protection, and it was widely expected that sooner or later tariffs would be introduced.

This expectation led to large orders for imports, in order to build up stocks before duties were imposed, and this in turn led to the Abnormal Importations Act, by which the President of the Board of Trade was empowered to impose duties up to 100 per cent ad valorem on manufactures. The Horticultural Products Act gave the Ministry of Agriculture the same powers over certain classes of fresh fruit and vegetables. Both these Acts were passed as temporary measures to meet an emergency, but they paved the way for a general and permanent tariff. With the Import Duties Act of February 1932 Great Britain became definitely protectionist, after surprisingly little discussion or opposition.

The main reason why the general public accepted protection was undoubtedly the great depression, and in particular the high level of unemployment. Arguments for protection always receive more sympathy during a depression. Home industries are in difficulties, men are out-of-work and plant is employed far below capacity, and it is claimed that this could be remedied, at least in part, if some protection were afforded against foreign imports coming in at "cut" prices. Possible adverse reactions on the export industries—which, after all, in Great Britain were among the most depressed—are either ignored or are expected to be relatively small.

The government doubtless hoped that once a tariff

was adopted it could be used as a bargaining weapon to extract concessions on British exports from other countries. Chapter V relates what was achieved in this way through trade treaties with foreign countries and Chapter VI includes an account of the negotiations with the Continental Steel Cartel, during which penal tariffs were used to bring pressure upon the cartel countries and to induce them to make terms, including quotas for British exports, which were deemed satisfactory. Moreover, the dream of imperial preference could now come true. Great Britain could at last give substantial concessions to Dominion imports, and the Dominions in return could maintain and increase the preferential treatment which they gave to goods coming from Great Britain.

We have already observed that after Great Britain had left gold, the public was more willing to adopt protection. The National Government which had been elected to maintain the gold standard had to abandon it after about a fortnight. A number of writers have since declared that this was a blessing: that Great Britain had previously been fettered by chains of gold. But this was certainly not the predominant view at the time. Serious efforts had been made to keep the pound on gold, and when they failed the public was fearful of the future. In these circumstances, a tariff appealed, not to people's reason but to their imagination and feelings, as a precaution and bulwark against unknown perils.

Yet the change to protection was not entirely due to the crisis. Faith in free trade had been weakening during the post-war years. This had very little to do with logical reasoning. It was simply that Great Britain was obviously lagging behind her rivals and was suffering from heavier unemployment. This might have been due to the over-valuation of the pound, or to the rigidity of incomes, or to the lack of enterprise and initiative shown by leaders of industry. Whatever the reason, it was happening under free trade, while other countries had advanced, and were advancing, under protection. The pseudo-monopoly which Great Britain had enjoyed during the Victorian era had passed away. There had been signs of its passing even before the war of 1914. During the first decade of the twentieth century real wages had failed to increase, and complaints were heard that the technical education and business methods of certain other countries were superior to those of Great Britain. During the post-war years, the economic *malaise* of Great Britain was apparent to the world. It clamored for a remedy, and the most attractive of the remedies offered was a tariff. The fact that a tariff would bring in perhaps £30 million of revenue made it particularly acceptable to a government faced with a deficit which it deplored.

The reader will notice that economic reasoning played very little part in causing protection to be accepted. About the only "respectable" economic argument put forward for protection was the proposal, mentioned above, made by some members of the MacMillan Committee for a general revenue tariff to reduce the adverse balance of trade. They considered this proposal as much superior to the alternative of devaluation. In fact, Great Britain did not devalue. She did what was even worse, according to the views held at that time by the members in question: she left gold without returning to it at a lower parity. The pound sterling was left free to find its own level—with some guidance, later, from the Exchange Equalization Fund. This meant that the balance of payments would automatically balance. Sterling would fall sufficiently low to keep down imports to the value which could be paid for. A tariff was no longer needed for that purpose. The lower exchange value of the pound discouraged imports and encouraged exports. The "balance of trade" argument for a tariff in order to keep the pound sterling on gold at the old parity completely vanished the moment that the pound left gold.

The great majority of economists, both in Great Britain and in the world as a whole, were and are in favor of free trade. Again and again international conferences have urged reductions in tariff barriers. Yet free trade would almost certainly have come in Great Britain in the nineteenth century if no abstract reasoning had ever been advanced in its favor, and all the economists—who, after all, are the specialists in this subject—were quite powerless to stem the tide of protection during and after 1931. It is a sad thought.

CHAPTER II

THE BRITISH TARIFF

1. THE MAIN FEATURES OF THE TARIFF

WE SHALL spare the reader anything like a full summary of the long list of import duties in force in the United Kingdom. The list is given in detail in *The Customs and Excise Tariff*, published every six months. The present section confines itself to a few broad generalizations, intended to give a bird's-eye view of the tariff as a whole.

The great bulk of the customs receipts still comes from duties whose main object is to raise revenue rather than to protect home production. In the year 1938 the gross amount received from customs duties was, in round figures, £264 million. Of this about £214 million came from "revenue" duties and only £50 million from "protective" duties. The distinction, of course, is not a clear-cut one. Protective duties do yield some revenue—in practice, this is a strong argument for imposing them and makes it difficult to get rid of them. And revenue duties are to some extent protective. This applies especially, in Great Britain, to the duty on sugar. Since 1924 the home production of beet sugar has been fostered both by an annual subsidy and by reduced excise duties. Imported sugar pays duty at a higher rate than home-grown sugar. Hence there is a protective element in the "revenue" duty on sugar. Even when the commodity is not produced at home, a "revenue" duty upon imports may give protection to home-produced substitutes. Thus the high duties on imported petrol give some protection to British coal. Petrol, or other oils, would replace coal to a greater extent if their prices were not raised by the duty. And even if there is no close substitute produced at home, the "revenue" duty keeps down the consumption of that product in favor of others. For example, more tobacco would be consumed if the duties on it were lower. Nevertheless our statement holds good: duties whose primary aim is protective yield less than a fifth of total customs receipts.

Most imports from the Empire are free. Most goods subject to "revenue" duties are taxed, even if they come from the Empire, but usually at lower rates. Thus fully-refined sugar from non-Empire countries pays 11s.8d. per cwt., but Empire sugar pays only 5s.10d., and Empire tobacco receives a preference of somewhat less than a quarter of the full duty. Empire dried fruits are an exception to this general rule: they come in free; and Empire petrol pays full rates. Goods which came under the "McKenna duties," first imposed in 1915, must pay two-thirds of the duty (that is, 22⅔ per cent) if they come from the Empire. The most important item under this head is motor-cars. All other goods from the Empire are free of duty. In practice, this applies mainly to foodstuffs and raw materials. In general, Empire manufactures, although they could come in free of duty, cannot compete with British manufactures in the British market.

Most imports of raw materials are free. The motive for this is plain. Great Britain herself produces few raw materials, and is a large exporter of manufactures. The finished product of one firm, however, may be the "raw material" of another, and thus a conflict of interests may arise between firms engaged in different stages of producing the same final products. The most important conflict of this kind in Great Britain was between firms producing mainly iron and steel and firms producing goods, such as motorcars, for which iron and steel are materials. It was won by the former—relatively high duties were imposed on iron and steel, including pig iron.

Some raw materials, including timber and vegetable oil, are subject to duty. As a rule, the object is to help Empire producers, whose products come in free. In 1938 productive duties on Class II goods ("Raw Materials and Articles mainly Unmanufactured") yielded about £5 million: the total value of Class II imports was nearly £250 million.

In order to prevent British exporters from being handicapped, "drawbacks" are given in a number of instances. Duties paid on, say, imported leather are refunded in so far as the leather is used in making boots and shoes which are exported.

Nearly all other imports are subject to duty. This is a slight exaggeration; it is made to stress the completeness of the swing to protection in 1931 and 1932. Before 1931, every import was free of duty unless listed in the tariff. Today every import from a non-Empire country is subject to duty unless it is listed as free.

Most foodstuffs are now subject to duty. Bacon, poultry, most canned meats, beef and veal (since 1936), dairy products, fruit, vegetables, and even feeding-stuffs for animals are all taxed. Wheat was taxed after Ottawa but was replaced on the free list by the American trade agreement of November 1938.

It is true that over half the receipts from protective duties come from manufactures, which form little more than a quarter of total imports. But this is because manufactures come mainly from foreign countries, while much of the foodstuffs come in duty-free from the Empire.

Most rates of duty are relatively moderate. In 1938 "protective" duties yielded about £50 million upon imports, excluding those subject to "revenue" duties, worth over £800 million. Clearly many goods came in free or at low rates of duty. A study of the tariff schedule confirms this. A number of duties are specific; for example, butter pays 15s. per cwt. Some duties, including those on "key industry" goods, non-licensed iron and steel, motorcars, and watches, are 33⅓ per cent or even higher. Twenty per cent is a fairly common rate for manufactures. But many goods still come in at the "standard rate" of 10 per cent. In 1937-38 duties under the Import Duties Act yielded £29.7 million, of which £11.6 million was raised at 10 per cent and £18.1 million at other rates.[1]

It is theoretically possible for a "low" rate of duty, such as 10 per cent, to be highly protective. It may cause home products to replace imports almost completely. In the same way, a low yield of protective duties may mean that they have succeeded in keeping out imports. But we know that this has not happened in Great Britain. The volume of imports has not been substantially reduced and, except in a few instances, home products have not displaced imports to any great extent. The British tariff, in fact, really is relatively moderate. This does not mean, we hasten to add, that its effects are small or unimportant. When a great nation, which imports one-sixth of all the goods entering into the international trade of the world, swings over to protection, the consequences for her foreign suppliers and the reactions upon trade policy elsewhere may be most serious and far-reaching, even if her rates of duty are not high. But at the moment our object is simply to give a broad picture of what the tariff is like, and it happens to be a fact that most rates are relatively moderate.

[1] *Twenty-Ninth Report of the Commissioners of His Majesty's Customs and Excise*, Cmd. 5876 of 1938, p. 151.

The tariff is not the only form of protection. We cannot conclude without reminding the reader of this very important truth. There are many other ways of keeping out imports. One important weapon may be monetary policy. If the exchange value of a currency is kept, say, 20 per cent below the equilibrium rate this is equivalent to a general duty of 20 per cent on imports. Another powerful weapon is the quantitative limitation of imports. Again, subsidies may be given in one form or another to home industries. We need not continue the list, which would range from veterinary regulations to exchange control. We discuss in the next chapters the more important forms of protection, other than import duties, applied by Great Britain.

2. A Brief History of the Tariff

At the outbreak of war in 1914 Great Britain had no protective duties. The import duties on goods also produced at home, such as spirits and beer, were accompanied by corresponding excise duties on home production. Customs and excise duties on alcohol yielded about £43 million, on tobacco about £18 million, and on tea, cocoa, coffee, sugar, and dried fruit about £10 million—all together over 40 per cent of the budget revenue.

Most of these duties have been changed several times since 1914. The alcohol and tobacco duties have been greatly increased. Thus the duty on spirits was 14s.9d. per proof gallon in 1914, 30s. in 1918, 50s. in 1919, and 72s.6d. in 1920 and thereafter, and the duty on tobacco was 3s.8d. per lb. in 1814, 8s.2d. in 1918, 8s.10d. in 1927, 9s.6d. in 1932, and 11s.6d. in April 1939. Before the war of 1939 revenue duties on imports yielded about £150 million and excise duties over £100 million (of which some £30 million from spirits and some £60 million from beer)—together, well over a quarter of the total budget revenue.

The main change in the picture—apart from the growing consumption of tobacco and the falling consumption of beer—was the rise of petrol as a revenue producer. The pre-1914 duty of 3d. a gallon on motor spirit yielded less than £1 million. In 1921 the customs duty (then 6d.) was repealed. It was reimposed, under the heading of "hydrocarbon oils," in 1928 at 4d. a gallon, raised to 6d. and then 8d. in 1931, and increased to 9d. in 1938, by which time it was yielding £50 million a year.

We now turn to protective duties. Only one set of such duties was imposed during the war of 1914-18. These duties, known as "McKenna Duties" (after Sir Reginald McKenna who was Chancellor of the Exchequer at the time), were imposed in 1915 at 33⅓ per cent ad valorem on motorcars and motorcycles, clocks and watches, and musical instruments, together with a specific duty on cinema films at ⅓d. per linear foot on blank, 1d. on positive, 5d. on negative. The purpose of the duty was to save cargo space: these goods were deemed luxuries. Nevertheless the duties have survived. They lapsed in 1924 but were reimposed the following year. Those on clocks and watches and musical instruments were somewhat reduced by the trade agreement with Germany in 1933. In 1937-38 the McKenna Duties yielded some £3 million, of which £1.7 million came from motorcars and motorcycles. They now come under the Import Duties Act.

The *"Key Industry" Duties* were first imposed by the Safeguarding of Industries Act of 1921. Their object was frankly protective. They applied to "certain articles of a pivotal character which were regarded as vital to the national safety in time of war or of outstanding importance to industry."[2] They were at first imposed for five years only. Mr. Baldwin said: "The object of fixing the period of five years is that that is the term of years which, after very careful consideration, we believe to be long enough for any industries that they may be able to stand and flourish at the end of that period. I think in specifying five years we have gone to the limit of what the industries may reasonably expect."[3] Nevertheless these duties have survived, with minor changes, to the present day. The Board of Trade has the power to issue lists of articles (within the general classes stated in the Act), subject to these duties. The rate of duty is 33⅓ per cent ad valorem except on optical glass and optical instruments (50 per cent) and on certain carbons (5s. or 7s.6d. per lb.). Among the numerous goods included are various precision instruments, many chemicals, wireless valves, and ignition magnetos. They yield about £1 million a year.

In 1925 a protective duty of 80s. per cwt. was imposed on imported *hops*. In the same year revenue duties, accompanied by excise duties, were imposed on *silk* (3s. per lb. on raw silk) and artificial silk (1s. per lb.). Silk was regarded as a luxury. In 1933 and 1934 these duties were made protective. The raw silk duty was reduced by half to 1s. 6d. and duties on more-finished silk products were increased.

In 1928 a 33⅓ per cent ad valorem duty was imposed on *buttons* and one of 25 per cent on *hollow ware*, largely in the hope of reabsorbing unemployed workers in these industries. These duties lapsed in 1933.

Thus the situation in September 1931 was as follows: There were the staple revenue duties, now including hydro-

[2] Cmd. 4066.
[3] 142, House of Commons Debates, 5.s., p. 877.

carbon oils and silk. There were protective duties on McKenna goods, key industry goods, buttons and hollow ware, and hops. Great Britain was still free trade. She had barely scratched the surface of protection.

During the crisis in the autumn of 1931 it became clear that the new National Government would consist predominantly of Conservatives and might well impose tariffs. British merchants and manufacturers gave large orders for imports, in order to forestall possible duties by building up stocks. To prevent this, the *Abnormal Importations (Customs Duties) Act* was rushed through in three days. Under this Act the President of the Board of Trade could issue orders imposing duties up to 100 per cent ad valorem on imports of manufactures. Three sets of orders were issued, in November and December, imposing duties of 50 per cent ad valorem on a wide range of manufactures.

Another measure passed at this time was the *Horticultural Products (Emergency Provisions) Act*. This enabled the Minister of Agriculture to make orders levying duties up to 100 per cent ad valorem on certain classes of fresh fruit, fresh vegetables, and similar products if they could be produced to a greater extent in the United Kingdom or if they were articles of luxury. Orders were made under this Act during January, February, and March 1932. One object of the duties seems to have been to prevent foreign growers of fruits and vegetables from "skimming the cream" off the British market by selling large quantities of their products before the British varieties were ready. Hence a number of the duties varied greatly according to the season of the year, being heavy during the "early" season of the products in question. This Act was revoked in September 1932 and the duties were continued under the Import Duties Act.

The basis of the present protective tariff is the *Import Duties Act* of February 1932. This imposed a general ad valorem duty of 10 per cent on all imports, except those specifically exempted, as from March 1. The free list, naming the articles which were exempted, consisted of some hundreds of items, including most raw materials. The Act did not apply to Empire products. It replaced the emergency duties levied under the Abnormal Importations Act, but all other duties remained in force. Under this Act, the Import Duties Advisory Committee, discussed in the next section, was set up. From April 1932 onwards this committee has from time to time recommended duties higher than 10 per cent upon a considerable number of items. Upon its recommendations orders have been issued imposing, for example, duties of 20 per cent upon many manufactures, of 30 per cent upon luxuries such as furs and jewelry, and of 33⅓ per cent on many iron and steel products.

The Ottawa agreements were signed in August 1932 and were followed by the *Ottawa Duties* upon foreign imports of a kind which the Empire could supply. They included duties of 15s. per cwt. on butter, 15 per cent ad valorem on cheese, and specific duties on eggs and apples, oranges, and certain other fruit. Wheat was removed from the free list and taxed 2s. per quarter.

From 1932 to 1938 the United Kingdom and the Irish Free State carried on a tariff war. The latter had not kept its agreement to pay certain sums due to the United Kingdom, which retaliated by imposing under the *Irish Free State (Special Duties) Act* additional duties of 20 per cent ad valorem on live animals, meat poultry, game, butter, eggs, and cream from that country. These duties were considerably increased as time went on and feeling became more bitter; and of course the Free State retaliated. In 1936 both sides reduced their duties and in 1938 a settlement was reached and these special duties were abolished. They had hit Eire hard, for Great Britain is her chief market, and they had led to a good deal of smuggling over the border into Northern Ireland.

In 1936 duties, the main one being ¾d. per lb., were imposed on beef and veal from non-Empire countries.

The table on page 35 shows the receipts from the various duties or groups of duties in 1936, 1937, and 1938.

3. How the Tariff Is Made

In the United Kingdom all import duties are imposed under the authority of Acts of Parliament. A trade treaty, provided that it did not change the law or impose taxes or public expenditure, could be made by the government without consulting Parliament, for the Crown has the sole right of making treaties. But it has become the custom in recent years to submit all treaties for parliamentary approval, so that tariff policy in all its aspects, including the quantitative limitation of imports, is subject to the control of Parliament. In the last resort, it is Parliament which decides whether a policy of free trade or protection shall be followed and, if the latter, how strong the dose shall be.

Revenue duties are imposed by the Finance Act. Most of them are imposed for one year only and renewed in the Finance Act of the following year, unless it is decided to abolish them or to change them. These decisions are made by the Chancellor of the Exchequer. Each year he has to determine how much revenue must be raised and what is the best way of raising it. His proposals, when they have been accepted by Parliament, become the Finance Act of that year. A special emergency may arise requiring,

GROSS RECEIPTS FROM CUSTOMS DUTIES[4]

Principal Articles	1936	1937	1938
	£millions		
Revenue Duties			
Tobacco..............................	105.4	112.0	115.4
Hydrocarbon oils......................	47.5	50.2	56.3
Sugar................................	14.5	13.4	15.4
Spirits...............................	4.7	5.0	4.6
Beer.................................	5.6	5.1	3.5
Wine.................................	5.0	5.1	4.8
Tea..................................	6.7	7.7	9.9
Cocoa................................	1.4	1.3	1.3
Coffee, etc...........................	.2	.2	.1
Dried fruits..........................	.8	.8	.7
Matches and mechanical lighters........	2.2	2.2	2.2
	194.0	203.0	214.2
Protective Duties			
Silk and artificial silk................	4.3	4.7	4.6
Hops, hop oil and hop extracts..........	.2	.2	.2
Key industry goods....................	.9	1.1	1.2
Goods liable under Import Duties Act, 1932:			
Cinematograph films...............	.2	.2	.2
Clocks, watches and parts..........	.6	.7	.7
Motorcars, motorcycles and parts...	1.6	2.0	1.4
Musical instruments and parts......	.1	.2	.1
Other goods......................	28.3	31.8	27.7
Goods liable under Ottawa Agreements Acts,			
1932.............................	7.7	8.1	8.6
Beef and veal........................	.1	3.2	3.5
Goods from Eire liable under the Irish Free State (Special Act, 1932) or the Import Duties Act, 1932......................	5.0	4.4	1.2
Other items..........................	.1	.1	.1
	49.1	56.7	49.5
TOTAL...............................	243.1	259.7	263.7

[4] Adapted from *Accounts relating to the Trade and Navigation of the United Kingdom,* December 1938, p. 275.

as it did in September 1931 and again in September 1939, a second set of proposals (a supplementary budget) embodied in a new Finance Act which replaces that of the previous April.

The Chancellor may decide that he can afford to repeal or to reduce some existing revenue duties. On the other hand, he may need more revenue than in the previous year and may therefore impose some new duties or increase some existing ones. The latter course does not always have the desired result. For example, in 1920 the duty on sparkling wines was increased from 2s.6d. a bottle to 5s. plus 33⅓ per cent ad valorem a bottle. Consumption fell off so much that the yield of this duty diminished and in the following year it was reduced to 12s.6d. per gallon. Most revenue duties, however, are levied upon goods whose consumption would not fall off much if their price were raised, so that an increase in the rate of duty does result in a larger revenue. The estimates of the revenue to be derived from the various duties are prepared mainly by the statistical staff (of the Board of Commissioners of Customs and Excise and of the Inland Revenue Department) of the Treasury, and these estimates are usually fairly near the mark.

Although the Finance Bill is debated in Parliament, the Chancellor of the Exchequer frames his budget as a whole and seldom alters any of his proposals in order to comply with the wishes of Parliament unless the feeling of many members on the point is very strong. He can, of course, get the bill through without amendment because his party controls the majority of votes in the House of Commons, whilst the House of Lords cannot hold up a "money" bill for any length of time and the assent of the Crown is never refused.

The procedure for protective duties is quite different. These are all imposed under the authority of some Act of Parliament, but as a rule they are not set out in detail, discussed by Parliament, and then embodied in an Act. Parliament simply would not have the time to discuss all the many hundreds of duties, not to mention exemptions and drawbacks, which have constituted the protective tariff since 1932. Changes are frequently made, and it would hardly be feasible to incorporate each of these changes in a bill which had to pass through all the various stages of procedure before becoming an Act. The practice, therefore, is for the Treasury to make an order stating in full detail the change to be made. This order is laid on the table of the House and from that moment has the force of law. If it imposes a duty it must be approved by the House within twenty-eight days or it then ceases to have effect. Other orders, however, continue in force unless the House annuls them within twenty-eight days. It seems beyond doubt that this system deprives Parliament of any effective control. There is seldom time for a full discussion of the orders. Probably the best way to restore real, as opposed to nominal, control by Parliament would be to create a small committee of members to consider the orders and to give them power to cross-examine the Import Duties Advisory Committee.

This body is of the greatest importance in shaping the protective tariff, for it advises the Treasury what orders to issue and its advice is usually taken. We must therefore discuss it at some length.

The Import Duties Advisory Committee was created by the Import Duties Act of 1932. It must consist of not less than three and not more than six members; appointments are made by the Treasury for three years, but can be renewed; and the remuneration of the members is decided by the Treasury. In fact, three members were appointed and have continued to constitute the committee up to the present time (spring of 1940). The chairman is an actuary, Lord May. The other two are Sir Sidney Chapman, at one time a professor of economics, and Sir George Allen Powell, a barrister and a former civil servant. The secretary is Sir Percy Ashley, who was seconded from the Board of Trade.

It will be remembered that the Import Duties Act of 1932 imposed a general ad valorem duty of 10 per cent with a free list and that the Ottawa Agreements Act of the same year imposed duties on certain products from non-Empire sources. The committee may make recommendations concerning all these articles.

It can recommend taking an article off the free list. It can recommend putting on the free list any article subject to the 10 per cent ad valorem duty. It can recommend granting or repealing drawbacks. It can recommend "additional duties" upon goods subject to the 10 per cent ad valorem duty, provided that they are not non-luxuries unlikely to be produced in substantial quantities in the United Kingdom; and upon goods subject to Ottawa duties provided that they were not on the free list before the Ottawa Agreements Act. Since 1936, it has had the power to recommend additional duties upon "key industry" goods and since 1938 upon goods previously subject to McKenna duties. It can recommend the importation by license of particular consignments of machinery, not procurable in the United Kingdom, either free or at reduced rates of duty.

Thus the committee has very wide powers of recommendation. But there are some things which it *cannot* recommend. It cannot recommend a reduction of duty on "key industry" goods or on McKenna goods. It cannot recommend additional duties on goods which were on the free list before the Ottawa Agreements Act. It cannot recommend reductions in Ottawa duties below the limit set by the Ottawa agreements or above the limit specified in the Act. It cannot recommend additional duties, above the 10 per cent of the 1932 Act, upon articles which are not articles of luxury and not likely to be produced in substantial quantities at home. And it has no power to recommend changes in the duties on foreign beef and veal, which were imposed under a special Act of Parliament in 1936. "Additional duties" may be recommended on either an ad valorem or a specific basis, but the 10 per cent ad valorem duty can be changed to a specific basis only if it can be "levied with greater advantage and convenience" in that manner.

The committee can only recommend. It is for the Treasury to decide after consulting with the "appropriate" department (the Ministry of Agriculture for agricultural products and the Board of Trade always) whether or not to accept its recommendations and embody them in an order. The Treasury, within limits, can make an order which differs from the recommendations of the committee. When the committee recommends an "additional" duty—"additional," that is, either to the 10 per cent ad valorem duty or to an Ottawa duty or to a key industry duty or to a McKenna duty—the Treasury cannot make the duty higher than recommended. This is a surprising surrender of power. But it can impose a duty at any lower rate down to, but not below, the basic duty on goods of that class. When the recommendation is to reduce an ad valorem duty, the Treasury may make a smaller but not a larger

reduction than that recommended. When the committee recommends adding an article to the free list, or
removing one from it, the Treasury can only accept or
reject the recommendation as it stands. The Treasury cannot impose a duty at a rate lower than 10 per cent unless
this is expressly recommended by the committee.

Before discussing on what lines the committee have
acted, a word should be said about *retaliatory duties*,
which do not fall within their sphere. These are imposed
against any foreign country which, in the opinion of the
Board of Trade, discriminates against imports from the
United Kingdom or its Colonial Empire. They are over
and above any other duties already levied on the same
goods, but they must not exceed 100 per cent. The Board
of Trade must get the consent of the Treasury before
imposing them, and the latter before giving its consent
must consult any other government department which
seems to it to be concerned. The Finance Act of 1933,
moreover, gives the Treasury, on the recommendation of
the Board of Trade, the power to repeal or reduce duties
in order to give effect to a commercial agreement. It may
be noted that the beef and veal duties have been modified
in this way. Tongues and jellied veal imported in air-tight
containers were exempted from duty in order to comply
with the terms of the Anglo-Polish trade agreement.

4. THE WORK OF THE IMPORT DUTIES ADVISORY COMMITTEE

The 1932 Act, which created this committee, gives it
the power to subpoena witnesses and to call for documents,
with the proviso that information about a business must
not be disclosed without the previous consent of its owner.
The Act leaves the committee a free hand to choose whatever procedure it thinks best, except that it is bound to

consider all representations made to it. Shortly after it was
set up, the committee made the following announcement:

The . . . Committee desire to announce that applications
should be made as far as possible by representative bodies of
the trade concerned. The Committee do not propose to pro-
ceed as a rule by formal hearings. Applicants, therefore, should
submit their case fully in writing, and the Committee will call
for supplementary statements, oral or written, as may be required. The Committee will from time to time give notice of
cases . . . which they are considering . . . in order that interested parties may have the opportunity of making representations.

Proceedings are held in *camera*. Those who oppose a
suggested change cannot insist upon cross-examining those
in favor of it. It is the usual practice of the committee to
set out their reasons for any recommendation which they
make to the Treasury. These statements are published
together with the corresponding orders.

A study of these statements reveals the main considerations on which the committee have based their decisions.
Their reason for recommending an increase in duty is
usually that the home industry is not flourishing or is
"endangered" or "in jeopardy" or that "home manufacturers are finding it difficult to secure a profitable outlet
for their production" or that there is considerable unemployment in the industry. The committee state why this is
so. It is often due to an increase of imports, although sometimes it is due mainly to a rise in the cost of materials
which does not seem to have raised import prices of the
finished products to a corresponding extent. In any event,
the committee hope that an increase in duty will help to
remedy the trouble. Their phrasing sometimes suggests
that they regard imports as a menace to the established

home industry. For example: "At the beginning of 1934 [imports] increased to well over 1,000 tons a month and in the second half of the year the position rapidly became worse. Imports on a substantial scale have continued and for the first nine months of this year they approach the high level of 1930. We are satisfied that the production of linseed oil in this country will be seriously endangered unless further assistance be accorded to it."[5] Sometimes they refer to the desirability, from a national point of view, of maintaining a sufficient output within the country. For example: "Yeast being essential to the production of bread, the maintenance of the domestic supply is a matter of national importance."[6] Or again: "The future of the wire industry in this country is closely bound up with that of the Iron and Steel industry, and no reorganisation of the latter can be regarded as satisfactory which leaves the former still dependent upon foreign sources for its main supplies of primary raw materials, viz. wire rod and rod-making billet."[7]

The committee sometimes refer to the probable effect which their recommendations will have upon the prices of the products in question, or of the consumers goods into which they enter. In some instances, they believe that prices will not be raised. The article may form only a small part of the total costs of the final product. A higher duty on doors should not raise the cost of building,[8] a duty on yeast should not increase the price of bread,[9] a duty on feathers should not adversely affect any other trade,[10] and

[5] Cmd. 5040 of 1935.
[6] Cmd. 4303 of 1933.
[7] Cmd. 4256 of 1933.
[8] Cmd. 4795 of 1935.
[9] Cmd. 4303 of 1933.
[10] Cmd. 4390 of 1933.

so on. There may be considerable unused capacity, so that an increased duty will make the industry more profitable and provide more employment by enabling fixed charges to be spread over a larger output without a rise in prices. Or again, "It is unlikely that producers would jeopardize the prospects of an expansion of demand by seeking to increase prices unduly."[11] In other instances, the committee believe that prices will be raised by adopting their recommendations but think this is necessary "to protect the home manufacturer against the uneconomic price cutting to which these goods are being subjected by foreign competition,"[12] or to safeguard the industry from "a severe setback." Occasionally the committee seem to wish to prevent consumers, in their own interests, from buying inferior goods from abroad. For example: "While these cheap pencils are generally inferior in quality to the British article, their sales have a damaging effect on the trade in the standard British article."[13]

The committee have been most favorable to applications for a reduced rate of duty when the article was a raw material or intermediate product and a reduction of duty would substantially benefit exporting industries or expand employment. Thus, in recommending that ferro-chromium should be placed on the free list they said: "The duty on imported ferro-chromium places the British Special Steel manufacturers at a disadvantage in the export markets as compared with their foreign competitors and we are of opinion that its removal is desirable until such time as sufficient home supplies are made available."[14] Clearly it requires a delicate judgment to decide whether to increase

[11] Cmd. 4405 of 1933.
[12] Cmd. 4405 of 1933.
[13] Cmd. 4764 of 1934.
[14] Cmd. 4330 of 1933.

a duty in order to call forth adequate home supplies or to reduce it in order to help the industry which uses the article. The committee have recommended a larger number of drawbacks in order to prevent exporting industries from being handicapped by duties on their materials.

Sometimes the committee, when considering an application for a change of duty on some particular product, have decided to review the rates of duty on a large number of related products. But on the whole they seem to have proceeded empirically and to have considered each case on its merits in the light of the situation existing in the relevant industry or industries. Nevertheless we can make the following tentative generalizations upon what they have done. They have tended to favor low rates of duty upon foodstuffs which are widely consumed by the working classes. They have tended to favor high duties of 30 or 33⅓ per cent upon luxuries and upon the products of what they regarded as key industries. On many manufactures they have not been averse from imposing an additional duty of 10 per cent, making the total duty 20 per cent. They have been most ready to grant a reduction of duty when a small reduction would considerably expand exports or employment. They seem never to have recommended a rate of more than 33⅓ per cent ad valorem on any article not subject previously to key industry or McKenna duties, but they have recommended a number of specific duties on low-priced imports which are equivalent to a higher rate than this.

An interesting solution was found in 1938 to a problem which duties or drawbacks could not adequately cope with. The growers of barley applied for an additional duty on barley and in particular on barley used for malting. Most imported barley is used as feed for cattle and it was not thought desirable to penalize the numerous cattle farmers for the benefit of the much less numerous barley growers. The other main uses of barley are in beer brewing and malting and whisky distilling. A duty on imported barley used for malting would have encouraged a greater use of home-grown barley for these purposes, but it was hardly practicable without an elaborate and expensive control of dealers to distinguish between this and other barley. The committee therefore entered into negotiations with brewers and distillers. The Brewers Society promised on behalf of its members that they would do their utmost to buy at least 7½ million cwts. of home-grown barley each year and to increase this amount if the output of beer increased. The chief distillers promised, unless market conditions changed, to continue to buy only home-grown barley. Hence the committee decided to regard the application for an increased duty as being in suspense.

It may be added that from time to time the committee have been asked by the government to make investigations outside their statutory province. Thus in 1932 the Chancellor of the Exchequer asked them to report upon the silk and artificial silk duties; in 1933 the President of the Board of Trade asked them to discover how far the Canadian Government was right in complaining that Russian timber was being dumped in the United Kingdom; in 1935 they were asked to consider whether the marketing arrangements in London for lead and zinc deprived Dominion producers of their preferential advantages; and in 1936 the Board of Trade requested them to examine the present position and future development of the iron and steel industry.

Chapter III

OTHER FORMS OF PROTECTION

1. Introductory

Import duties are not the only form of protection. There are many other ways of directly or indirectly restricting imports.

It can be argued that every kind of state action may have some effect in favoring home products relatively to imports, or conversely. If the result is to promote exports and to increase the proportion of total output which is sold abroad, the presumption is that imports also will tend to increase. But it would lead us much too far afield to consider from this standpoint all that the state has done in Great Britain during recent years. The favorable or unfavorable effect upon imports of most of its activity is either negligible or purely a matter of conjecture.

Let us take an example. The Derating Act of 1929 was an important piece of legislation. In Great Britain, the revenue of local authorities is derived largely from taxes on the value of buildings. A firm must pay this tax whether it is making large profits or small profits or losses. The tax is an overhead cost which must be met. These local rates, as they are called, clearly tend to discourage investment in building and to penalize firms, notably those in the heavy industries, whose premises are of necessity large and valuable relatively to their profits. The 1929 Act was an attempt to remedy this. It reduced the rates on certain types of buildings and is estimated to have lessened the burden of rates on industry by some £29 million a year. Did this assist home producers to compete more successfully against imports? It can be argued that it merely relieved them of a burden which ought never to have been placed upon them. It can be argued that the relief to industry was less than it seemed, since the central government had to compensate the local authorities by increasing its annual grant to them and therefore had to raise more in taxation than it would otherwise have done. It can be pointed out that some of the industries were export industries. It can be urged that local rates did not affect output anyway, since they were fixed charges which did not vary with output. We do not propose to discuss how much truth there is in any of these arguments. Our object is to point out that such a discussion would be long and would probably lead to no very certain or definite conclusion. We shall therefore confine ourselves to the more important actions of the state which have obviously either restricted imports directly or assisted home producers to compete against imports.

Nevertheless a few words may be said here about monetary policy. Monetary policy can be made the most powerful instrument of protection. This had happened during recent years in a number of countries, notably Germany, which have adopted more or less complete exchange control. They have been able by this means to decide which goods shall be imported and in what quantities, and to cut down their total imports to any extent desired. Great Britain has not done this. She has placed no obstacles in the way of British importers who wish to pay their foreign suppliers. But it might be suggested that British policy as to the exchange value of sterling has indirectly restricted imports. The Exchange Equalization Fund, it might be urged, has kept down the exchange value of sterling over a considerable period and has thus tended to keep out foreign goods by making them dearer in terms of sterling. It might also be suggested that the voluntary ban on loans to foreign countries has acted as a brake on world trade. The borrowing countries, if they could have raised loans in London, would have bought more from Great Britain and elsewhere. Imports into Great Britain would subsequently have increased owing both to the general stimulus to international trade resulting from the loans and to the interest payments due to her upon them. We discuss these two points in the chapter on monetary policy. But we may point out at once that to some extent they cancel out, for if Great Britain had lent more abroad this would have had a downward effect on the exchange value of sterling.

2. Assistance to Home Producers Competing Against Imports

In some countries a definite and substantial preference is given to home firms and home materials on public contracts. In Great Britain public and semi-public bodies do tend, under the influence of sentiment and of public opinion, to favor British firms in placing their contracts. But there is no law about this;[1] the Treasury acts as an alert watch-dog to prevent unnecessary expenditure by the departments of the central government, and the discrimination exercised is slight and negligible compared with that which takes place in a number of other countries.

The Merchandise Marks Acts require certain articles to bear an indication of their origin. This assists home pro-

[1] It is interesting to note, however, that the sugar commission set up under the Sugar Industry Reorganization Act of 1936 may forbid the British Sugar Corporation to install or use any class of equipment, plant, material, or other article not wholly manufactured in the United Kingdom.

ducers in so far as consumers prefer to buy British. But the total effect is probably small, and it is doubtful whether this measure should be termed protective.

During recent years most of the subsidies paid by the state have gone to agriculture. During the years 1932 to 1938 inclusive beet sugar received £18.6 million, land fertilization £2.0 million, and oats and barley £164,000. The only other subsidies of any size over this period were £4 million to tramp shipping, £3.5 million to civil aviation, and £110,000 to herring fishing. Agriculture, which employs less than three-quarters of a million people out of a working population of over 21 million, is also assisted in other ways, in addition to subsidies and duties and restrictions on various imports. Farmers can choose any of three bases of assessment for their income tax, and this is a valuable concession. Agricultural land is free from local rates. Wheat farmers are helped by the wheat scheme, which does not appear in the above list of subsidies because the cost is borne not by the taxpayers but by the consumers. We devote a special chapter to agriculture, but it is relevant to note here the assistance it receives, for nearly all its products compete with imports.

The beet sugar subsidy and the wheat scheme are discussed in this chapter, instead of being considered together with other forms of assistance to agriculture in Chapter VIII, because they have an obvious and substantial effect in keeping down imports of wheat and sugar. We also give a brief account of the shipping subsidy. Although shipping services are an "invisible export" and help to cover the adverse balance of trade, British ships do compete with other ships for passengers and freight. We discuss also the quota scheme for British cinematograph films.

3. QUANTITATIVE LIMITATION OF IMPORTS

For various reasons the importation of a number of products into Great Britain is prohibited. Examples are prepared opium, white phosphorus matches, parrots, musk-rats, lottery advertisements, and indecent or obscene articles. Some prohibitions apply only to goods from certain countries: for example, to shaving brushes from Japan. Some articles—for example, cocaine, vaccines, dogs and cats, and fire-arms—can be imported only under special license. Others, such as live cattle, tobacco, and saccharine, must go to special ports.

We shall concern ourselves only with restrictions imposed as protective measures in order to help home producers or to give preference to imports from certain countries. It may be thought that the powers bestowed on the Ministry of Agriculture and the Ministry of Health to restrict imports, in order to prevent disease, could be used as instruments of protection. In fact, they do not seem to have been used in this way. When it was desired to give preferential treatment to Canadian cattle, a special Act of Parliament, the Importation of Animals Act 1922, was deemed necessary. This Act permitted Canadian store cattle, if certain specified conditions were fulfilled, to be exempted from the law requiring cattle to be placed in quarantine at a special port and to be slaughtered there within ten days of landing.

The limitation of imports on particular goods can be a most effective way of protecting home producers. It may be thought that if imports of bacon and hams, for example, are restricted to, say, 7.6 million cwts. a year, this has precisely the same effect as an import duty which results in a total import of only 7.6 million cwts. But this is not so.

In the first place, producers feel more secure than they would under the import duty. They know that however much prices may fall abroad only the quantity fixed will come in. To that extent, their market is assured.

In the second place, an import duty brings in revenue to the government. Every unit which enters pays the duty. Under an import quota the government gets nothing unless it sells or taxes import licenses. The extra profit per unit, due to the excess of the home price over the world price, upon the imports goes to importers or exporters or both. If *import* licenses are granted and exporters compete with one another it goes to importers. If exporters are organized for the purpose of selling in the importing country, and the limitation is administered by the issue of *export* licenses to exporters, it goes to the latter.

In the third place, the total permitted quantity of imports is usually divided among the exporting countries on some basis, such as the proportion of total imports which they supplied in some preceding period, and any such basis must be more or less arbitrary. This enables a restricting government, if it wishes, to evade its obligations under the most-favored-nation clause and to discriminate in favor of certain countries by choosing a basis which gives them a relatively high proportion of the total quota.

In the fourth place, a quota has certain advantages, as a protective device, over an import duty. Consumers, not fully realizing its effects, do not object to it as much as they would object to a tariff which raised prices to the same extent. A quota can often be altered more rapidly and easily than an import duty. This makes it both more flexible as a means of protection and more powerful as an instrument of bargaining with other countries for trade concessions.

From the standpoint of free traders, import quotas are worse than tariffs. They cut off the home market from the influence of the world market. Home prices may be rising, owing to an increase in home costs, while world prices are falling. This would not happen under a fixed tariff, provided it were not prohibitive. Import quotas tend in practice to lead to monopolies of importers: it is often difficult for new firms to get the right to become importers of "quota" products. And in some countries import quotas lead to a certain amount of corruption.

Of course a product may be subject both to quota and to an import duty. In some countries the "tariff quota" is often used. A certain quantity from particular countries is admitted at a relatively low duty; additional imports can come in, perhaps without limit, on payment of a much higher duty. This applies to most iron and steel products entering Great Britain. Again, the restriction may be imposed voluntarily by the exporting countries. But this will succeed in keeping down their exports to the desired level only if there is some organization for doing so and the countries fear that worse will befall them if they fail. The voluntary restriction of meat exports from the Dominions was not very successful. On the other hand, the present voluntary restriction, by exporting countries, of exports of canned beef and processed milk to Great Britain seems to be working satisfactorily.

The commodities whose import into Great Britain is restricted by prohibitions or compulsory quotas are dye-stuffs, bacon, meat, potatoes, and sea-fish. We discuss them briefly below, together with the "tariff quota" on most iron and steel products.

It may be added that these devices can be employed as a means of exerting political pressure. This has happened twice in Great Britain during recent years. The Irish Free State (Special Duties) Act of 1932 besides imposing extra duties on Irish goods also prohibited the importation of beef and veal and restricted by quota the importation of cattle from the Irish Free State. The dispute lasted until 1937-38, when these restrictions were removed. In 1933 a dispute arose with Russia over the imprisonment by that country of certain British nationals. In consequence the Russian Goods (Import Prohibition) Act of 1933 was passed, giving power to prohibit by Proclamation the import of any goods produced in Russia. A Proclamation was made in April prohibiting the import of timber, petroleum, butter, wheat, and certain other goods. It was revoked in July, the prisoners being released.

4. BEET SUGAR

The subsidy on beet sugar dates from 1924. At that time a few thousand acres were under beet and there were three factories. The government decided to subsidize the industry, the money being paid to the factories on sugar produced, for various reasons. It wished to help arable farming, which was declining and in some difficulty. Sugar beet is a good cleaning crop; it frees the soil from weeds. It needs a considerable amount of fertilizer. Hence other crops, notably wheat, which follow sugar beet in rotation on the same land benefit from a clean and fertile soil. Another reason for the subsidy was the desire to give employment, especially in East Anglia where most of the beet is grown. Sugar beet requires a great deal of labor, although this is mostly casual labor employed during the season to hoe and gather the crop. But the main reason was probably the wish to be less dependent on imported sugar in time of war. It should be remembered that before 1914 about half Britain's imports of sugar had been beet sugar from Germany and Austria.

It was hoped that the industry would need less and less assistance as it became established. Accordingly the subsidy was a tapering one: 19s.6d. per cwt. of sugar in 1924-27; 13s. in 1928-30; 6s.6d. in 1931-34. The excise duty was reimposed at the same rate as the customs duty on Empire sugar.

A rapid expansion followed. The acreage under sugar beet rose from 22,000 in 1924 to a peak of 396,000 in 1934 and the number of factories rose to 18. The output of sugar rose from 24,000 tons in 1924 to 615,000 in 1934. The cost to the Exchequer over these ten years was £40 million— £30 million in subsidies and £10 million representing the difference between the excise duty on home-produced sugar and the customs duty on foreign sugar. It is right to include this £10 million, for half the imports come from non-Empire sources despite the preference on Empire sugar, so that if the home industry were not there the gap would be filled by imports paying the full rate.

Over these ten years both the growers and the factories had increased their efficiency. Nevertheless the industry was little nearer standing on its own feet than in 1924. For over this period great technical improvements had been made —notably the discovery in Java of a very prolific type of cane—in the production of cane sugar. For a number of years hardly any beet sugar, wherever grown, has been able to compete without a subsidy against the cheap cane sugar from the tropics. One result of this technical progress has been a considerable fall in the world price of sugar and a marked increase in its consumption.

In 1935 the Greene Committee, which had been set up by the government in the previous year to review the question, published its report. Two of the three members were in favor of abolishing the subsidy altogether. But the Government followed the advice of the third member to continue the subsidy. It passed the Sugar Industry Reorganization Act of 1935. This continued the subsidy but limited the amount of home-produced sugar to a maximum of 560,000 tons a year, the estimated product of 375,000 acres. It amalgamated the sugar factories into the British Sugar Corporation and limited its profits. It set up a permanent Sugar Commission which determines the rate of subsidy. This is fixed in such a way as to call forth rather less than 560,000 tons of sugar a year. During recent years the subsidy and the revenue abatement together have cost some 5 or 6 million pounds a year. The amount of home-grown sugar has been around 450,000 to 500,000 tons and of retained imported sugar around 1.5 or 1.6 million tons. Since 1928 there has been a protective duty on sugar-refining and over 300,000 tons of refined sugar are exported from Great Britain. The large refineries are more efficient at refining than the sugar beet factories, but to protect the latter an industrial agreement was negotiated giving them the right to refine about a quarter of the total sugar requirements of the country. They have not always fully used their quota: when the margin on refining has been small they have sold part of their quotas (at about 1s.4d. per cwt.) to the large refineries.

5. WHEAT

The Wheat Act of 1932 was passed at a time when the price of wheat had fallen greatly. It was feared that unless something was done to help wheat farmers some of the land normally under wheat would be put down to grass or would go out of cultivation altogether. There was also a desire to maintain and increase employment; a vague belief, quite unfounded, that wheat was in some sense the backbone of agriculture; and a feeling that it was unwise to let Great Britain become almost entirely dependent on imports from overseas. At the time, some 85 per cent of her wheat was imported. The acreage under wheat had been tending to shrink ever since the war. In 1931 it was only 1.25 million acres, the lowest recorded.

The Act set up a Wheat Fund from which "deficiency payments" are made in order to bring the price received by wheat farmers up to 10s. per cwt. (equal to 45s. a quarter), which is a little below the average price over the ten years before the Act. But a limit was placed on the subsidy. If the total sales[2] exceeded 27 million cwts., the amount of the subsidy would be sufficient only to bring the price up to 10s. on 27 million cwts. But in any event the whole subsidy was to be pooled evenly; every cwt. of wheat sold by a registered grower would receive the same deficiency payment, or subsidy, as every other. In 1937 the limit was increased from 27 to 36 million cwts.

The subsidy is not paid by the government out of general revenue and therefore does not appear in the budget. It is paid out of the proceeds of a "processing tax" levied on millers and known as a "quota payment." Every sack of flour milled in Great Britain pays this levy, which (together with a similar levy on the small amount of flour imported) constitutes the income of the Wheat Fund. Flour exported or sold to ships for stores receives a rebate. There is a Wheat Commission which determines what the average

---

[2] Some wheat is used by the growers and not sold to millers. This wheat receives no subsidy.

price actually realized for British wheat has been, what was the total volume of sales of British wheat, and what, therefore, must be the deficiency payment per cwt., and which can adjust the levy on flour from time to time in order that the receipts of the fund shall cover its payments.

This scheme has led to a marked expansion of wheat growing. Although the market price during recent years has averaged only about 7s.6d. per cwt., the acreage under wheat has increased from 1.25 million acres in 1931 to over 1.80 million acres,[3] and the output (for sale) from 20 to 30 million cwts. The total subsidy was £4.5 million in 1932-33, £7.2 million in 1933-34, £6.8 million in 1934-35, £5.6 million in 1935-36, and £1.3 million in 1936-37. Clearly the burden is borne, except in so far as part of it falls on wheat growers overseas, by British consumers of flour and bread or other products embodying flour. But the burden is not very obvious. In the first place, the proportion of wheat consumed which is grown at home and therefore gets the subsidy is less than 25 per cent. In the second place, the subsidy falls as the price of wheat rises. When it rises above 10s. per cwt. no subsidy is paid. The Wheat Commission points out[4] that when the quota payment was at its highest level (4s.3d. per 28 lb. sack of flour), in 1933-34 and 1934-35, the price of bread was only 7½d. to 7¾d. per 4 lb. loaf and when in 1936-37, owing to high wheat prices, the quota was entirely suspended the price of bread rose to 9d. Nevertheless the levy-subsidy (provided that wheat is below 10s. per cwt., so that the scheme is in operation) does act as a brake upon falling prices and does make the price

[3] The increase took place during 1932-34. In 1934 the acreage under wheat was 1.87 million.
[4] 1938 Report, p. 130.

of bread a little higher, at any given time, than it otherwise would be.

6. SHIPPING AND SHIPBUILDING

In 1934 the North Atlantic Shipping Act was passed. This authorized the Treasury to make advances up to £9.5 million for the construction of one or more large vessels for the North Atlantic service and for the provision of working capital. The object was to get the Cunard Company to continue with the construction of the liner afterwards named the *Queen Mary*. Work on the liner had been abandoned owing to the fall in passenger traffic across the Atlantic. Half the workers in shipbuilding and 30 per cent of those in shipping were unemployed. The main motive of the government was to reduce unemployment.

The subsidy to the company took the form of a loan at a much lower rate of interest than they would have had to pay on the market. In return, the company agreed to merge their North Atlantic business with the Oceanic Steam Navigation Company. The government hoped that this would reduce competition and benefit both the companies.

It is interesting, although perhaps irrelevant, to note that the government protected its interests as a first mortgagee towards the close of 1934. A British concern was going to buy the ships of the Red Star Line from the International Mercantile Marine of New Jersey in order to run a "ferry service" at cut prices across the Atlantic. The Treasury expressed its disapproval and this stopped the deal.

The British Shipping (Assistance) Act of 1935 granted two separate subsidies: the tramp shipping subsidy and the "scrap and build" scheme.

The main object of the former seems to have been to

raise freight rates, which at the time were at only 77 per cent of their 1929 level, by restricting competition for freight among tramps. The scheme did not apply to passenger ships or tankers (already covered by an international cartel arrangement which compensated owners for idle tonnage) or to ships with refrigerator space. A committee was set up which gave a kind of quota to each tramp owner by advising him what proportion of his tonnage (or, rather, ton-days) he should allow to be occupied. He received a subsidy only on that quota. The total amount of the subsidy was not to exceed £2 million and was granted for one year. The subsidy was continued, again with a maximum of £2 million, for another year. The full amount was paid out in both years. It was again extended in 1937 but nothing was paid out as freight rates were well above the 1929 level and the scheme contained a proviso that the subsidy should taper off to zero as freight rates rose above 92 per cent of the 1929 level.

The "scrap and build" scheme was for making loans up to a maximum of £10 million to shipowners for building new ships or modernizing old ones. Proposals for advances had to contain a promise to scrap two tons for every one ton of new building or to scrap one ton for every ton modernized. Foreign ships could be purchased for scrapping as well as British. Only £3.5 million was actually advanced under this scheme, which came to an end in February 1937, by which time the whole situation had changed and instead of a surplus of shipping there was a shortage.

By the end of 1938 British shipping was again depressed and the government in March 1939 put forward a new series of proposals to aid it. Briefly, these included up to £2.75 million a year for tramps, up to £500,000 a year for owners placing new orders for tramps or cargo liners, up

to £2 million for purchasing vessels which would otherwise be sold abroad for breaking up but which could serve
as British reserve, and loans on favorable terms up to £10
million to shipowners for the building of tramps and cargo
liners.

These proposals were defended on the grounds that
much foreign competition was subsidized and that it was
vital for Great Britain to have sufficient shipping in time
of war.

7. Cinematograph Films

The Cinematograph Films Act of 1928 established two
quotas, one for "renters," who hire out, or "rent," films
to exhibitors, and one for exhibitors. A minimum percentage of the films rented by any renter during a "quota
period" had to be British. Similarly a minimum percentage
of those exhibited by any exhibitor had to be British.
Offenders were subject to heavy fines. The quotas were
laid down for ten years ahead and increased as time went
on. The quotas were further separated into long films, of
over 3,000 feet, and short films.

Thus, in addition to the $33\frac{1}{3}$ per cent duty on imported films, an increasing share of the home market was
reserved for British films. Under this stimulus there was a
gradual increase in their output, which was usually well
above the quota minimum. But the number of films imported also increased year by year owing to the rapid
growth of the cinema habit.

One somewhat unfortunate consequence of this scheme
was that a number of British films of little merit were produced cheaply to enable renters and exhibitors to comply
with the quota requirements. The Act of 1938 aimed at
preventing this. In order to count as a quota film a picture

must be proved to have cost at least £7,500 and £1 a foot in labor costs. This condition, however, may be relaxed if the Board of Trade considers that a film has special entertainment value. On this matter the Board must consult the Cinematograph Films Council, consisting of twenty-one persons appointed by the Board, eleven being independent persons and the others representing different interests of the trade.

The Act of 1938 reduced the renters' quota, which was then 20 per cent, to 15 per cent for both long and short films. The quota was to rise over the next ten years by prescribed stages to 30 per cent for long films and 25 per cent for short films. The exhibitors' quota was fixed at 12½ per cent for both long and short films, and was to rise to 25 per cent for long and 22½ per cent for short.

An inducement was given to British companies to produce expensive films suitable for export. A film which costs at least £22,500 and £3 a foot in labor costs may count as double its length for quota purposes, and one which costs at least £37,500 and £5 a foot in labor costs may count as treble its length. This Act has so far led to a considerable fall in the number of British films produced but to a rise in the number of first-class films likely to find a market overseas.

8. DYESTUFFS

The Dyestuffs (Import Regulation) Act of 1920 was originally passed for ten years but it was renewed from time to time until 1934, when it received slight amendments and was made permanent. It prohibits the import of synthetic organic dyestuffs, at any stage of manufacture, except under license from the Board of Trade. A license may be granted either for particular consignments or for particular classes of dyestuffs. The Board of Trade are advised in this matter by a committee of eleven persons, three independent, five from the trades using dyestuffs, and three representing home manufacturers. If the committee finds that the goods to which the application refers are wholly manufactured in one of the Dominions the Board cannot refuse a license. In other cases it may act as it thinks fit.

The main motive behind this prohibition is strategic. The war of 1914-18 showed that Great Britain relied on imports, mainly from Germany, for such dyestuffs. But of course the same can be said of certain key industry and other duties, such as those on optical glass. The result has been to promote the production of dyestuffs in Great Britain although costs of production are considerably higher than in Germany.

9. Bacon and Hams

In November 1932 voluntary agreements were made with eleven foreign countries to restrict their exports of bacon and ham to the United Kingdom. The agreements were for the period November 1932 to September 1933. Total imports from these countries were to be 20 per cent less than in the corresponding period of the previous year, when imports had been unusually large. Each country was alloted a certain percentage of the total: for example, 61.1 per cent to Denmark and 6.4 per cent to the United States. In fact, imports over this period were 2 per cent greater than allocations.

Owing to a considerable increase in the British output of bacon, it was decided to reduce imports still further. The eleven countries agreed to a reduction of 11 per cent but when a further reduction of 16 per cent was requested

Denmark objected. Compulsion was therefore introduced by the Bacon (Import Regulation) Order of November 1933, issued under the Agricultural Marketing Act. This order prohibited the import of bacon and ham, except under license, from any foreign country which sent more than 400 cwts. a week to the United Kingdom.

As bacon is almost the leading British import commodity in value, we give below a table showing imports from 1932 onwards. It will be seen that total imports have fallen from some 12 million cwts. to 7½ million cwts. Imports from foreign countries have been cut down by more than half. This has particularly hit Denmark, which had specialized in supplying bacon to the British breakfast and obtained a considerable part of her national income from that source. But Denmark, and other foreign suppliers, have not suffered as much as they might have done in that the limitation is administered by export licenses issued to the governments of the exporting countries and almost the whole of the price difference due to the restriction of imports has gone to the foreign suppliers. They have received around £1 a cwt. more than the price ruling in their own countries.

It will be noted from the table that imports from Canada have greatly increased. No restrictions have been imposed on Empire countries, but it was agreed with Canada in 1932 that she could export up to 2,500,000 cwts. As her exports to Great Britain had averaged 201,000 cwts. in 1929-31, this gave rise to the joke that an extra nought had got in by mistake. But imports from Canada rose so rapidly that in 1936 a new agreement was made which gave the United Kingdom the right, not yet exercised, to restrict imports from Canada if they were "expanding at an abnormal rate" towards the agreed maximum of 2,500,000 cwts.

After import regulations had been working for some

UNITED KINGDOM—IMPORTS OF BACON AND HAMS

	Av. 1929-31		1932		1933		1934		1935		1936		1937		1938	
	cwts. '000	per cent	cwts. '000	per cent	cwts. '000	per cent	cwts. '000	per cent	cwts. '000	per cent	cwts. '000	per cent	cwts. '000	per cent	cwts. '000	per cent
TOTAL............	10,489	100.0	12,192	100.0	9,983	100.0	8,327	100.0	7,604	100.0	7,241	100.0	7,600	100.0	7,533	100.0
From British countries....	595	5.7	541	4.4	911	9.2	1,457	17.5	1,589	20.9	1,898	26.3	2,227	29.3	2,060	27.3
Of which																
Canada..........	201	2.0	324	2.6	687	6.8	1,075	12.9	1,110	14.6	1,370	18.9	1,702	22.4	1,508	20.0
Eire...........	391	3.7	215	1.8	225	2.4	380	4.6	479	6.3	528	7.5	525	6.9	552	7.3
From Foreign countries...	9,394	94.3	11,651	95.6	9,042	90.8	6,870	82.5	6,015	79.1	5,343	73.8	5,373	70.7	5,473	72.7
Of which																
Denmark........	6,147	58.6	7,677	63.0	5,524	55.5	4,288	51.5	3,827	50.3	3,374	46.6	3,429	45.0	3,389	45.0
U.S.A...........	1,188	11.3	529	4.3	627	6.3	517	6.2	439	5.8	350	4.8	319	4.2	438	5.8
Netherlands......	916	8.7	977	8.0	873	8.8	608	7.3	500	6.7	485	6.7	481	6.3	314	6.8
Poland..........	680	6.5	1,253	10.3	858	8.6	497	6.0	452	5.9	421	5.8	445	5.9	457	6.1
Sweden.........	502	4.8	424	3.5	403	4.0	297	3.6	257	3.4	242	3.3	250	3.3	251	3.3
Lithuania........	147	1.4	512	4.2	416	4.2	252	3.0	163	2.2	194	2.7	188	2.5	190	2.5

time it was found that unusually large amounts of bacon were coming in from some countries whose exports had previously been less than 400 cwts. a week and were therefore not restricted. It was believed, for example, that Danish pigs were being sent to Germany to be cured and that in this way Danish bacon was escaping the quota restriction by coming in through Germany. In 1935 an order was made to stop this loophole by prohibiting the import of any bacon produced in a foreign country from pigs bred in any other foreign country.

Until 1938, the aim of the scheme was to stabilize the total British consumption of bacon at 10,670,000 cwts. a year. The quotas allotted to foreign countries depended on the expected British output and the expected imports from the Empire. An increase in either led to a cutting down of foreign imports.

One result has been a large increase in the number of pigs in Great Britain and in the amount of bacon cured in Great Britain, although the scheme has not been altogether successful because the pork market was left unregulated. The price of Wiltshire bacon has risen from 86s. 6d. per cwt. in 1932 to 101s. in 1937, but the price of Danish bacon has risen more: from 61s. 6d. to 99s. 6d. The price of pigs, first quality baconers, has risen from 10s. 4d. to 13s. 2d.

10. MEAT

Great Britain imports over half her meat. The imports are chilled or frozen and are consumed mainly by the poorer classes. Naturally consumers prefer fresh meat if they can afford it, and it commands a higher price. Nevertheless British meat and imported meat are substitutes for one another and if abundant and cheap supplies from abroad are available this tends to keep down the price of British meat. The live-stock output of Great Britain, including pigs and poultry, represents about a third of the total value of all agricultural products. Hence restrictions on the import of meat were imposed primarily in order to help the home live-stock industry, which was in a state of depression. Another object, however, was to give Dominion producers a bigger share of the British market at the expense of foreign suppliers.

Compulsory restrictions on imports from foreign countries date from the Ottawa Agreements Act. The twelve months from July 1931 to June 1932, known as the "Ottawa year," were taken as a basis and foreign imports were restricted to a percentage of what they were in that year.

The restrictions on *chilled beef* were not severe, for the Dominions exported very little chilled beef before 1933 and the chief foreign supplier, the Argentine, is a large purchaser of British goods and a country in which much British capital is invested. A trade agreement with the Argentine provided that the quantity imported should not be reduced below 90 per cent of the Ottawa year level unless similar reductions were imposed on the Dominions also. In December 1936 a new agreement was signed by which the Argentine was guaranteed a minimum quantity and also a minimum proportion of foreign imports, but her quota was reduced a little. The net result has been that since January 1, 1933, when compulsory regulation began, foreign imports have been fairly stable at just over 8 million cwts. a year, which is about 10 per cent below the previous level. Imports from the Empire, previously quite small, have increased until they now exceed 900,000 cwts. a year. They come mainly from Australia and New Zealand, who have improved their technique of chilling beef. Empire imports were regulated by voluntary agreement in 1935.

Restrictions on *frozen beef* were more severe because a substantial proportion came from the Empire, mainly from New Zealand and Australia. Hence foreign imports were compulsorily cut down, from January 1, 1933, on a scale agreed upon at Ottawa. It began at 90 per cent of Ottawa year imports and fell by a further 5 per cent each quarter to 65 per cent in the second quarter of 1934. It remained at this level until July 1937, when an increase of 20 per cent was permitted. Empire suppliers agreed to do their best to prevent their exports to Great Britain from exceeding those of the Ottawa year by more than 10 per cent, but in fact they have been considerably larger than that. The 1936 trade agreement with the Argentine guaranteed her a minimum quantity of 124,600 cwts. a year during 1937-38.

Empire countries, notably New Zealand and to a less extent Australia, are important suppliers of *frozen mutton and lamb*. The Empire supplied two-thirds of British imports in 1929-31. Hence restrictions on foreign imports have been severe. The same scale was applied to them as to frozen beef, and the level of 65 per cent of the Ottawa year quantity, reached in the middle of 1934, has remained in force ever since. The Empire now supplies four-fifths of total imports.

Imports of *frozen and chilled pork* from foreign countries have been prohibited since 1935 except under license. Allocations are made quarterly and the quotas have remained stable at the average 1932-34 level, which is well below the pre-Ottawa level as there was voluntary restriction before 1935. Australia, New Zealand, and Canada made voluntary agreements to limit their exports. In 1932-34 imports from these countries averaged 361,000

cwts. a year. The voluntary quota agreed upon was 363,-
300 for 1935, 487,400 for 1936, and 465,000 for 1937. Actual imports were considerably higher, reaching 834,000 in
1937.

11. Potatoes

In November 1934 an order was made prohibiting the
importation of potatoes from foreign countries except
under license. This applies both to the main crop and to
earlies. The potato crop is very variable and the price of
potatoes tends to fluctuate a good deal. The object of the
restriction is to limit imports to the quantity by which
British output falls short of normal consumption. It might
be thought that this would stabilize prices, but in fact in
1936 and 1937 they were nearly double the prices of
1933-34, which were abnormally low. The total quantity
of permitted foreign imports is fixed periodically. No allocations are made between countries. Licenses are issued
to importers up to the total fixed and they are free to buy
where they please.

12. Sea-Fish

Import quotas for sea-fish were imposed under the Sea-
Fishing Industry Act of 1933. This Act also attempted to
limit the supply of British fish by enforcing a certain size
of mesh for the nets, forbidding the sale of fish below a
minimum size, and prohibiting the landing of fish, caught
in Northern waters, during certain periods. Fish are thrown
back into the sea in the hope that this will help the fishing
industry. Actually, largely owing to bigger landings of cod
from distant waters, the price of wet fish has tended to fall
during recent years.

Annual import quotas have been allotted to each of the

supplying countries. For quota purposes, cod, haddock, hake, plaice, soles, dabs, and herrings are lumped together, but Belgium, France, Germany, and Norway have separate quotas for herrings. In 1936 wet-salted split codfish were taken out of the quota and kippered herrings were put in. The total quota, for all the countries taken together, has remained stable at just below 2½ million cwts., about 10 per cent below the 1930-32 level. In fact, for one reason or another, most countries have not supplied their full quota. Germany, with a quota of 660,000 cwts., plus 27,000 cwts. for herrings, landed only 86,000 cwts. in 1937, and total landings were only 1,414,000 cwts. The scheme is administered like the bacon scheme in that licenses are sent to the governments of the supplying countries.

On balance, Great Britain is a considerable exporter of fish, notably herrings. Foreign landings in Great Britain are only a small part of total landings. Nevertheless restrictions on imports do safeguard the home market for British fishers, although restrictions have been little needed during recent years.

13. STEEL

In July 1935 an agreement was concluded between the British Iron and Steel Federation and the International Steel Cartel, consisting of Belgium, France, Germany, and Luxembourg. As a result, Section 6 of the Finance Act of 1936 provided for a system of licensing on most iron and steel products. This came into operation in November 1936. The scheme provides "tariff quotas." Each supplying country can provide a certain quota of each product at a low rate of duty. The quotas for the four cartel countries, who are the chief suppliers, were laid down in the agreement named above. For any other country the quota ton-

nage is that imported from that country in 1934. By special
arrangement between the Federation and the Cartel, a
tonnage in excess of the quota (but not greater than the
1934 imports from that country) may be imported under
license from each of the four countries. The quota certificates are issued by organizations in the supplying countries.

Duties on licensed imports were at first fixed at 20 per
cent, but the greatly increased demand for steel and the
resulting shortage of "semis" caused them to be reduced
to 10 per cent in March 1937 and to 2½ per cent in July.
Duties on unlicensed imports were 20 to 33⅓ per cent
ad valorem with higher specific duties on the cheaper products—for example, £2 per ton on blooms, billets, slabs
and bars, not over £4 per ton in value and £3 per ton on
plates and sheets not over £7 per ton in value.

CHAPTER IV

IMPERIAL PREFERENCE

1. THE BRITISH EMPIRE

THE BRITISH EMPIRE may be divided into four groups, which we shall call briefly Great Britain, the Dominions, the Colonies, and the Mandated Territories.

The United Kingdom of Great Britain and Northern Ireland imports more than all the rest of the Empire put together. Over one-sixth of all the goods which enter into international trade are sold to Great Britain. She buys mainly foodstuffs and raw materials and is therefore far and away the biggest single market for most of the products of her Empire. Of course there are exceptions. In particular, most of the rubber and tin of Malaya goes to the United States. But for all the Dominions the largest single customer is Great Britain. This applies even to Canada, with the great market of the United States next door to her.

Great Britain always has a large surplus of imports over exports. For example, in 1937 her imports were £1,029 million and her exports and re-exports only £597 million. This import surplus represents interest on her overseas investments, payments to her for shipping and insurance services, and so forth. In terms of the crude and short-sighted notions which have again become fashionable in recent years, she could complain to each of her Dominions that it buys less from her than she buys from it, and could try to use this as an argument for obtaining "better" treatment. But of course the sensible answer would be that if she chose to give up the interest and profits on her overseas investments, over half of which are in the Empire, most of her import surplus would disappear. How can the Dominions pay their interest if Great Britain wants to export as much as she imports? Her import surplus is, in fact, a sign of prosperity and not something to complain about.

We shall use the term "Dominions" to cover Eire, Canada, Newfoundland, Australia, New Zealand, the Union of South Africa, Southern Rhodesia, British India, and Burma. British India and Burma were united until 1937. They have not yet full dominion status, but we include them with the others because they are free to pursue whatever tariff policy they please. Since 1930, when the Finance Member of the Indian Central Government, acting on the Indian Tariff Commission's recommendation, accepted duties of 15 per cent on British and 20 per cent on foreign imports of cotton goods, India has been free in practice to impose whatever tariffs she pleases. All these countries can and do impose duties upon British goods. The conference at Ottawa was between Great Britain and these countries, and in August 1932 she concluded separate Agreements, known as Ottawa Agreements, with each of them except Eire, with whom she was conducting a trade war.

It is more difficult to generalize about the Colonies and Protectorates. The extent to which they are permitted to frame their own tariffs varies a good deal, but if Great Britain holds strong views on any point there is no doubt that any Colony will do as the British Government "invites" it to do. Some members of this group had protective tariffs before 1931.[1] For example, most of the West Indies, Fiji, and British North Borneo had fairly substantial duties.

[1] See U.S. Senate Document No. 31 of 71st Congress, 1929.

But most of the Colonies and Protectorates were on the whole free trade, with customs duties for revenue only. They were not represented at Ottawa, but since Great Britain turned to protection their goods have enjoyed the same privileges in the British market as those of the Dominions. The East African colonies and Tanganyika are bound by the Congo Basin Treaty to maintain the open door, and the *entrepôt* trade of Gibraltar, Aden, and Hong-Kong is too valuable for them to indulge in protection. The others were "invited" shortly before the Ottawa Conference to give preference to Empire products. Some did so already: for example, the most common rates of duty in Fiji were 20 per cent on British goods and 35 per cent on foreign; Trinidad and Tobago gave a preference equal to half the general duty on nearly all Empire products, which was equal to 10¾ per cent ad valorem on most manufactures; and British North Borneo gave Great Britain a preference of about 25 per cent on certain goods. But the response to the "invitation" meant a general increase in duties upon foreign goods, with a rebate, varying between Colonies from one-sixth to two-thirds of the total duty, upon Empire products. This was not always done with the full consent of the Colony; in Ceylon, for example, the legislative assembly voted against it.

In May 1934 the Colonies, with the exceptions noted above, applied quotas to imports of foreign textiles. These were aimed mainly at Japanese products, and therefore the basis was generally the period from 1927 to 1931, before imports from Japan began to increase rapidly. In the West African colonies quotas were imposed against Japan alone.

The Mandated Territories and Territories under condominium do not necessarily enjoy the same privileges as the Colonies. Thus it is a grievance of Palestine that her oranges are not admitted freely into the British market.

A Dominion or a Colony need not treat all Empire countries alike. Thus, before the depression Canada made a trade agreement with Australia giving preference to her mutton and dairy produce in exchange for Australian preferences on her timber, pulp, paper, and certain manufactures, including automobiles, but she scrapped a similar agreement which she had made with New Zealand because her farmers resented the competition of New Zealand butter and cheese. Again, in 1920 Canada made a trade agreement, renewed in 1925, with the West Indies by which the latter agreed to grant preferences (varying from 50 per cent in Trinidad to 25 per cent in Jamaica) upon imports from Canada in return for an undertaking by Canada that her duties on West Indian goods (other than tobacco and spirits) should not be more than half those charged on foreign goods.

Great Britain maintains the view that preferences granted by herself or a Dominion or Colony to other parts of the Empire need not be extended to foreign countries although these may have by treaty the right to most-favored-nation treatment. A Dominion is a separate country for purposes of voting in the League of Nations but for tariff purposes the British Empire is a mystic unity confronting the rest of the world. At the same time, Great Britain claims that any tariff concession made by a foreign country with whom she enjoys most-favored-nation status must be extended to her also. This attitude of hers prevented Belgium and Holland from making the mutual reductions in tariffs which they agreed upon at the Ouchy Convention in 1932. They wanted to form a low tariff group, and were willing to make similar concessions to any country which cared to join them. But Great Britain insisted that any concession made, for example, by Belgium (with whom she had most-favored-nation status) had to be extended to her although she made no new concessions to Belgium. The Ottawa Conference upheld this attitude, concluding that preferences granted between members of the Empire need not be generalized to foreign countries enjoying most-favored-nation treatment but that concessions made by members of a regional group, such as the Oslo Powers or the Danubian States, to one another must be generalized to countries enjoying most-favored-nation privileges.

Some indication of the relative importance to world trade of the four groups into which we have divided the British Empire is given by the values of their exports of domestic produce. In 1937 these were: Great Britain £522 million, Dominions £737 million, Colonies £203 million, and Mandated Territories £25 million. These figures include, as they should, exports of gold by gold-producing countries: £83 million for South Africa, £27 million for Canada, £12 million for Australia, £6 million for Southern Rhodesia, and £4 million for the Gold Coast.

In 1929, 74.3 per cent of the foreign trade of the British Empire was with foreign countries and 25.7 per cent was inter-imperial trade. By 1937 the former percentage had decreased to 68.6. This, however, somewhat exaggerates the fall, as Hong-Kong trade is not included in the 1929 figures and the separation of Burma from India apparently increased inter-imperial trade. The true figure is 69.9 per cent. Even so, this is a quite considerable change. It was due at least in part to the extension of imperial preference after the Ottawa Conference.

2. The Concept of Imperial Preference

It has often been suggested that the British Empire, with a total area of over 12 million square miles, a total population of some 500 million, and a great variety of natural resources, could somehow benefit by binding itself more closely together with economic ties. Thus Mr. Joseph Chamberlain in 1903 declared that "here we have an Empire which with decent organization and consolidation might be absolutely self-sustaining. Nothing of the kind has ever been known before. There is no article of food, there is no raw material of your trade, there is no necessity of your lives, no luxury of your existence which cannot be produced somewhere or other in the British Empire if the British Empire holds together and if we who have inherited it are worthy of our opportunities."

In fact, the British Empire could not be self-supporting. It is short, for example, of petroleum and cotton. But let us leave that on one side. Our purpose is to discuss the possible meanings of imperial preference.

The ideal at which Mr. Chamberlain was aiming was, as he said in 1896, "a true Zollverein for the Empire," "free trade established throughout the Empire." He thought this would be "the greatest advance that free trade has ever made since it was first advocated by Mr. Cobden." But he admitted that it would involve the imposition of duties against foreign countries. It would have put a ring fence of tariffs round the Empire. It would have meant that Great Britain, the most important market of the world, would turn from free trade to protection. How exactly this would have been a great advance for free trade is not clear. If the Empire was going to trade more with itself it would have to trade less with the rest of the world. It was not obvious, nor is it today, how the Empire would gain if, for example, Malaya sold less rubber to the United States or Australia less wool to Japan, or if England, in order to encourage cotton growing in the Empire, deprived its own cotton industry, to a greater or less extent, of cheap American cotton.

Nevertheless this rather confused notion of Empire free trade continued to exert a powerful influence, and as recently as the decade after the world war it was loudly advocated by the big newspaper owners, Lord Beaverbrook and Lord Rothermere. Apart from its merits or defects, there are great practical difficulties in the way of an Empire customs union. The customs unions which have hitherto been formed, such as the German Zollverein, or the United States, or Australia, have been formed by the union of contiguous states, whereas the British Empire sprawls across the globe. Moreover, in every such union the central government is supreme in customs matters. The Dominions, however, have acquired complete self-government and India and other territories are moving towards that goal. For them to surrender an important part of their sovereignty would probably be distasteful to them. Again, Empire free trade would mean a permanent fall in their revenues from customs duties and the gap would probably be filled largely by new or increased excise duties. This would raise difficult administrative problems, for consumption habits are different in different parts of the Empire and there would be problems of excise drawbacks and allowances for exports from one Empire country to another. But the biggest obstacle of all to Empire free trade is the determination of the Dominions, or rather of most of them, to safeguard their own manufacturing industries. These are now far more important than they were forty years ago. They are also protected by much higher duties, even against British goods. In most cases by far the most powerful competitor which Dominion manufacturers have to face is Great Britain. There is no hope whatever that the Dominions would sacrifice their manufacturing industries, or rather that part of them which can survive only under protection, by permitting the free entry of British goods. The prospects of Empire free trade were poor enough in Mr. Chamberlain's time; when Lords Beaverbrook and Rothermere were sponsoring the idea, they were quite hopeless.

Hence for a long time advocates of imperial preference have had in mind not an Empire customs union but preferential treatment by Empire countries for Empire products. This implies duties upon foreign goods in order that similar Empire goods shall come in at a lower duty or free. Until 1931, the great obstacle to this was that Great Britain remained free trade. The Dominions could grant reduced duties on British products, but Great Britain herself admitted most goods free and could therefore give preference to Empire products only on a few goods such as sugar and tobacco. It is true that she listed most Dominion and colonial loans as trustee securities, thereby enabling the Empire to borrow from her somewhat more cheaply: according to one estimate, on the average about one-half per cent more cheaply. It is true that she bore the whole cost of the British Navy. But this was not enough for the advocates of closer economic union between the mother country and the Dominions. They paid no heed to the warning that bargaining and wrangling over tariff concessions might lead to some ill-feeling instead of promoting harmony. They wanted a wide range of concessions on both sides and this became possible only when Great Britain embraced protection.

The technical meaning of "preference" is usually the margin between the duty on foreign goods and the duty on British goods. Thus Australia charges 65 per cent as her general tariff on apparel but only 45 per cent on apparel from Great Britain. She is said to give Great Britain a preference of 20 per cent on apparel. Some countries, for example Canada, have a three-decker tariff. The highest duties constitute the general tariff, then comes the intermediate or most-favored-nation tariff, and below that is the British preferential tariff. If, as is now[2] the case with Canada, most of her imports of manufactured products of a kind exported by Great Britain come from countries to whom she gives most-favored-nation treatment, in so far as they come from foreign countries and not from Great Britain, the preference to Great Britain is the margin by which the intermediate tariff exceeds the British tariff.

It was calculated, some years before Ottawa, that the preferences granted to Great Britain by the Dominions were worth £14 million a year whereas those granted by Great Britain to the Dominions were worth only £2 million a year, most of which went to Australia. Such figures represent the total amount of extra duty which these products would have paid if the same quantities had entered but had paid the full rate of duty instead of the preferential rate. They therefore had little meaning. It is impossible to say how much any given Empire import would have been reduced had it been compelled to pay the full duty or to what extent the prices received by ex-

[2] Since her agreement with the United States of November 15, 1935, which was superseded by the agreement of November 17, 1938.

porters would have changed had less been sold to the Empire.

Most British economists were slightly annoyed by these calculations. They pointed out that British manufacturers would be in a much better position if the Dominions allowed all manufactured goods to enter free and did not in effect reserve a large part of their home market for the products of their own protected industries, some of which could doubtless stand on their own feet if compelled to do so without the support of a tariff but others of which could not. They said that a Dominion preference which really consisted of a fairly high duty on British goods and a still higher one on foreign goods was like giving two blows to foreign products and one to British, and calling this a British preference. They claimed that Great Britain, by permitting free entry for all, treated the Dominions better than they treated her. But of course such arguments were seldom advanced by politicians, because if the Dominions had taken offense and charged the full duty on British goods, British exporters would have been still worse off. And so long as Great Britain was determined to remain free trade there was nothing which she could use as a bargaining weapon against the Dominions. They knew very well that she would continue to maintain her fleet in order to protect her trade, and that her fleet would incidentally protect them, whatever tariff policy they followed, and that in any event Great Britain would wish them to be prosperous because she had so much capital invested in them. Only when Great Britain swung over to protection did she acquire a "big stick" to flourish.

One very important consideration affecting the value of the preference often escapes notice. The Empire as a whole produces more than it consumes of a number of its main products. Hence the Empire as a whole exports more of them than it imports: it has an "export surplus" of these products. It has been argued that a preference on such products would really be without any value at all. Take, for example, wheat. The Dominions and India export more wheat than Great Britain and other Empire countries import. What, then, will happen when Great Britain grants a preference on Empire wheat? Suppose that, as a result of the preference, all her imports come from Empire sources, foreign wheat being completely shut out by the duty upon it. There will still be a substantial quantity of Empire wheat which must find a market in foreign countries. It will have to be sold in foreign countries at the same price as foreign wheat. But will Dominion producers be content to accept a lower price for the wheat they sell in foreign countries, in competition with foreign wheat shut out from the British market, than other Dominion producers are getting on the wheat which they sell to Great Britain? Surely not. So long as the British price of Empire wheat is above the foreign price, all Empire wheat will tend to seek a market in Great Britain rather than elsewhere, until its price in Great Britain is forced down to the same level as its price in foreign countries, and Empire producers therefore have nothing to gain by selling within the Empire rather than outside it. Such a state of affairs would mean that the value of the British preference on Empire wheat was zero. Indeed, in so far as it encouraged Empire producers, in the false hope of getting a more remunerative price, to expand their production, its value would be negative, for it would tend to bring about a fall in the world price of wheat.

This reasoning assumes that Empire producers would compete freely against one another. If they chose to organize themselves into an Empire wheat monopoly, they could, it is true, obtain some benefit from the British preference. They could do this by restricting the quantity which they sold to Great Britain to the amount which Great Britain would import at a price exceeding the world price by slightly less than the British duty on foreign wheat. The rest of their wheat would be sold for whatever price they could get in foreign markets. But clearly the British public would not consent to be exploited in this way by the Dominions. As soon as it became known that the Dominions were charging a higher price to Great Britain and were dumping their surplus in foreign countries at lower prices, there would be an indignant outcry from British consumers. Hence this possibility was ruled out. At Ottawa, Great Britain tried to make this clear by declaring that preference would be given to Dominion wheat and certain other products of which the Empire had an export surplus only so long as the Dominions supplied adequate quantities at prices which were not above the world level.

In fact, the argument as we have stated it above goes rather too far. Wheat, for example, is not a homogeneous commodity. There are many varieties and grades. The British public has acquired a taste for a certain type of bread, and millers were therefore averse from making too marked a change in the proportions of different types of wheat which they used. Thus a considerable amount of Argentine wheat continued to enter Great Britain after a duty had been imposed upon it. This means that the British preference was of some value to Dominion producers, although of much less value than might be supposed at the first blush. Again, Great Britain exports considerably more cotton piece goods, for example, than the

Empire imports, but nobody with experience in the cotton trade would deny that the preference given to her by the Dominions and India are of value, mainly for the reason stated above, although their value is often exaggerated. An interesting example of Empire producers being disappointed at the result of the British preference is that of lead. The Empire as a whole has an export surplus of lead. Great Britain had therefore inserted in some of the Ottawa agreements a clause providing that Great Britain could remove the general ad valorem duty on lead if at any time the Empire producers were unable or unwilling to offer their metal on first sale in the United Kingdom at prices not exceeding world prices and in quantities sufficient to supply the requirements of United Kingdom consumers. Empire producers nevertheless could not understand why foreign lead, which was subject to 10 per cent duty, obtained more or less the same price as Empire lead in the London market. They were also displeased because the London price of lead had actually fallen from £18 1s.6d. in 1930 and £11 18s.3d. in 1932 to £10 18s.8d. in 1934. They therefore complained and the matter was investigated by the Import Duties Advisory Committee.[3] Although the report of this committee does not analyze the situation very clearly, it is plain that the root of the difficulty was that the Empire had an export surplus of lead. As the committee pointed out, "almost all the [British] demand was met from Empire sources" and some Empire sales had to be made to foreign countries: for example, Canada sold substantial quantities to Japan. This meant that the British preference on lead was almost useless to Empire producers and was likely to remain so. Much the

[3] Cmd. 4983 of 1935.

same applies to zinc, which was considered by the committee at the same time.

Another consideration which affects the value of a preference is whether the production of the commodity can be expanded in Empire countries without a substantial increase in costs. Take, for example, currants and raisins. There is no question here of an Empire export surplus. But it is doubtful whether the benefit of British preference on these commodities is as great as might be supposed. For the preference has tended, in Australia particularly, to divert land towards grape-growing which is not very suitable for that purpose. The producers probably make incomes which are little higher than they could make if they used the land for other purposes, and the gain to them is certainly much less than the loss of customs revenue to Great Britain due to the grant of free entry to Empire currants and raisins.

Some of the Dominions protect their own producers of certain products enjoying British preference by levying a kind of "processing" tax, or using some similar device to keep home prices of such products at a relatively high level. They then dump the surplus abroad, mainly on Great Britain. A leading example is Australian sugar. Australia, following her "White Australia" policy, has for many years fostered the cultivation of cane sugar in Queensland with white labor. The costs of producing it are far higher than in Cuba, Java, and the West Indies. Nevertheless she grows much more than sufficient for her own needs, exporting the rest to Great Britain. During recent years she has produced 12 to 15 million cwts. a year and has exported 4 to 8 million cwts. to Great Britain. Australian consumers have been paying some £25 a ton but the price obtained for the sugar dumped on Great

Britain has been around £8 or £9 a ton. Of course if Australia is determined to produce at a high cost more sugar than she needs, the British preference is a help to her, but in so far as it encourages her to produce sugar to be exported well below its cost of production it can scarcely be deemed a great benefit. In the same way, Australia makes her own consumers pay considerably more for butter and raisins than British consumers pay. She is of course suited to produce these commodities, but it has often been suggested that she has encouraged them too much. Some other Dominions have similar schemes, notably for butter. An argument often put forward in favor of such schemes is that manufacturing in, say, Australia is highly protected and that to assist, for example, producers of butter does something to redress the balance. But this argument does not seem very strong. What happens is this. Each producer of butter pays a levy of so much per pound of butter produced. The price of butter in Australia is fixed at a relatively high level and the proceeds of the levy are used in effect to subsidize the export of the surplus butter which cannot be sold at home.[4] There is, of course, a tariff to keep butter from New Zealand or other countries from entering Australia. It is the Australian consumers who suffer, and this includes most of the farmers, for only a minority is engaged in dairy farming. In so far as the scheme causes more butter to be produced than would otherwise be produced, it can be claimed that land and labor are diverted from uses which are really more profitable to the nation into the production of butter and that, in so far as this is en-

[4] Thus in 1934-35 the home price of Australian butter was 1s.3d. per lb., but over half her output was exported at 10d. per lb.

couraged by the British preference, the latter is not much of a real benefit.

These various considerations perhaps explain in part why the Dominions are nowadays regarding imperial preference with less favor than formerly. There was very little regret, for example, when Great Britain in 1939 abandoned her duty on foreign wheat. But the main reason is probably that the Dominions are looking ahead. Their populations are increasing and they must seek expanding markets. There does not seem much hope of further expansion in the British market. The population of Great Britain has ceased to grow to any significant extent and in time will begin to fall. There have as yet been few signs that Great Britain will cease to protect her own farmers or will reduce still further imports of, for example, Argentine meat or Danish butter in order to provide a bigger market for Dominion produce. Hence the Dominions must look elsewhere if they wish to expand their exports, and the Ottawa agreements, in so far as they promised minimum margins of preference to British goods, tied their hands. The feeling has been growing in the Dominions that it would not be such a bad policy to break away to some extent from the lines laid down at Ottawa in order to be free to offer concessions to other countries.

3. IMPERIAL PREFERENCE BEFORE OTTAWA

The first practical step towards imperial preference was taken by Canada, who in 1898 gave a preference on goods from the British Empire. At the Colonial Conference of 1902 there was general agreement that imperial preference was desirable. The representatives from Australia, New Zealand, The Cape, and Natal promised to recommend their various Parliaments to grant preferences. Preferential rates in favor of most Empire products, and varying from 5 to 15 per cent, were in fact introduced into the tariffs of New Zealand in 1903, South Africa in 1904, and Australia in 1907.

In the following year, 1903, Mr. Chamberlain, who had been Colonial Secretary, resigned because he was unable to persuade the Cabinet to give any preferences to Empire products. He devoted himself to intensive propaganda in favor of imperial preference. He founded the Tariff Reform League, to spread the doctrine, and the Imperial Tariff Commission to study the details of protection and preference. The free-traders conducted an equally intensive campaign of propaganda in opposition to Mr. Chamberlain. The general election of 1906 was fought largely on this issue. It resulted in an overwhelming defeat for protection and left many observers with the conviction that the electorate would never accept protective duties on foodstuffs. It took the great depression of 1930 onwards to overcome that conviction. Even so it must be remembered that food prices were low and tending to fall when food imports were restricted by duties or quotas. It remains to be seen whether the British public will accept any considerable rise due to protection in the cost of living.

At the conference of 1907, the last to be called a Colonial Conference, Mr. Deakin of Australia and some of the other Dominion Prime Ministers again requested that Great Britain should consider giving them some preferences in exchange for those which the Dominions gave to her. The original notion of the Dominions that their preferences were in the nature of something freely offered in gratitude for the protection of the British fleet and advantages on the British capital market was tending to disappear. This tendency has grown stronger in the years that have elapsed since. The request of Mr. Deakin was met with a blank refusal. In the words of Mr. Winston Churchill, at that time one of the triumphant Liberals, Great Britain "banged, barred, and bolted the door."

It was not opened until after the world war. The Finance Act of 1919 gave preferences to Empire products for the first time. On McKenna goods the preference was one-third. Foreign motorcars, to take the main commodity affected, paid 33⅓ per cent but Empire motorcars thenceforward paid only 22⅔ per cent. One result of this was that motorcar factories under American control were established in Canada to take advantage of the preference. On Empire wines the preference varied from 30 to 50 per cent. On spirits a preference was given by adding 2s.6d. per proof gallon to the basic rate on spirits imported from foreign countries. This benefited mainly West Indian rum, but the market for rum in Great Britain was declining. On most other goods subject to revenue duties, the most important by far being sugar, a preference of one-sixth was given.

In 1921 a duty of 33⅓ per cent was imposed on various key industry goods from foreign countries and similar Empire goods were allowed to come in free.

In October 1923 there was an Imperial Conference. Once again the question of imperial preference was discussed. It was realized that in order to give substantial preferences to the Empire, Great Britain would have to adopt protection and to impose duties on some foodstuffs from foreign countries. This the Conservative Party was prepared to do, and it appealed to the country to support its program. It was defeated. It came into power again in October 1924, but it had pledged itself not to impose any new taxes on food. Accordingly, Mr. Baldwin compro-

mised by granting £1 million a year to an Empire Marketing Board, one of whose aims would be to assist the
marketing of Empire products in the United Kingdom
and to encourage, by research and advertisement, the consumption of Empire goods rather than foreign goods. Mr.
Baldwin also, in 1925, gave preferences on Empire products coming under the new protective duties. They received a preference of one-sixth on the raw silk and of
one-third on the "safeguarding" duties on lace and em-
broidery, cutlery, gloves, incandescent mantles, and im-
pregnated hose. The safeguarding duties lapsed in 1930.
It should perhaps be mentioned that there has been no
"reciprocity" about any of the preferences granted by
Great Britain either before, during, or after 1925. Some
parts of the Empire, as we have seen, gave preferences to
British goods at this time but others, including India and
Newfoundland, gave no preferences at all. Nevertheless
British preferences applied to products from any Dominion
or Colony or Protectorate.

Another change made in 1925 was that the preference
on sugar was increased and put on a specific basis. It had
previously been one-sixth: that is to say, Empire sugar
had paid five-sixths of the duty on foreign sugar. Owing
to the reduction on the sugar duties, the value of this
preference had fallen from 4s.3½d. per cwt. to 1s.11½d.
per cwt. It was now stabilized at a minimum of 4s.3½d. per
cwt. for ten years. If the duty on foreign sugar became
less than this, Empire sugar was to come in free. This
stabilization of preferences was extended to all products
receiving imperial preference by the Finance Act of 1927,
which declared that the existing margins would be regarded as a minimum for ten years.

All the various preferences granted by Great Britain

before 1931 did not amount to very much. Tobacco-growing was stimulated in Rhodesia and Nyasaland and preference on sugar was undoubtedly a help to the West Indies. If the value of British preferences is calculated by the method described above, it amounted to some £2 million a year, of which most went to Australia, mainly on sugar.

When Great Britain turned to protection, she imposed duties on a wide range of foreign goods but permitted similar Empire goods to continue to come in free for the time being, without pledging herself to continue granting them this privilege. She could and did use the threat of taking away some of these preferences as a bargaining weapon at Ottawa.

The extent of these new preferences, as they were just before the Ottawa Conference, is best shown by the following facts. On the basis of retained imports coming into Great Britain in 1930, over half the sales of Canada and Australia to the British market received preference, and over 30 per cent of the sales of other British countries received preference. This was imperial preference at last on the grand scale. The immediate result was that in the March-June quarter of 1932, 38 per cent of British imports came from the Empire as against 30 per cent in the same quarter of previous years.

4. THE OTTAWA AGREEMENTS

Great Britain and the Dominions met at Ottawa in the summer of 1932. The great depression had reduced the volume of world trade to three-quarters of its previous level. It had been most severe on countries, such as the Dominions, which specialized in raw materials and grain. The prices of most of these products were about half

what they had been in 1929. In so far as they were produced by farmers and their families, the quantities produced and exported did not fall much. The reduced demand from Europe and the United States, partly due to
drastic restrictions on imports by Germany, France, and
other European countries, therefore led to a great drop
in values. Hence the Dominions were anxious mainly to
get the prices of their chief exports back to a more remunerative level. They hoped to achieve this by maintaining and increasing the preference given to them in the
great market of Great Britain.

Great Britain was in a rather different position. Her
exports consisted mainly of textiles, machinery, and other
manufactures. Their prices had not fallen so much, but
sales had been greatly diminished owing to the reduced
purchasing power of countries overseas, including the Dominions. There was very heavy unemployment in her
main export industries. At Ottawa, therefore, she was seeking above all greater outlets for her exports. She hoped to
find them in the Dominions, and she now had a tariff she
could use as a bargaining weapon.

Mr. Baldwin, head of the British delegation, spoke of
cleaning out the channels of trade and the conference recorded its convictions "that by the lowering or removal
of barriers among themselves provided for in these Agreements the flow of trade between the various countries of
the Empire will be facilitated and that by the consequent
increase of purchasing power of their peoples the trade
of the world will also be stimulated and increased." But
it was clear from the start that the result would almost inevitably be to raise tariff barriers rather than to reduce
them. In order to give effective help to the Dominions,
Great Britain would be obliged to retain most of her

existing duties, probably to increase some of them, and to impose new duties or quantitative restrictions upon other foreign imports which competed with Dominion products in her market. The Dominions, for their part, had sought to shelter themselves to some extent from the depression by giving more protection to their own manufacturing industries. The chief competitor to their own manufactures was Great Britain. If they were going to give more preference to British goods, they were more likely to maintain or increase their duties on foreign goods than to reduce substantially their duties on British goods. And this, on the whole, is what happened.

The Ottawa agreements were signed in August 1932. Great Britain made five concessions.

In the first place, she promised that all Dominion products then admitted free would continue to be admitted free. This covered over 80 per cent of all imports from the Empire. The rest were subject to revenue duties or to pre-1931 protective duties. This promise held good for five years, except for dairy produce. The British government reserved the right to review the situation as to dairy produce at the end of three years. It might then either impose a duty on imports from the Empire, raising the duty on imports from foreign countries in order to preserve the existing margin of preference, or else impose quantitative regulation.

In the second place, new or revised duties, the "Ottawa duties," were imposed on a number of goods coming from foreign countries. These were products in which the Dominions were especially interested. Thus the duties on butter, various fruits, and eggs were raised from 10 per cent to 15 or 20 per cent or more and three commodities previously on the free list—wheat, linseed, and unwrought copper—were subjected to duty. The duty on foreign wheat was 2s. a quarter.

In the third place, Great Britain agreed to maintain the general 10 per cent duties for five years on a wide range of foreign goods. In 1930 her imports of these goods had amounted to £101 million, of which only a quarter had come from the Dominions. On these goods Great Britain promised not merely that the Dominions should have free entry but also that similar foreign goods would be taxed at least 10 per cent for at least five years.

In the fourth place, Great Britain agreed, as we saw in the last chapter, to restrict the quantities of chilled and frozen beef, frozen mutton and lamb, and bacon and ham which she imported from foreign countries. But she was concerned to protect her own farmers as well as to provide a larger share of her market for Dominion meat. She therefore reserved her rights to impose quantitative restrictions upon imports from the Dominions if these entered in too large quantities. Australia undertook to do her best to limit her exports of frozen mutton and lamb to those of the Ottawa year and of frozen beef to 110 per cent of those of the Ottawa year. New Zealand undertook to give reliable estimates of her exports as early as possible in each export season (October 1 to December 31). Only for bacon and ham was any large expansion agreed upon: Canada was to be allowed to export up to 2½ million cwts. a year and New Zealand was to have a reasonable share of the expansion caused by cutting down foreign imports.

In the fifth place, certain other undertakings were given. The existing preference on Empire tobacco was guaranteed for ten years to Canada, South Africa, and India. The preference on coffee was increased, for the benefit of India, from 3s.4d. to 9s.4d. per cwt. Southern Rhodesia was assured the same preferences on tobacco and coffee as those promised to India. The arrangements for importing live cattle into Great Britain from Canada were to be modified at a later date. The agreement with Canada further stated that if state action in any country were to frustrate the intentions of the preferential tariff, imports would be prohibited from that country. Canada had this inserted in order to prevent her timber from being undercut by Russian timber: exported, of course, by the Soviet government. This meant that Great Britain had to denounce her 1930 agreement with the U.S.S.R.

At Ottawa, Great Britain concluded a separate agreement with each Dominion. But in fact she subsequently gave to all Empire imports the same preferences as those which she promised to one or other of the Dominions in her agreement with that Dominion.

What did the Dominions give her in return?

Canada had a high protective tariff and in order to get revenue during the economic crisis she had imposed a sales tax of 6 per cent and a general surcharge of 3 per cent on all imports. Moreover, she was applying, in effect, "dumping duties" on British goods by converting sterling values into dollar values at a higher rate than the rate ruling in the market.

At Ottawa, she promised to abolish surcharges on British imports and to consider the abolition of exchange dumping duties. She undertook to give tariff protection only to industries which seemed to have sound prospects of survival, to keep her tariffs sufficiently low (except on goods competing with her "infant industries") to enable efficient British producers to compete, to set up a tariff board and not to increase duties on British goods without an enquiry

by the board at which British producers should be entitled
to a hearing.

She added a number of British goods, previously subject
to duties mostly ranging from 5 to 15 per cent, to the free
list. She gave increased preference to Great Britain on
over 200 items, either by reducing the duty on British
goods or by raising the duty on foreign goods or by doing
both. This sounds impressive, but in fact most of the new
or increased preferences were not of much use to Great
Britain. The great bulk of her duties on British goods remained appreciably higher, and on foreign goods very
much higher, than they had been under the Liberal tariff
which Mr. Bennett inherited and revised upwards in September 1930.

Australia also had followed a policy of high protection
before the world depression. The total value of her exports fell from £138 million in 1928-29 to £75 million in
1930-31, owing mainly to the great fall in the prices of her
wool and other exports. She owed Great Britain some
£25 million a year in interest charges. In order to cut
down her imports, she imposed some import prohibitions
and made some drastic increases in her duties. She imposed a surcharge of 50 per cent on the duties on a number
of luxury and other imports, and a general tax, known as
a primage duty, on all imports: she raised this to 10 per
cent in July 1931. Her tariff was one of the highest in the
world in 1929; these "crisis" additions made it almost
prohibitive on many goods.

At Ottawa, she agreed to abolish import prohibitions
and surcharges and to reduce or remove the primage duty
as soon as financial conditions permitted. She gave an
undertaking similar to that given by Canada to protect only
industries reasonably sure of survival, and so forth. She

granted increases in the preferential margin to Great Britain on a number of goods, the most common margins being 15 to 20 per cent. But these increased preferences were granted mainly by increasing the duties on foreign goods, so that her general tariff after Ottawa was higher than in 1929 and her duties on most British goods remained formidable. For example, her general tariff on woolen piece goods was 50 per cent and her British tariff was 35 per cent, giving a preferential margin to Great Britain of 15 per cent; corresponding figures for machinery n.e.i. were 50 per cent and 45 per cent; for galvanized or corrugated steel plates and sheets 130s. and 90s. per ton.

South Africa had followed a policy of moderate protection. Although her duties under the 1925 tariff went up to 30 and even 40 per cent, a large proportion of her imports came in free. She gave preferences to Great Britain and also to Canada and New Zealand. The preferential margin was about 5 per cent on many manufactures and she promised at Ottawa that the existing preferential margins would not be lowered. She also gave preferences for the first time, or increased existing preferences (usually raising them from 5 to 10 per cent) on a short list of manufactured articles. This had to be done mainly by increasing the foreign duties. But even her general tariff remained fairly moderate. For example, on cotton piece goods costing less than 1s.3d. per yard the general duty was 1½d. per yard and the British duty 5 per cent; and on iron and steel products the general duty was 15½ per cent and the British 12½ per cent.

New Zealand before the world depression had a moderate tariff with considerable preference to Great Britain. For example, much of the machinery and the iron and steel coming from Great Britain was not subject to duty; if from foreign countries it paid 20 per cent. Foreign motor vehicles paid 35 per cent and British 10 per cent; foreign woolen piece goods paid 40 per cent and British 20 per cent. With the crisis of 1931 she increased her duties somewhat on a large number of goods without changing the British preferential margin; and she imposed a surtax and primage duties.

At Ottawa, she agreed to abolish the surtax, of about 5 per cent, on British goods and to remove the 3 per cent primage duty on "duty-free" goods as soon as possible. She gave an undertaking similar to those of Canada and Australia about protecting only industries with a reasonable chance of survival. She promised to maintain her existing preferences on British goods unless they were over 20 per cent. She reduced her duties on British clothing and hosiery from $32\frac{1}{2}$ per cent to $27\frac{1}{2}$ per cent and on British confectionery from 30 per cent to $27\frac{1}{2}$ per cent; and British silk and rayon piece goods, which had previously paid 10 per cent, were to be admitted free.

Newfoundland, where the main occupation is fishing, had a customs tariff mainly for revenue purposes. It provided three-quarters of her revenue. No preferences had been granted on British goods. At Ottawa, she promised to grant preferences of 10 per cent on sixty-one classes of goods with the proviso that she could reduce this margin if her revenue fell off considerably.

India had a protective tariff in which the commonest rate was 25 per cent. Some goods, including machinery, paid 10 per cent and some semi-luxuries 50 per cent. British cotton piece goods paid 25 per cent or $4\frac{3}{8}$ annas per lb., whichever was higher; foreign, paid $31\frac{1}{4}$ per cent or $4\frac{3}{8}$ annas. India gave few preferences on British goods.

At Ottawa, she undertook to give Great Britain a 10 per cent preference on a large number of manufactured goods and a 7½ per cent preference on motorcars, accumulators and omnibuses. On the whole, this meant raising foreign duties unless customs revenues were to fall off considerably. The agreement between Great Britain and India could be terminated by either at six months notice.

Southern Rhodesia had a fairly low tariff. The most common rate was 10 per cent on British goods and 20 per cent on foreign. At Ottawa, she gave increased preferences to Great Britain on a few goods, including cotton, silk, and rayon piece goods, mainly by raising the foreign duties.

5. Changes Since Ottawa

The Dominions kept their pledges to remove crisis restrictions. Canada halved the surcharge on British goods in 1934 and abolished it in 1935. She ceased to apply exchange dumping duties against Great Britain in March 1933. Australia removed most of her import prohibitions at once. She gradually abolished her surcharge on imports. She introduced imperial preference into the primage duty in 1933 and most British imports are now exempt from it or pay only 5 per cent. South Africa abolished her 7½ per cent surcharges and 5 per cent primage duty when she left the gold standard in January 1933. New Zealand abolished her surtax, but her revenue needs compelled her to retain the 3 per cent primage duty on goods which otherwise were duty free. Most of such goods come mainly from Great Britain.

The undertakings given by Canada, Australia, and New Zealand to protect only industries which had a reasonable chance of survival, and to keep duties on British goods sufficiently low (except in so far as they were protecting infant industries) to permit efficient British firms to compete, did not lead to any substantial changes. An undertaking given in such general terms can of course be interpreted much as the government or the tariff board pleases. It can be used as a pretext either for reducing duties or for maintaining them or increasing them. In Canada, there were long judicial enquiries by the tariff board into relative costs of production, leading for the most part to the negative result that it was difficult to find exactly similar products manufactured in both Great Britain and Canada or to compare the cost of production of those which could be found. If these difficulties had been surmounted, the imposition of a duty on British goods just high enough to equalize costs of production, which was apparently the object aimed at, would have killed, instead of increasing, imports from Great Britain, for of course international trade takes place only because and precisely because there are differences between countries in costs of production. In Australia, the tariff board interpreted its instructions in a sensible, and not a literal, manner and on the whole exerted a downward influence on the level of duties on British goods. Similarly in New Zealand.

In 1936 India denounced her agreement, but it proved difficult to make a new one and by consent the provisions of the old one were temporarily retained. A new one was made in March 1939.

In February 1937 Canada and Great Britain signed a new pact to replace their Ottawa agreement. A Liberal Government was in power in Canada and the general revival of trade helped it to follow its inclinations and to make a more liberal agreement. But the new concessions were made almost entirely by Canada. She reduced her duties on many British goods, mainly by 2½ to 5 per cent but a few by percentages ranging up to 20. These reductions covered 40 per cent of all imports from Great Britain previously subject to duty. A number of articles were placed on the free list. Canada also transferred many commodities from the list guaranteeing a minimum percentage margin of preference to a list guaranteeing that the preferential duty would not exceed a certain rate. This, of course, opened the door to Canada to make reductions in foreign duties if she wished. In return, Great Britain guaranteed not to increase the duty on Canadian motorcars above 22⅔ per cent and reduced her preferential duty on silk stockings and placed reed organs from the Empire on the free list. She also pledged herself in no circumstances to reduce the existing duties, which applied of course to foreign goods only. Canada promised to continue extending preferences to the colonies and in return some of the Colonies were "invited" to grant certain specific preferences to Canada.

In 1937 another Imperial Conference was held. It was expected to result in new agreements, as the 1932 ones were made for five years. But in fact it did nothing and the old agreements temporarily remained in force.

In April 1938 the trade war between Great Britain and *Eire* was formally brought to an end, and Eire was given the same preferences as the rest of the Dominions. She in turn abolished her special charges on British goods and agreed to admit a number of them, including machinery and many iron and steel products, free of duty. Great Britain guaranteed Eire minimum preferences on butter, cheese, eggs in shell, and a few other commodities. Eire promised to retain her existing preferences on British goods, and to grant British preferences of one-third the rate on foreign goods or 10 per cent ad valorem, whichever should be the greater, on any new duties which she imposed in the future. There were various other provisions, including a promise by Eire that either British coal and coke should enter freely or at least 3s. a ton should be charged on foreign coal.

The British-American Trade Agreement of 1938 made certain changes necessary. Canada agreed to a substantially reduced preference on timber and apples and Great Britain agreed that certain preferences (covering over £2 million of her exports to Canada) guaranteed to her by Canada should be reduced, mostly by 2½ per cent ad valorem. The main items affected were chemicals and rugs, tin plates, Diesel engines, and certain iron and steel products. The 1938 agreement between Canada and the United States provided for reductions in duty on a wide range of United States goods, and this involved reductions in the preferences previously granted by Canada to Great Britain. Canada consented to reductions in the preferences she enjoyed in the British market on wheat, apples, pears, honey, chilled or frozen salmon, and patent leather. Great Britain followed her usual practice of not discriminating between her various Dominions and Colonies or between different foreign countries. Hence her duty on wheat, to take the most important example, was completely abolished. Of course these two agreements—the British-American and the Canadian-American—were in a sense supplementary to one another and were negotiated more or less simultaneously.

On one point Great Britain does discriminate between the various parts of her Empire otherwise than by granting a preference to all, which in fact (as for example that on tobacco or coffee) benefits only a very limited number of Dominions or Colonies. The great depression plunged the West Indies into considerable distress. In 1932 Great Britain assisted them by granting an extra preference upon sugar, up to a certain maximum amount, coming from specified Colonies in the West Indies. Thus the rates per cwt. on fully refined sugar were in 1939:

> 11s.8d. non-Empire
> 5s.10d. Empire
> 4s.7d. excise
> 2s.4.7d. Colonial quota

The outbreak of war in September 1939 led Great Britain to impose restrictions on various exports and to control imports through exchange control without immediately modifying her tariff or imperial preference.

6. THE RESULTS OF IMPERIAL PREFERENCE

The proportion of British imports coming from the Empire rose from 29 per cent in 1930 to 35 per cent in 1932 and 38 per cent in 1935. In 1938 it was 40 per cent.

It may be of interest to give a few figures to illustrate the main changes in the sources of supply of bacon, beef, mutton, butter, and wheat, between 1930 and 1938.

In 1930 imports of bacon and hams were 10.2 million cwts., costing £46.1 million; 5.0 million cwts. came from Denmark, 1.3 million from the United States and 0.2 million from Canada. In 1938 total imports were 7.5 million cwts., costing £33.9 million; 3.4 million cwts. came from Denmark, 0.4 million from the United States, and 1.5 million from Canada.

In 1930 imports of chilled and frozen beef were 11.6 million cwts., costing £30.0 million; 8.4 million cwts. came from the Argentine, 1.1 million from Uruguay, 0.8 million from Australia, and 0.3 million from New Zealand. In 1938 total imports were 12.3 million cwts., costing £23.7

million; 7.5 million cwts. came from the Argentine, 0.7 million from Uruguay, 2.3 million from Australia, and 0.9 million from New Zealand.

In 1930 imports of frozen mutton were 6.4 million cwts., costing £19.7 million; 1.5 million cwts. came from the Argentine, 0.4 million from Uruguay, 3.3 million from New Zealand, and 0.8 million from Australia. In 1938 total imports were 6.9 million cwts., costing £19.2 million; 0.9 million cwts. came from the Argentine, 0.2 million from Uruguay, 3.7 million from New Zealand, and 1.9 million from Australia.

The diversion of imports of these three commodities from foreign towards Empire sources was of course due to the quantitative restrictions on imports from foreign countries. It will be noted that total imports of beef and mutton have risen a little. Total imports of bacon have considerably fallen, owing to the encouragement given to the production of pigs and bacon in Great Britain.

In 1930 imports of butter were 6.8 million cwts., costing £46.9 million; 2.3 million cwts. came from Denmark, 1.6 million from New Zealand and 1.0 million from Australia. In 1938 total imports were 9.5 million cwts., costing £50.0 million; 2.4 million cwts. came from Denmark, 2.6 million from New Zealand, and 1.8 million from Australia. The consumption of butter in Great Britain has increased by 50 per cent over the last ten years or so. Despite the tariff, leading foreign suppliers, notably Denmark, the Netherlands, and Sweden, are sending more butter than in previous years. The Netherlands sent only 0.1 million cwts. in 1930 but 0.7 million in 1938. Imports from the Argentine, however, have fallen from 0.3 million cwts. in 1930 to 0.1 million in 1938.

Imports of wheat in 1930 were 104.8 million cwts., costing £43.1 million. In 1938 imports were 101.6 million cwts., costing £38.6 million. Imports from leading supplying countries, in millions of cwts., were as follows:

	1930	1938
Australia	26.2	31.0
Canada	12.7	28.9
British India	3.3	4.4
U.S.A.	21.0	15.8
Argentine	15.2	5.8

There have been considerable variations from one year to another in sources of supply. For example, Canada sent 41 million cwts. in 1928 and the Argentine 45.4 million in 1929. These figures were exceptionally high, but the 1930 figures for these two countries were unusually low. Again, the United States sent very little from 1933 to 1936. Nevertheless the years chosen, 1930 and 1938, give a picture which is not misleading. We have already put forward the view that the duty on foreign wheat was not really of much value to the Empire. It also created some difficulty in that it is cheaper to send some Canadian wheat via Buffalo and an American port, but the British customs authorities ruled that such wheat, although Canadian, had to pay duty unless shipped from an Empire port. The abandonment of the duty caused few regrets.

The change in the direction of British exports was somewhat less striking. The proportion going to the Empire rose from 43.5 per cent in 1930 to 48 per cent in 1935 and 50 per cent in 1938. The table on page 105 shows some of the changes between 1930 and 1936.

It will be seen that British exports of machinery to British countries have risen while exports to foreign countries have fallen, that nearly all the increase in exports of motor-cars has gone to the Empire, and that exports of textiles

BRITISH EXPORTS OF CERTAIN COMMODITIES[5]

Commodities	1930		1938	
	Total export	To British countries	Total export	To British countries
	£Million			
Iron and steel products...	59.5	30.2	42.2	26.5
Agricultural implements and machinery........	2.4	1.5	2.2	1.2
Electrical machinery and apparatus.............	18.2	10.3	15.2	10.9
Other machinery........	44.1	19.0	36.0	19.7
Motorcars, etc., and parts	12.6	7.9	16.2	11.3
Other metals and manufactures thereof........	13.6	5.1	13.5	4.8
Yarn and thread, including wool tops..........	33.8	7.6	29.9	7.9
Piece-goods: cotton.......	61.3	30.3	40.3	22.5
Piece-goods: woolen......	23.5	6.6	18.0	6.1
Piece-goods: other........	10.7	5.0	9.8	4.2
Apparel, except footwear..	16.0	11.0	10.6	7.2
Other textiles............	19.7	10.9	16.4	9.8
Chemicals, drugs, dyes, etc.	18.3	9.1	18.1	10.5

to the Empire have fallen considerably, although not quite as much as to foreign countries.

The various statistics which we have given above tend somewhat to exaggerate the extent to which diversions of trade took place owing to imperial preference. In the first place, for one reason or another a number of countries were taking a smaller part in world trade than they did before the world slump. This applies, for example, to the United States and Italy and France. Great Britain and the Empire as a whole (with some exceptions, notably Canada) are

[5] From the *Statistical Abstract for the British Empire,* 1938.

taking a greater share of world trade than formerly. In the second place, the percentages for inter-imperial trade were somewhat lower in 1930 than in the immediately preceding years. The world slump depressed first and most deeply the prices of foodstuffs and raw materials, and therefore hit the Dominions and Colonies. Hence the values of their exports fell considerably in 1930, and their purchases fell also.

What main changes have taken place in the trade between Great Britain and the leading Dominions?

Great Britain's imports from *Canada* in 1938 formed over 8 per cent of her total imports as against less than 4 per cent during 1929-31. It has sometimes been suggested that this in part arises from arrangements by which goods originating in the United States have had finishing processes applied to them in Canada. But in fact the increased imports from Canada have consisted of foodstuffs and non-ferrous metals rather than manufactures. The proportion of Great Britain's exports going to Canada has remained roughly stationary, at about 5 per cent. This, however, is because total imports into Canada have remained low. Canada has been taking a somewhat bigger percentage of her imports from Great Britain during recent years. For example, she used to take less than 80 per cent of her woolen piece goods from Great Britain, the rest coming mainly from France. During recent years she has taken almost all from Great Britain. Again, she used to take her cotton piece goods mainly from the United States, but during recent years Great Britain has supplied most of them —more than twice as much as the United States. Similarly, the great bulk of her iron and steel goods used to come from the United States but during recent years imports from the United Kingdom have doubled in value, and have been nearly as large as those from the United States.

Until Canada made her first agreement with the United States in November 1935, goods from the United States had to pay the full, and not the intermediate rates of duty. This gave a considerable preference to British goods, paying the lowest of the three rates (general, intermediate, and British) although the duties on textiles were fairly high.

Great Britain's imports from *Australia* in 1938 formed over 7 per cent of her total imports as against less than 5 per cent during 1929-31. The percentage of her imports coming from *New Zealand* has also risen—from about 4 per cent to about 5 per cent. The percentage of her total exports going to Australia fell heavily in 1930 and 1931 but has since risen to about the pre-slump level of over 7 per cent. The percentage of her total exports going to New Zealand has risen from about 3 per cent to about 4 per cent.

There has been some dissatisfaction among British exporters, especially of cotton goods, at the trend of trade between Great Britain and India, and the new agreement of March 1939 aroused no enthusiasm. The percentage of Great Britain's imports coming from India has risen from below 5 per cent to about 7 per cent, but the proportion of her exports going to India has fallen from nearly 11 per cent in 1929 to less than 8 per cent in 1938.

Some dissatisfaction with the working of the Ottawa agreements has been expressed in *South Africa*. This Dominion has now become the largest single customer of Great Britain, taking over 8 per cent of her total exports. This has been due largely to the prosperity arising from the high price of gold. But Great Britain's imports from South Africa have fallen from 2 per cent in 1929 to just over 1½ per cent of her total imports. It has been argued that these latter percentages give a misleading picture since they relate to merchandise only and do not include gold. It is true that in 1937-38 Great Britain sold £40 million of merchandise to South Africa and bought only £16 million of merchandise from her but, it is urged, she bought also £79 million of gold. It is doubtful whether this argument has any weight, for the United States has always been prepared to buy gold without limit at a fixed price.

By 1939 there was not much enthusiasm for imperial preference either in Great Britain or in the rest of the Empire. British farmers were annoyed that meat and dairy produce from the Dominions continued to come in free and the British manufacturers were disappointed that leading Dominions and India insisted upon giving fairly high protection to most of their own manufactures, so that British sales of a number of products, especially textiles, tended to fall off despite the preference. The British government had found it embarrassing when seeking expanding outlets for British exports in foreign countries to find their hands tied by pledges given to the Dominions which prevented them from making concessions to other countries. The Dominions, for their part, were somewhat disappointed that the benefits of preference on commodities such as wheat, of which there was an Empire export surplus, had been so slight, and although Australia and New Zealand were pleased with the preferences on their meat and dairy produce they were apprehensive of being requested to restrict their exports of these goods in the interest of British farmers. The manufacturers in the Dominions resented such reductions as had been made in the duties on competing British goods. And, in spite of Empire preferences, Great Britain was not an expanding market for Empire or, indeed, any other produce. If the Dominions wanted to increase their sales, they would have to look to other countries and free themselves to some extent from their undertakings to Great Britain. As for the Colonies, the main result of the change in British policy has been to keep up their cost of living. For example, the 1932 agreement with Canada had imposed an extra duty of 1s. per pair on the cheap canvas rubber-soled shoes from Japan and other foreign countries; and textile quotas since 1934 kept out cheap cotton and other clothing from Japan.

Chapter V

TRADE AGREEMENTS

1. The Most-Favored-Nation Clause

THE USE of the most-favored-nation clause in trade agreements between countries dates back to at least the seventeenth century. It has been a leading feature of international trade relationships, and especially of those between Great Britain and foreign countries, since about 1860. Most British trade agreements—a term which we shall use to include commercial treaties, conventions, and so forth—with foreign countries are based upon the principle of most-favored-nation treatment.

In addition to specific concessions, or instead of them, one country may grant another the general privilege of holding a certain kind of status in their trade relations. There are three such kinds of status, to each of which corresponds a certain type of clause in a trade agreement: the parity clause, the reciprocity clause, and the most-favored-nation clause. The parity clause gives the other country treatment not worse than that received by the citizens of the first. The reciprocity clause gives the other country treatment not worse than the other country gives to the first. The most-favored-nation clause gives the other country treatment not worse than that given to any third country.

The most-favored-nation clause has two forms: the conditional and the unconditional. The latter, which is the more common and is employed by Great Britain, is essentially a pledge not to discriminate against the other country: to treat it at least as well as the most-favored other country is treated. This pledge is usually given with respect to a number of matters, such as the rights of foreign persons and companies and the treatment of foreign shipping, as well as with respect to trade. A typical most-favored-nation clause relating to trade is: "Articles produced or manufactured in the territories of one of the two contracting parties imported into the territories of the other, from whatever place arriving, shall not be subjected to other or higher duties or charges than those paid on the like articles produced in any other foreign country."

The conditional form of the clause has been adopted at times by some countries, notably France and the United States. The latter adopted it in all its trade agreements before 1922, when it changed to the unconditional form. The conditional form has the superficial appeal that under it a country need not give something for nothing. Any concession which it makes to a second country in return for a concession granted to it by that country will be extended to a third country only if the third country makes a concession of the same or equal value. This is quite opposed to the true most-favored-nation spirit of non-discrimination; it is practically a refusal to grant most-favored-nation treatment at all.

The conditional most-favored-nation pledge is not worth much. Let us take a hypothetical example. Suppose that the United States, before 1922, reduced its duties on silk from Japan in return for a reduction by Japan in its duties on American steel. If China enjoyed conditional most-favored-nation treatment from the United States could China demand the same reductions in duty on its silk? Only in return for a concession of the same or equal value. But what is a concession of "the same or equal value?" Suppose that China imported no steel from the United

States or that she already allowed steel to enter free. In the last resort, only the United States could decide whether a concession was of equivalent value to that given by another country, and therefore her use of the conditional clause led to numerous disputes and bad feeling.

The unconditional form means that any concession, usually a reduction in tariffs, granted to another country must at once be applied, automatically and without compensation, to every other country which has been granted most-favored-nation privileges by the first. In this way, countries may receive concessions for which they give nothing in return. It was this feature of the clause which caused discontent with it to grow during the post-war years. In particular, there was considerable annoyance with the United States, which until 1935 maintained very high tariffs and yet reaped the benefit of all concessions made by other countries, with whom she enjoyed most-favored-nation treatment, without herself conceding anything. It was pointed out that at least it was an advantage, and reduced the risks of exporters, to know that the United States, for example, would not discriminate against the country to whom she gave the most-favored-nation treatment. She might raise her tariffs but they would be raised to all alike. Nevertheless the feeling was growing that most-favored-nation treatment was too valuable a privilege to be granted lightly and that it should be given only to countries which followed a tolerable tariff policy.

It may be thought that the widespread use of the most-favored-nation clause must make for lower duties all round, since any concession made to any country is generalized. It certainly led to more freedom of trade in the latter part of the nineteenth century and possibly in the twentieth also. But it may have the opposite effect. A may refuse concessions to B which she would otherwise grant because she knows that if she grants them to B she must grant them to all the other letters in the alphabet also, or, in general, a country may increase its duties to a high level as a preliminary to entering into tariff negotiations with others and in the end may not reduce them much. The truth seems to be that most-favored-nation treatment may lead either to low duties or to high ones: in the last resort, everything depends on whether the countries concerned favor greater freedom of trade or greater protection.

The spirit of the most-favored-nation clause can be evaded in various ways. One method is for A to draw up a very detailed and intricate tariff schedule, so that the carefully specified classes of goods on which it reduces its duties in favor of B exclude very similar goods coming from other countries. Another ingenious method, formerly practised by Austria in her trade relations with Hungary and Italy, is as follows. One country, say Austria, subsidizes her exports of a particular product to the other country, say Hungary, and Hungary gives an equivalent subsidy to her exports of something to Austria. This operates in the same way as a mutual reduction of duties which is not extended to third countries despite their most-favored-nation status.

During and since the world slump, the spirit of the most-favored-nation clause has been widely evaded by means of import quotas and exchange control.

On what basis can import quotas be granted in order to avoid discrimination? If "global" quotas are used, which allow imports to come in from anywhere until the quota is filled, this favors neighboring countries, besides leading to uncertainty among importers as to whether each will get his supplies and to goods being refused at the frontier because the quota for the period is filled. If exactly the same quota is given to all countries, this is clearly unfair to those countries which are normally the chief suppliers. If the quotas are allocated between supplying countries in proportion to the relative amounts which they supplied to the restricting country during some year or years chosen as the base period, this leads to disputes over the choice of the base period. One country may claim that its exports to the restricting country were showing an upward trend and would form a bigger proportion of her total imports, if there were no quota, than they did during the base period; another country may say that for one reason or another her exports of that commodity to the restricting country were unusually low during the base period; and so forth. The fact is that there is no method of complying with the spirit of the most-favored-nation clause if import quotas are imposed on commodities, even if the country imposing them wishes to avoid discriminating.

In fact, during recent years restricting countries have not infrequently wished to discriminate, and have used import quotas to evade their most-favored-nation obligations. For example, in 1929 Germany raised her import duty on cattle from 16 RM. per 100 kilos to 24.50 RM., but allowed Sweden to export to Germany her quota of 5,000 head, to increase later to 7,000 head, at the old rate of duty. The quota of 5,000 head covered Sweden's exports of cattle to Germany in the preceding years. Germany then interpreted the most-favored-nation principle in such a way that Denmark was allowed a quota of the same absolute number, 5,000, at the lower duty. But Denmark had sent 260,000 head to Germany in 1928. Again, when quotas on textile imports were imposed in a number of British colonies in 1933 and 1934, the base period chosen was a period before the slump. This was deliberately aimed at

Japanese imports, which had increased greatly during 1930-34, after Japan had been compelled to switch over to other exports owing to the great fall in the American demand for her silk. To take a final example, Great Britain induced Denmark in 1933 to purchase at least 80 per cent of her coal imports from Great Britain, although the 80 per cent had no basis in past experience.

The same situation arises to a still greater extent under exchange control. Germany, for example, can restrict her imports from any particular country more or less as she pleases by refusing to grant import licenses to more than a certain value for goods coming from that country, on the ground that to do so would reduce her reserves of foreign exchange. In practice, a country with complete exchange control can discriminate between its different sources of supply much as it chooses without breaking the letter of its most-favored-nation treaties. Great Britain, in her agreements with some exchange control countries, has obtained from them the promise of favorable treatment in their allotment of foreign exchange.

A very thorny question is that of exceptions to most-favored-nation treatment made by a country which wishes to grant exceptionally favorable treatment to some other country or countries. If two countries unite in a complete customs union, such as that between Belgium and Luxembourg, it is universally agreed that they may grant one another whatever special privileges they choose, without extending them to third countries. The same is usually held to apply to the trade relations between a country and its colonies. Again, it is generally agreed that the United States is entitled to make a similar exception for Cuba. But what about Norway, Sweden, and Denmark? After the world war these three countries agreed to try to limit the most-favored-nation clause in all trade agreements which they made in future by introducing a Scandinavian reservation clause, by which they could grant one another concessions not granted to third parties. In fact, this reservation clause has been ineffective because Great Britain and Germany refused to recognize its validity. These three countries, together with Belgium and Holland, met at Oslo in 1930 to try to stabilize, and later to reduce, import duties among themselves. Little came of this, but in 1932 two of the Oslo powers, Holland and Belgium, drew up the draft treaty of Ouchy. Under this, each was to reduce its duties to the other by 10 per cent a year, so that in five years they would be only half as high (with a few exceptions) as they were in 1932. Further, they were prepared to extend these concessions to any country which would do the same to them. It is doubtful whether much progress would have been made at the time, nevertheless this might have meant the beginning of a low-tariff *bloc* which would gradually expand as new countries joined it. But Great Britain made it known that she would insist upon her most-favored-nation rights. Any duties which Belgium and Holland reduced to one another they would have to reduce to Great Britain also, although she gave no concessions in return.

The Danubian countries have from time to time proposed the formation of a regional pact. This was strongly advocated at the conference of Stresa in August 1932. The essential feature of the proposed scheme was that neighboring wheat-importing countries should grant subsidies to the depressed Danubian countries in the form of preference on their wheat. This would have helped the latter to pay their debt charges and in return they might have lowered their duties upon manufactures instead of turning, as they did, to greater industrialization behind high tariff barriers. Great Britain, presumably in the interest of her wheat-exporting Dominions, let it be known that she would consider such preferences as a breach of most-favored-nation obligations, and this killed the scheme. At Ottawa a formal resolution was passed declaring that countries could not avoid their most-favored-nation obligations by forming a regional pact of this kind, and the Danubian countries were specifically mentioned.

Great Britain has always insisted that her Dominions, even after they had acquired in other respects the status of independent nations, were entitled to grant preference to her despite their most-favored-nation obligations. Other countries did not think this altogether justifiable, but were constrained to accept it. Hence, when Great Britain herself adopted protection and gave preferences to her Dominions as well as to her Colonies, this was logically an extension of a principle which she had always maintained. At Ottawa, a resolution was passed declaring that imperial preference within the British Empire was not counter to most-favored-nation obligations. Great Britain bases her legal position on the fact that in her trade agreements she grants the other party the same privileges as any *foreign* country: "foreign" meaning "not British." But the world thought it odd that a regional pact among the members of the British Empire, who between them performed 30 per cent of the trade of the world and who sprawled all over the globe, was not contrary to the most-favored-nation clause, whilst a regional pact between a few neighboring countries was inconsistent with their most-favored-nation obligations.

2. Bargaining Power

Before we consider some of the most important trade agreements made by Great Britain during recent years, it will be useful to discuss what factors place one country in a strong bargaining position relatively to another with whom she is negotiating a trade agreement.

A country may be able to impose its own terms upon another by threatening to invade or to blockade the other if she refuses. Of course such a threat can succeed only if it could be carried out fairly easily and if the other country is not subjected to equally strong pressure by a third Power. Such threats are rare in times of peace and will be neglected in what follows.

A free trade country is in a weak bargaining position unless other countries are convinced that it will impose tariffs against them if they are not reasonable. As a free trade country has no concessions to offer, its best course is to try to secure unconditional most-favored-nation treatment for its exports. Great Britain even before 1931 followed this course with success: there was no discrimination by other countries against her exports. It can be argued that her success was due to her political power and, to some extent, to the fear that a country might not be able to borrow easily in the London market if it discriminated against her. Smaller free trade countries, such as Holland and Belgium, shared in the benefits of the most-favored-nation system which Great Britain favored and supported. The world slump, however, produced a great increase in protectionist feeling and in restrictions on imports. Then the small countries fared rather badly and Great Britain undoubtedly found her tariffs and quotas useful in extracting concessions. In most of her trade agreements she obtained concessions mainly by promising not to raise her duties on particular products above a certain level, and not to restrict particular imports from particular countries to more than a certain extent, rather than by relaxing her existing measures of protection. Her promise not to restrict her imports of Argentine chilled beef, for example, by more than 10 per cent below the 1931-32 level was of real value because she had already embarked on a policy of restricting foreign supplies and there was no knowing how much further she might travel in that direction. Similarly, her promise to Denmark to take at least 2,300,000 cwts. of butter a year from her was of real value, although in fact she did not impose quotas on imports of butter. For she had adopted quantitative restrictions, and in the future might well have applied a quota to butter.

A country cannot as a rule exert much pressure by threatening to withhold its exports. Even if A is the main source of supply of an important raw material essential to B's industries, B could usually get supplies from an alternative source or could purchase some of A's exports through a third country. For example, Great Britain has no pull over France because she supplies her with coal. France could buy her coal from Germany instead, or could use Belgium as an intermediary. It is rather Great Britain who would suffer if she refused to supply an important customer with coal, for this would lead to unemployment and reduced profits in her important coal-mining industry. It is true that in recent years the spread of exchange control enhanced the importance, to an exchange control country, of supplies of certain commodities to be paid for in her own currency instead of in free exchange. Rumania has found a bargaining weapon in her oil, of which Germany has wished to obtain as much as possible in exchange for marks; Germany has granted Bulgaria the privilege of receiving a certain amount of cotton in exchange for leva; and so on. But in general it is the consuming country which has the upper hand in bargaining.

During recent years the crude notion that A is conferring a benefit on B if she buys more from B than B buys from her has played a considerable part in trade negotiations. Great Britain, anxious, like every other country, to increase her exports, has frequently drawn attention to the fact that she buys much more from the country with which she is negotiating than that country buys from her. The balance of trade between the two countries is said to be "unfavorable" to Great Britain and the conclusion is drawn that the other country should buy more from Great Britain. Great Britain certainly has a large surplus of total imports over total exports. If she had not, how would she be paid interest (of over £200 million a year) on her overseas investments, and how would she receive payment for her shipping services and for the banking and insurance services performed for foreigners by the City of London? Since her total trade must show a large surplus of imports, this is naturally reflected in her trade with most individual countries. Even if a country A has not a surplus of imports on its trade as a whole, it is almost certain to have such a surplus with some particular countries. The cheapest source of certain supplies may be B, but B may not want most of the goods which A supplies or may be able to get them more conveniently and cheaply from C and D. C and D may use the purchasing power thus obtained from B to buy more from A than they sell to her, and so the trade between the four countries may balance. Attempts to make the trade between each pair of countries balance is bound to rob international trade of much of its advantages, by making countries buy less from their best sources of supply, and is bound to keep down the total volume of world trade. One would have thought that Great Britain, whose prosperity depends on international trade, would have refrained from employing the argument that trade between herself and the Argentine or Denmark or a number of other countries was too "one-sided." In fact it was frequently employed in her Parliament and Press.

Analytically, however, the mere fact that Great Britain is a large market and has an import surplus does not in itself give her a pull over other countries. This point can be illustrated from the trade dispute between Australia and Japan which began in May 1936, when Australia imposed heavy duties and, later, severe quantitative restrictions on her imports of Japanese cotton and rayon piece goods. Japan bought two or three times as much from Australia as Australia bought from her, but this did not give Japan any bargaining advantage. Japan was a large buyer of wool from Australia, and by way of retaliation she went elsewhere for her wool. Australian wool growers did not suffer. As Sir Earle Page pointed out, when Japanese purchases were diverted to South Africa, raising prices there, other buyers who usually bought in South Africa switched over to Australia for their supplies. "No matter where one particular section of the demand goes, the remainder of the demand must be satisfied—if not from the usual source, then from another." So long as Japan bought the same amount of wool from somewhere Australia was not injured. She could readily sell her wool elsewhere.

One or both of two conditions must be fulfilled if A is to injure B by buying less of a certain commodity from B. A's action must either cause the world consumption of that commodity to fall or cause the production of it in countries other than B to increase. Consider, for example, British purchases of Danish bacon. If Great Britain simply bought less bacon from Denmark and correspondingly more from elsewhere, production and consumption in the rest of the world remaining the same, Denmark would suffer very little. She would merely switch over her exports of bacon to other consuming countries in order to fill the gaps left by Great Britain's increased purchases from other exporters. In fact, the quantity of Danish bacon exported was considerably reduced by British action. In the first place, this pushed up the price of bacon in Great Britain and prevented British consumption of bacon from increasing. In the second place, it led to a considerable increase in the production of bacon outside Denmark: in Great Britain herself and in Canada and other Dominions.

Where Great Britain has succeeded in recent years in inducing countries to make trade agreements with her tending to increase their purchases of British exports it has not been because her balance of trade with them was one-sided, although that argument was used, but because she has been in a position to hit some of their chief exports (notably meat and dairy produce) by causing more of them to be produced either in Great Britain herself or, through preferential treatment, in her Dominions or Colonies. This explains her "success" with the Argentine and the Scandinavian and Baltic countries in contrast to her failure to obtain substantial concessions from, for example, Germany. But this is not quite the whole story. A country such as Denmark would not have been in such a weak bargaining position relatively to Great Britain had she been able to switch over without much loss from supplying bacon or butter, or whatever the threatened commodities were, and instead to produce something else for her own consumption or for export. In fact, this was not so. The countries with whom Great Britain had the most success in her trade agreements had specialized in supplying certain products, notably meat and dairy produce, to the British market. Although some of them were constrained to switch over to some extent—Denmark, for example, considerably reducing the number of her pigs and growing more grain—this reduced their profits, and they were anxious not to be compelled to switch over still more. Again, it is conceivable that the other country might have been able to use a similar counter-threat against Great Britain. In fact, this was not so. The British market was of vital importance to the countries in question but they themselves took a relatively small proportion of British exports.

Another factor, however, is international investment. Until recently, Great Britain has been on balance a lending country. Capital has been relatively more abundant and therefore cheaper in Great Britain than in most overseas countries. Hence Great Britain was able, if she chose, to obtain concessions in exchange for the promise of a loan on favorable terms—made possible, for example, by a British government guarantee that the interest would be paid. But once heavy investments have been made, the boot is on the other foot. Unless the debtor country needs a new loan from its creditor, it can obtain relatively favorable treatment on the ground that otherwise it will not be able to continue paying interest in full. It has been said that during recent years the economic world has been a debtor's paradise. This is an exaggeration but it contains some truth. We may surmise, for example, that Great Britain might have restricted her imports from the

Argentine more than she did if there had not been over £500 million of British capital invested in that country.

When two countries make a trade agreement without either having an economic pull over the other or exerting any kind of pressure, presumably each country thinks it benefits. But what constitutes a benefit is a matter of opinion. If both countries have liberal ideas they may both be pleased at mutual reductions of tariff even if these have to be generalized to other countries. But if a country believes in protection, it will grudge any tariff reduction which it has to make and will regard it as a concession given only because the benefit to its own export industries from the other country's reductions of tariffs are thought to outweigh this "loss." It will probably try to prevent its own concessions from being extended to other countries to whom it gives most-favored-nation treatment by stating them in a very specific form which includes the goods of the other party but not most of those of competing countries. If both countries favor high protection, the agreement may really be an excuse for raising tariffs. Country A may agree to particular increased duties by country B, which were forbidden by the A-B agreement previously in force, provided that B agrees not to protest against certain increases in A's tariff. It is an error to suppose that trade treaties always mean lower duties and increased trade between the two contracting countries.

3. Exchange Control

During the great depression a number of countries adopted exchange control. Broadly speaking, this meant that all exchange transactions had to pass through the central bank. For example, an exporter had to surrender all the foreign exchange which he received, giving it to the central bank at the official rate in exchange for local currency. Similarly, an importer could not pay his foreign supplier unless the central bank let him have the foreign exchange.

This system was adopted for various reasons. Some of the countries adopting it were afraid that the alternative of letting the exchange value of their currencies depreciate, in order to stimulate exports and check imports, would make their citizens fear that inflation was taking place and would lead to financial panic and withdrawals from their banks. Some, notably Germany, wished to use exchange control as an instrument of national planning. Somehow or other their imports had to be reduced or their exports expanded in order to make their international transactions balance. Exchange control, with its apparatus of export and import permits, enabled them to control all foreign trade and to determine, for example, what quantities of various imports could enter, and from what countries. Again, nearly all the countries adopting this system were debtor countries. They were enabled to reduce their debt payments to other countries without technically defaulting. They transferred only a part of the sums due, the rest being paid into "blocked accounts," in the local currency at the central bank. Some countries allowed some of these blocked balances to be invested in local industries or to be used by the owners to pay their expenses while traveling in the country or to be sold for free exchange at a heavy discount, the "profits" being used to subsidize exports from the exchange control country.

Exchange control implies, for otherwise it would not be necessary, that the official value of the local currency is well above its equilibrium value. Hence all sorts of devices became incorporated into or encrusted upon the system.

For example, some countries subsidized certain exports to free exchange countries; some countries demanded that all or part of the payment for certain commodities such as petrol and wheat and copper should be made in free exchange, even if the commodities were bought by another exchange control country; some countries permitted "private compensation trade" in certain commodities: their exporters could sell all or part of the foreign exchange obtained to local importers for what it would fetch, which was usually much more than its official value in terms of the local currency.

One early result of exchange control was the arrangement of "clearing" agreements. Most of these are rather complicated, but the essential principle may be illustrated by a simplified example. British exporters to an exchange control country, for example, Rumania, found that they were not receiving payment. The Rumanian firms who owed them money were honest and solvent but could not get sterling: the sums due were paid into blocked accounts. But Great Britain bought more from Rumania than she sold to Rumania. Hence she was in a position to insist that all payments due to Rumania should go into a special "clearing account" and that payments due by the Rumanian government and Rumanian firms to British exporters should come out of the clearing account. This would still leave a balance in the clearing account (for British purchases exceed British sales) and the complicated provisions of the agreement related to how much of this balance should go to pay off accumulated trading debts due to British exporters who had exported to Rumania before the agreement was made and had thereby acquired blocked lei, how much should go to pay debt charges due by Rumania to Great Britain, and which particular debt charges should have priority, and how much should be placed at the free disposal of the Rumanian government.

A clearing agreement often does not work smoothly. For example, take that between Great Britain and Turkey. Great Britain normally buys more from Turkey than she sells her. But after the 1935 and 1936 agreements, Turkish firms bought more heavily from Great Britain, paying "through the clearing," and the balance of trade moved the other way. In the summer of 1939 there was over £2 million sterling owing to British exporters and they had to wait over two years before receiving payment from the clearing. Hence one country may have to make a whole series of clearing agreements, over a period of time, with another in order to try to remedy defects as they become apparent. Great Britain, for example, has made some half-a-dozen or more clearing or payments or transfer agreements with Germany, and also with Italy and Rumania over the last few years.

Most of the British agreements are called "payments agreements." The distinction between a clearing agreement and a payments agreement is not very clear but it may be said that the latter is an improved form of the former. The essential improvement may be illustrated by the Anglo-German payments agreement. Germany agreed to restrict her imports from Great Britain during any months to 55 per cent of the value of German exports to Great Britain in the month-but-one before. This made it certain that there would be enough in the clearing account to pay British exporters to Germany without more than three months delay at the outside. And this enabled the ordinary facilities of the banking system to be used—a British bank would without hesitation discount a bill due to an English firm from a sound German firm because it knew that there would be no trouble about "transferring" the money to Great Britain. Another advantage was that firms could deal with one another instead of everything being lumped together in a general clearing account. Moreover, a definite proportion of the total—in this case 45 per cent of the value of German sales to Great Britain —was available to pay old commercial debts, interest on the external public debt of the exchange control country, and so forth.

Great Britain now has agreements as to clearings and payments of commercial debts with the Argentine, Brazil, Germany, Hungary, Italy, the Soviet Union, Spain, Turkey, Uruguay, and Yugoslavia. In addition, there may be explicit or implicit understandings in a British trade agreement with an exchange control country that Great Britain will not be discriminated against in the distribution of import licenses by the latter. For example, there was such a clause in the supplementary agreement of 1936 with Denmark.

4. British Trade Agreements 1933-38

After she had adopted protection and concluded her arrangements with the Dominions, Great Britain was ready to negotiate trade agreements with other countries.[1] Some of those concluded during the years 1933 to 1938 were little more than exchanges, or renewals, of assurances of

[1] Great Britain is a party to some four hundred bilateral agreements, many of long standing. She has unconditional most-favored-nation agreements with most countries. A number of the four hundred relate to specific problems such as the legal position of joint-stock companies and the relief of distressed seamen. She is also a party to nearly thirty multilateral agreements on subjects (such as copyright, the safety of life at sea, and international navigable waters) of common interest to a number of countries.

most-favored-nation treatment.[2] There were also a number
of clearing and payments agreements.[3] These were discussed
in general terms in the preceding section and need not be
considered here. The most important of the others were
those with the Argentine, the various Scandinavian and
Baltic States, France, Germany, the Soviet Union, and the
U.S.A.

The main object of British policy in negotiating these
agreements was to try to expand the sales of British exports.
We shall therefore ask what kinds of concessions she obtained, with this object in view, and what kinds of concessions she granted in return. She was most successful in
obtaining concessions from countries which relied largely
on the British market as an outlet for their produce.
Agreements were concluded during 1923 and 1934 with a
number of countries which were in this position, namely:
the Argentine, Denmark, Sweden, Norway, Iceland, Finland, Estonia, Latvia, and Lithuania. The agreements with
the Argentine and Denmark are summarized in some detail in the following sections. The others were all on much
the same pattern and will therefore be considered in general terms.

All the countries named sold much more to Great Britain
than they bought from her and this fact was stressed by
the British negotiators. It was explicitly stated in the pro-
visional agreement with Estonia in July 1933. "Both Governments undertake to keep in view the balance of trade
between the United Kingdom and Estonia, and the Es-
tonian Government recognise that it is in the interest of
both countries that the present disparity in that balance

[2] For example, those with the Netherlands (1934), Uruguay (1935),
Brazil (1936), Chile (1937), and Cuba (1937).

[3] Made at various dates with Brazil, Germany, Hungary, Rumania, Spain,
Turkey, Uruguay, and Yugoslavia.

should be readjusted as far as possible by the increase of the sales in Estonia of goods the produce or manufacture of the United Kingdom." After that, it became usual for some such reference to be inserted in the protocol to an agreement, the other government promising "to encourage and promote by all means at their disposal" the sale of British goods.

With all the countries named Great Britain obtained most-favored-nation treatment for her exports, not only as to tariffs but also—at any rate, in general terms—as to any import quotas that might be imposed and as to import licenses for British goods if a country practised exchange control. At this point, we may mention that the exchange of notes with the Netherlands in July 1934 contains an attempt to apply the most-favored-nation principle to import quotas. We may mention, in order to show that Great Britain was fully aware of the damage which might be done to her export industries by quantitative discrimination against them, that the agreement with France (June 1934) ended a dispute over quotas. Great Britain had claimed that the French import quotas discriminated against her goods and had retaliated by placing a 20 per cent surtax on her imports from France. By the agreement Great Britain removed the surtax and France undertook to allocate quotas for British goods according to the proportions entering France in the base period, which for most goods was 1928-30.

Great Britain did not succeed in obtaining any reductions in duties, apart from a tariff quota on British herrings granted by Finland, from any of the countries named except Denmark. Any reductions granted to her would probably have had to be granted to other countries under most-favored-nation arrangements, and would have meant a loss of revenue too large to be faced during a depression. What she did obtain, as a rule, was an assurance that duties on a number of British goods would not exceed stated maxima.

A special feature of the agreements with Scandinavian and Baltic countries was the concessions obtained for British coal. Great Britain could terminate her agreement with each of the following countries if at the end of any period of twelve months the percentage of its total coal imports coming from Great Britain was less than the figure shown:

Denmark.....	80 per cent	Finland.......	75 per cent
Iceland.......	77	Lithuania.....	80
Norway.......	70	Estonia.......	85
Sweden.......	45	Latvia........	70

Thus Great Britain secured for herself a predominant position in the Scandinavian and Baltic markets for coal. The quotas granted were considerably higher than the proportions of British coal imported in previous years. This aroused some indignation in some other countries, who claimed that Great Britain had imposed arrangements contrary to the most-favored-nation spirit.

The same objection was raised against the "purchase agreements" of which the two governments "took note" in the protocol to some of the agreements. These were private arrangements made by British firms with local firms to facilitate and promote the sale of certain British products. For example, for Finland the British products were flour, creosote, iron and steel, commercial vehicles, wood-working tools and machinery, jute wrappers for bacon and hams, and salt.

In return for these various concessions, general and specific, to British exports, Great Britain usually gave most-favored-nation treatment—but, of course, only with non-British countries—as to tariffs and import quotas which she was imposing or might impose in future. An interesting statement of how the most-favored-nation principle would be applied to quotas occurs in Article 4 of the Agreement of September 1933 with Finland. It reads: "In the event of such regulation of imports being introduced in the case of all or any of these products, the following provisions shall have effect in so far as they may be applicable. . . . The Government of the United Kingdom will, in such event, in making allocation to Finland, take into consideration the position which Finland has held in past years as a supplier of these products to the United Kingdom market. Allocations to Finland will be made on the same basis as, and on conditions not less favourable than, allocations to any other foreign country." Great Britain did not reduce any of her duties in any of these agreements. She was bound by her Ottawa pledges to keep her duties on a number of goods, including butter and eggs, exported from these countries at certain minimum levels. But she did promise that her duties on a number of products would not exceed stated maxima.

We have already mentioned the agreement with *France* signed in June 1934. Great Britain was not in a strong bargaining position with France, and did not succeed in getting an increase in the French quota on British coal or even unconditional most-favored-nation treatment for British exports. Indeed, this agreement is a remarkable exception to the usual British practice in this respect. It is true that most-favored-nation treatment in tariff matters was granted but it was explicitly stated, *inter alia,* that this did not mean treatment as favorable as that received by countries with which special arrangements had been made, that if one country stimulated its exports, "directly or indirectly" by "abnormal and artificial means," the other could take measures to counteract this, and that certain stated goods would not get most-favored-nation treatment.

The 1930 agreement with the *Soviet Union* had provided for reciprocal most-favored-nation treatment and led to the placing of Soviet contracts (guaranteed by the Export Credit Guarantee Department of the Board of Trade) and a consequent increase in British exports to the Soviet Union from £3.7 million in 1929 to £9.2 million in 1932. But Canadian timber interests, relying on the clause in the British-Canadian agreement by which the British government undertook to prevent dumping in the British market of goods produced by state-controlled industries, renewed their protests against the dumping of Russian timber and the British government had to denounce this 1930 agreement in October 1932.

A new agreement was concluded in February 1934. This contained an attempt to regulate the balance of payments between the two countries. "The payments of the Union of Soviet Socialist Republics in the United Kingdom . . . shall bear to the proceeds of the Union of Soviet Socialist Republics in the United Kingdom . . . the following proportions:

In the year ending December 31, 1934	1:1.7
In the year ending December 31, 1935	1:1.5
In the year ending December 31, 1936	1:1.4
In the year ending December 31, 1937	1:1.2

"Thereafter an approximate balance of payments measured by the ratio 1:1.1 shall be maintained."

It is doubtful whether the agreed balance of payments was reached. For example, in 1937 gross imports from the Soviet Union were £29.1 million, domestic exports £3.1

million, and re-exports £16.4 million. In any event, British exporters complain that Russia has not kept the spirit of the agreement, for most of her purchases have been purchases of imported copper, tin, rubber, nickel, lead, and other goods not produced in Great Britain. At the outbreak of war in 1939 Russia owed several million pounds on credits guaranteed by the Export Credit Guarantee Department.

The agreement with *Poland* in 1935 is remarkable in that it is one of the few agreements by which some duties were reduced. Poland made reductions in textile duties in return for guarantees regarding the restriction of British imports of her bacon, butter, and eggs.

The trade agreement with *Germany* in 1933 is about the only instance before the Anglo-American agreement of 1938 of reductions in duties made by Great Britain. In return for a minimum coal quota of 180,000 metric tons per month, Great Britain made some reductions in her duties on certain goods of a type exported by Germany, including toys, musical instruments, gramophones, clocks, jewelery, enameled hollow ware, and safety razor blades. There were various payments agreements with Germany during the following years. In January 1939 representatives of the British and the German coal-mining industries concluded an *Anglo-German coal agreement* by which selling prices would be fixed and British exports would bear the relation to German exports of 65 to 35. Conversations took place at Düsseldorf in March 1939 between representatives of the Reichsgruppe Industrie and of the Federation of British Industries, resulting in an agreement to replace competition in common export markets by price-fixing and marketing arrangements. The stage seemed set for a comprehensive commercial treaty but both these agreements were suspended after German troops marched into Prague in March 1939.

The agreements with Argentine and Denmark and the Anglo-American trade agreement of November 1938 are so important that separate sections are devoted to them.

5. AGREEMENTS WITH THE ARGENTINE

By the treaty of 1925 the United Kingdom and the Argentine assured one another most-favored-nation treatment in matters of trade and shipping.

It will be remembered that the British livestock industry was considerably depressed during the slump. Prices of beef were especially low in the autumn of 1932. In November 1932, therefore, Great Britain obtained a voluntary agreement from South American exporters to cut down their exports to her by 10 per cent. The Argentine, confronted with the Ottawa policy of restricting imports of foreign meat and fearing that her import quota might be reduced much further, sought to obtain some kind of guarantee for her producers.

Great Britain, for her part, wished to increase her exports to the Argentine and to make arrangements for the "unfreezing" of about £16 million which had accumulated in blocked peso balances since the Argentine adopted exchange control in October 1931. A convention was signed in May 1933 and a supplementary agreement in September 1933.

The most important type of meat exported by the Argentine is chilled beef. The convention contained an undertaking by Great Britain not to reduce her imports of Argentine chilled beef below the quantity imported in the Ottawa year "unless, and then only so far as, it appears to the Government of the United Kingdom after consulting and exchanging all relevant information with the Argentine Government to be necessary in order to secure a remunerative level of prices in the United Kingdom market." This undertaking was not of great value. British beef prices were not "remunerative" and imports from the Argentine were kept nearly 10 per cent below the Ottawa year level. But Great Britain gave a further undertaking that if a reduction below 90 per cent of the 1931-32 level was imposed on the Argentine, British imports from other countries, including British countries, would be reduced by the same proportion. This apparently meant that if, for example, British imports of Argentine chilled beef were reduced to 81 per cent of the 1931-32 level, British imports of Dominion beef would be reduced by 10 per cent. This was a very valuable promise. Lord Beaverbrook doubtless had this in mind when he said that the convention meant "the granting of Dominion status to the South American republic."

The same concession could not be granted on frozen beef and frozen mutton and lamb. The Dominions were leading exporters of these commodities, but at the time they exported comparatively little chilled beef. Hence the Ottawa scale was applied to these commodities: British imports were to be reduced by the middle of 1934 to 65 per cent of the 1931-32 level.

A protocol to the convention contains a paragraph declaring that the Argentine Government, "fully appreciating the benefits rendered by the collaboration of British capital in public utility and other undertakings," intends to give those undertakings "such benevolent treatment as may conduce to the further economic development of the country, and to the due and legitimate protection of the interests concerned in their operation."

The supplementary agreement provided for maximum rates of duty on about three hundred items imported into the Argentine from Great Britain. The Argentine undertook not to levy any duty on coal or on any other article which she admitted free from the United Kingdom on May 1, 1933. The United Kingdom agreed to admit Argentine maize and meat free of duty and not to impose quotas on Argentine cereals. The British duty on linseed was to be 10 per cent and on wheat 2s. per quarter. The two governments were to consult together if the Argentine market for British coal and coke was not maintained.

Arrangements were made for the gradual transfer to Great Britain of the blocked balances. A loan of £13½ million was raised in London in the form of 4 per cent Argentine government bearer bonds, to be repaid over the next twenty years. The sterling thus obtained was used forthwith to transfer blocked balances due to British short term creditors.

Arrangements were also made to ensure that payments falling due in the future to British investors and shipping firms, as well as to British exporters, should be transferred (and not blocked) as fully as possible. By Article 2 of the convention all the sterling received from British purchases in the Argentine was to be earmarked for this purpose, after deducting "a reasonable sum"—fixed at £3 million a year—towards the service of Argentine public debts owing to other countries. Great Britain was to receive most-favored-nation treatment in the allotment of foreign exchange to would-be Argentine importers.

In fact, the Argentine exchange control worked, or rather was worked, very favorably to Great Britain. The Exchange Control Commission tended to ration foreign exchange to would-be importers not according to the proportion of purchases made from different countries in the past but according to the purchases made from the Argentine by different countries. Great Britain of course was by far the biggest purchaser. Moreover, a 20 per cent surcharge was imposed in April 1935 on goods imported without prior exchange permits. This also favored Great Britain, as it was easier to obtain permits to import from Great Britain than to obtain them to import from other countries.

British imports from the Argentine fell from £50.87 million in 1932 to £43.99 million in 1935, but British exports to the Argentine rose from £10.66 million in 1932 to £15.26 million in 1935. This was just the kind of result which Great Britain had hoped to achieve.

The 1933 agreements were for three years. In 1936 the Dominions pressed Great Britain to restrict still further her imports of meat from the Argentine. Owing to technical improvements it had become commercially possible to send chilled beef from Australia and New Zealand and the quantities they sent had increased rapidly since 1932. Although Empire producers had been asked to keep down their exports of frozen beef (their exports of chilled beef being relatively unimportant) to a maximum of 10 per cent above the amount sent in the Ottawa year, total imports of beef (frozen and chilled) from these two countries increased from 1.6 million cwts. in 1932 to 2.5 million in 1934.

The 1936 agreement therefore made another turn or two of the screw upon the Argentine. There was now to be a duty of not more than three farthings a pound on chilled beef, but there were to be no duties on mutton, lamb, and pork. British imports from the Argentine of chilled beef were to form at least 88.6 per cent, of frozen beef at least 60.6 per cent, and of mutton and lamb at least 70 per cent, of all foreign imports subject to regulation. In no event were British imports to be less than a certain minimum. For chilled beef, this was for 1937 the quantity imported in 1935 less 138,700 cwts.; for 1938 the quantity imported in 1937 less 138,700 cwts.; for 1939, the quantity imported in 1938 less 138,700 cwts., but the 1939 imports were in no case to be less than 6,590,000 cwts. For frozen beef, the minimum was 124,600 cwts. per year. For mutton and lamb, the minimum was 886,000 cwts. for 1937 and 797,400 cwts. for 1938. These figures represented reductions of a few per cent on the previous levels but on the other hand limits were set to the amount of future reductions. It might have been a good deal worse. As a matter of fact, imports considerably in excess of the minimum were permitted in the following years.

Great Britain undertook once again not to impose a duty on maize, not to increase her duty on wheat, and not to impose quotas on cereals. The Argentine reduced the £3 million deductions for foreign debt service to £1½ million.

6. Agreements with Denmark

The fall in prices which began in 1929 was much greater at first for vegetable produce than for animal produce. Denmark profited by the cheapness of feeding stuffs and considerably increased her output of pigs and butter. Her exports of bacon and butter to Great Britain increased greatly. The prices of these commodities fell and British farmers demanded some restriction of imports. A section of the British press attacked Denmark on the ground that her purchases from Great Britain were little more than a quarter of her sales to Great Britain and that she used much of her receipts from the latter to pay for manufactured goods which she imported from Germany.

Denmark was in a very weak bargaining position. Great Britain was far and away her largest market. Her second market, Germany, had greatly stiffened its restrictions on Danish produce in 1932. And there were no substantial British investments in Denmark, as there were in the Argentine. When negotiations for the trade agreement began in December 1932 the question which Denmark asked herself was how much more Great Britain would demand in addition to what had been arranged in Ottawa.

The agreement was signed in April 1933. There was to be no British duty on bacon and hams, but Denmark was unable to secure the right to export a stated minimum quantity, for Great Britain intended to cut down imports in order to encourage a greater home production. However, Denmark was given the right to supply 62 per cent of the total permitted imports from foreign countries.

Butter and bacon were about equal in importance to Danish exporters. Great Britain undertook not to raise her duty on butter above the 15s. per cwt. "Ottawa duty." But she reserved the right to impose import quotas on butter. For butter, in contrast to bacon, Denmark was given a minimum quota of 2,300,000 cwts., equal to the quantity which she supplied to the British market in 1930. Similar arrangements applied to eggs. In fact, Great Britain has not imposed import quotas on butter or eggs, so that these quota provisions did not become effective. Nevertheless they were a valuable safeguard to Denmark.

Denmark made a series of important concessions, which were of course extended to other countries under most-favored-nation clauses, on various goods. The most important were the promises to reduce and bind the tariff on a number of textile goods.

A protocol was attached to the treaty. Denmark undertook to purchase at least 80 per cent of her total coal imports from Great Britain. The two governments "took note" of private arrangements which had been or were being concluded between British sales organizations and Danish trade organizations to ensure that the salt, salt-petre, and jute cloth used in the treatment and packing of Danish produce exported to Great Britain should be purchased in Great Britain. It was also noted that Denmark would take steps to increase its imports of British iron and steel.

No explicit mention was made in the treaty of the Danish exchange control office, but it was undoubtedly assumed that this would continue to promote imports from Great Britain.

It will be remembered that in November 1933 the 62 per cent of foreign imports of bacon and hams granted to Denmark was reduced, without the consent of Denmark, to 47 per cent. But the fact that export licenses for bacon were distributed by Denmark, and that her exporters were organized and did not undercut one another, meant that the difference (which rose to over one pound per cwt.) between the British price and the Danish price went to Denmark. Her exports of bacon to Great Britain in 1938 were well below half her exports in 1932, but her receipts were only 4 or 6 per cent lower. There were supplementary agreements with Denmark in 1936 and again in 1938. The latter gave her a bacon quota of at least 68.95 per cent of the total imports from non-British countries and a ham quota, corresponding to the very small exports in the past, of 0.4 per cent.

The change in Denmark's trade with Great Britain is shown by the following figures:

	Imports from Great Britain		Exports to Great Britain	
1929	263 million Kr.		963 million Kr.	
1932	255	" "	728	" "
1935	479	" "	731	" "
1937	638	" "	824	" "
1938	567	" "	861	" "

7. THE AGREEMENT WITH THE UNITED STATES

The British agreement with the United States was signed at the White House on November 17, 1938. An agreement between the United States and Canada was signed at the same time. The two agreements were complementary in that some of the concessions made by Great Britain— notably the abolition of the wheat duty and reductions in the duties on soft woods and on apples—required the consent of Canada to a diminished margin of preference in the British market. By an exchange of letters with Great Britain on the previous day Canada had agreed to this and in return Great Britain had agreed to receive smaller margins of preference in Canada on certain chemicals, steel manufactures, internal combustion engines, and one or two other items. This enabled Canada to reduce her duties on these commodities for the benefit of the United States. Both Canada and Great Britain expected to gain more by the concessions granted to them by the United States than they would lose by a diminution of imperial preference.

These agreements were made possible only by the liberal attitude adopted by both Mr. Cordell Hull and Mr. Mackenzie King. All three countries made real concessions by granting reductions in some duties and undertaking not to increase a number of others. Moreover, Newfoundland and the Colonies were included in the British agreement. The United States sells much more to Great Britain than she buys from her but she buys about three times as much from the Colonies as she sells them. Hence the provisions relating to the Colonies are valuable, for they included undertakings by the United States not to increase her duties on many of their products, which meant that most of them would continue to enter free of duty.

Great Britain was not prepared to forgo revenue by reducing her duties on tobacco, but she did promise that the existing imperial preference would not be increased until 1942, when a reduction would be considered. Nor was she prepared to reduce the protection given to the British motor industry, although she promised not to increase the existing duty on cars of 25HP and over. But she did reduce her duties on various commodities representing a total value of over £10 million of her imports from the United States in 1936. The duty of 2s. per quarter on wheat, which dates from Ottawa, was abolished.[4] The 10 per cent duty on lard and the duties on canned grape fruit, grapefruit juice, and orange juice were abolished. The duties on a number of other products, including apples, soft wood, and many canned and dried fruits were reduced. The continued free entry of raw cotton, sulphur, resin, and fur skins was guaranteed. Hams also were to remain on the free list and the American quota was increased.

In 1936 British exports to the United States amounted to some £40 million. Of these, about £17 million remains on the free list, over £11 million is given reduced duties,

[4] One result of this is that Canadian wheat can once more be shipped, if desired, through New York and Boston.

and existing duties are stabilized on a further £6 million. This last category includes whisky, which is the chief single item exported by Great Britain to the United States. The duty on it is stabilized at the low level to which it was reduced by the American agreement with Canada in 1935.

The most important American concessions relate to textiles, on which the duties were very high. Duties on most cotton piece goods were reduced by 20 to 30 per cent, on high grade woolen goods from 60 per cent to 35 per cent ad valorem, and on many ranges of linen goods from 35 to 20 per cent ad valorem. Duties were reduced on a number of other commodities also, including earthenware, china, glass, specialized metal products, leather goods, sports goods, pipes, and marmalade.

The two countries grant one another most-favored-nation treatment, but Great Britain may grant more favorable terms to the Empire, and the United States to its territories, to the Panama Canal zone, and to the republic of Cuba. Moreover, the agreement contains a provision which has become usual during recent years in American agreements but has never before appeared in a British agreement. It is to the effect that any concession may be withdrawn or modified if it happens that some third country, to which it is extended, obtains the major benefit and in consequence increased imports threaten serious injury to home producers. The agreement may be terminated "if there should be a wide variation in the pound-dollar rate of exchange."

The concessions made by both sides in the agreement were real, if limited, and the agreement was greeted with approval by all who favored greater freedom of trade. They hoped that it would mark a turning point in tariff policy and would lead to a general reduction of protection.

It was certainly an important move away from the Ottawa system—and a move to which the Dominions and India agreed. Great Britain and the United States together perform well over a quarter of the trade of the world. This agreement between them, naming long lists of items with many reductions and stabilizations of duties but not a single increase, is indeed a remarkable and encouraging document.

8. The Results of British Trade Agreements

The various British agreements, with the notable exception of the recent one with the United States, brought about remarkably few reductions in import duties. An apparent exception is the agreement with France in 1934, by which Great Britain reduced by 50 per cent her duties on raw silk and artificial silk yarns. But these reductions had been recommended, in the interest of British manufacturers, by the Import Duties Advisory Committee in May 1934.

The chief exports of most of the countries with which agreements were concluded were agricultural products, and in so far as these were subject to British duties Great Britain was unable to offer concessions, even if she wished, without breaking her pledge to one or other of the Dominions to maintain a stated minimum margin of imperial preference. The best she could offer was that her existing duties would not be increased.

The limitations which she imposed on her imports of various kinds of meat from foreign countries tended to reduce the total volume of world trade. This was particularly true of bacon. Total British imports of bacon were considerably cut down, being replaced by home-produced bacon. It was much less true of meat. Total British imports of meat were not reduced. Australia and New Zealand increased their exports, and despite their promises and endeavors to set limits to this increase in fact it filled the gap in British consumption caused by the reduction in imports from the Argentine and other foreign countries. The pig population of Great Britain increased considerably, but the other sections of the livestock industry remained depressed.

As time went on, British exports expanded to most of the countries which had made her substantial concessions and were able and willing to promote the sale of British goods through their exchange control or in other ways. It is not easy to judge how much of this expansion of British exports was due to a recovery of the prices of foodstuffs and raw materials, and the consequent increase in the purchasing power of the countries in question, and how much was due to the trade agreements and all that they implied. The table on page 147 perhaps affords some indication. The trend of trade with Holland, which had refused to give any special concessions to Great Britain, may be contrasted with the trend for the other four countries.

The increase in British exports to the Scandinavian and Baltic countries and to the Argentine can certainly be attributed partly, although not entirely, to the trade agreements and to the measures taken by these countries to divert their purchases towards Great Britain. But it seems very probable that British exports to other non-Empire countries would have expanded more if these trade agreements had not been made. Other manufacturing countries, finding that certain markets were largely closed to them and reserved for Great Britain, competed more fiercely for sales elsewhere.

A good illustration of this is provided by the history of

BRITISH TRADE WITH CERTAIN COUNTRIES
£ Thousands

	1931	1932	1933	1934	1935	1936	1937
Sweden							
Imports	17,342	13,424	15,938	17,956	17,009	20,628	26,231
Exports	7,743	6,885	7,175	9,082	9,723	10,386	13,019
Norway[5]							
Imports	8,630	8,282	6,961	8,442	8,213	8,940	11,577
Exports	7,559	5,801	5,553	6,289	6,619	7,146	8,936
Denmark							
Imports	49,695	40,569	35,428	32,875	32,037	33,235	36,551
Exports	8,656	9,852	11,797	13,354	13,759	14,943	16,881
Finland							
Imports	11,630	11,733	12,766	15,232	14,914	18,145	22,452
Exports	1,603	2,263	2,845	3,611	4,152	4,217	5,963
Holland							
Imports	35,198	22,029	18,602	20,973	23,065	25,088	32,016
Exports	13,701	12,106	12,371	12,092	11,657	12,343	15,031

British exports of coal. It will be remembered that "coal clauses" in the protocols were a special feature of all the agreements made in 1933 and 1934 with Scandinavian and Baltic countries. Great Britain was assured, by the large quotas granted to her, of a predominant position in these markets. As a result her coal exports to them rose from 4.9 million tons in 1932 to 8.5 tons in 1936. British and Polish coal producers came to an understanding towards the close of 1934, but no understanding was reached with German producers, who had been powerful rivals of Great Britain in these markets. German coal, largely excluded from these markets, began to displace British coal in France, Belgium, Italy, and other European markets. The total exports of British coal (excluding bunkers) fell from 38.9 million tons in 1932 to 34.5 million tons in 1936, and their value fell also although the total value of British exports of merchandise was considerably higher in 1936 than in 1932. Such figures can

[5] After 1932 without Spitzbergen.

never be very conclusive. Great Britain's coal might have fared much worse without these agreements. The big fall in her exports to Italy—from 5 million tons to 60,000 tons—was largely due, it could be argued, to the imposition of economic sanctions by Great Britain after the commencement of the Abyssinian war. Nevertheless German coal exports rose from 22 million tons in 1934 to 28.7 million tons in 1936 and to 37.6 million tons (as against 40.3 million tons exported by Great Britain) in 1937.

It may be added that one result of the change in the distribution of British coal exports was considerable distress in South Wales. It was the East Coast which gained by the expansion of sales to Scandinavia and the Baltic. South Wales, however, suffered by the fall in exports to western and southern Europe.

It would be ridiculous to attribute the slow rate of expansion of international trade entirely or even mainly to the Ottawa system and to British trade agreements. The strength of protectionist feeling in many countries, uncertainty as to how exchange rates would vary in the future, and policies of exchange control, were all potent influences which slowed down the revival of foreign trade. But British trade policy played its part. The Ottawa agreements tied the hands of Great Britain by preventing her from reducing her duties on a number of important commodities, and equally tied the hands of the Dominions. The attitude adopted by the Empire towards regional pacts effectively prevented the formation of low tariff *blocs* between neighboring countries. And the British drive towards a reduction in her import surplus from various countries inevitably tended, in so far as it was successful, to make international trade more bilateral and therefore less in volume than it would otherwise have been.

Chapter VI

MONETARY POLICY

1. The Significance of Exchange Rates

This chapter discusses the external monetary policy of Great Britain. It deals, that is to say, with the measures taken to control the exchange value of sterling in terms of other leading currencies, such as the dollar and the franc.

If we can take money incomes and money costs in Great Britain as given, then a low exchange value of sterling tends to promote British exports. Suppose, for example, that British exporters of some commodity can make a reasonable profit by selling it for £1 per unit. If the pound is worth 5 dollars, they must ask 5 dollars per unit in the United States, but if the pound is worth only 4 dollars, they need ask only 4 dollars, and if they are competing with one another for the American market, the price will be driven down to about 4 dollars. Moreover, a number of British goods which could sell for, say, a pound, at a profit but which, owing to competition of other countries, would fetch only, say, 4.50 dollars abroad, cannot be exported, except at a loss, when the pound is worth more than 4.50 dollars. Thus a fall in the exchange value of the pound tends to increase the range of goods which can be profitably exported. Of course, if the value of sterling is deliberately kept down, this means that Great Britain is in a sense making a present to the rest of the world. In technical terms, she is turning the terms of trade against herself. By selling British goods more cheaply, she is giving a larger quantity of exports than before in return for any given quantity of imports. But few countries during recent years have paid much attention to this aspect of the matter. They have all been anxious to promote their exports, partly in order to reduce their unemployment, and partly because the old mercantilist belief that exports are somehow good and imports somehow bad is still very much alive..

A low exchange value of sterling tends also to check imports into Great Britain. People tend to spend less upon, say, American goods at 5 dollars a unit when a unit costs 25 shillings than when it costs £1. Thus a low exchange value of sterling is equivalent to a general tariff.

If the value of sterling is kept unduly low, the sums received from abroad in payment for British exports and shipping services, as interest on British overseas capital, and so on, tend to exceed the sums paid out for imports into Great Britain, foreign loans made by Great Britain, and so on. Under a free exchange rate, this would tend to push up the value of sterling again, but under some form of exchange control this situation can continue provided that the controlling authority is prepared to acquire increasing balances of foreign currencies—which it can usually turn into gold if it wishes.

This, of course, is not the whole story. An unduly low value of sterling tends to raise money incomes and money costs within Great Britain. Higher prices for imported food raise the cost of living and lead to demands for increased wages. Higher costs, in sterling, of imported materials raise the costs of manufacture. Nevertheless the above conclusions are broadly true: exports are promoted and imports are checked.

Hence the device of exchange depreciation, or devaluation (returning to gold at a lower parity), has a special appeal for any country which wishes to improve the position of its export industries. The exporters gain, because they get more in terms of their own currency, and purchasers of imports lose, because they have to pay more in terms of their own currency. But this "advantage" disappears if more and more countries follow suit. And if the depreciating country is, like Great Britain, an important exporter, other countries may be bound sooner or later to follow suit. For the lower prices at which British goods are being offered in the markets of the world will compel the exporters of other countries to reduce their prices also, and unless they were making large profits before, this means that they will now be selling at prices which do not cover their full costs, while some will be driven out of the exporting business altogether. The obvious remedy is for their governments also to depreciate or devalue their currencies.

Hence when an important country deliberately undervalues its currency this is likely to lead to a period of competitive exchange depreciation, with the volume of international trade kept down by the exchange risks due to uncertainty and fluctuations in exchange rates, and in the end the "advantage" of the first country may have quite disappeared because other countries have reduced the exchange value of their currencies to an equal or greater extent.

2. THE GOLD STANDARD: 1925 TO 1931

After 1920, Great Britain adopted a deliberate policy of deflation. The volume of money was reduced year by year in order to bring down prices and to make possible a return to the gold standard at the old parity. This was carried out on May 1, 1925.

As we showed in Chapter I, Great Britain was not happy on the gold standard during these post-war years before the crisis of September 1931. It was expected that American prices would continue to rise after the spring of 1925, but in fact they tended rather to fall. Later, a number of other countries, including France, returned to gold at a rather low parity, thus increasing the difficulties of British exports. Great Britain found herself in the opposite position to that discussed in the preceding section. The pound sterling was pegged to gold at 84s.11½d. an ounce (equivalent to £1 = 4.866 dollars) and this rate was too high. Given the level of money incomes and costs, sterling was overvalued. British exporters could not quote sufficiently low prices in foreign currencies to enable Great Britain to retain her previous share of the world's exports.

The orthodox remedy was deflation. If money incomes had been reduced, British consumers would have curtailed their demand for imports; and if costs, notably wage rates, had been reduced this would have encouraged British exports. But there were great objections against this course. Great Britain imports mainly foodstuffs and raw materials. A fall in money incomes would cause people to economize more on luxuries and semi-luxuries produced at home than on imports. In order to cut down imports by 10 per cent, a cut of considerably more than 10 per cent in money incomes might have been necessary. Moreover, wages in the export industries were already very low, and the trade unions seemed to be taking a firm line against wage reductions. The orthodox remedy of a high bank rate and a contraction of the quantity of money would probably have considerably increased unemploy-

ment—and there were already over a million unemployed
—and caused great discontent.

Possibly this course should have been adopted, despite
these objections to it. The advantages of fixed exchange
rates to a great trading nation like Great Britain are extremely large. Moreover, a reduction in the value of
sterling reduces the real return on sums, amounting to
some £100 million, representing that part of her overseas
interest income which is fixed in sterling. And in any event
the British economic system clearly lacked flexibility and
adaptability. More transfer of persons was needed between
districts and industries. A reduction in the exchange
value of sterling might have done something to promote
British exports but it would not have gone to the root of
the trouble.

What actually took place was a typically British policy
of compromise. Great Britain did not deflate. Losses of
gold were not allowed to have their "normal" effect of
reducing the quantity of money, and thereby money incomes. "You will find," said Sir Ernest Harvey, Deputy
Governor of the Bank of England, in his evidence before
the MacMillan Committee (Question 353), "if you look at
a succession of Bank returns that the amount of gold we
have lost has been almost entirely replaced by an increase
in the Bank's securities." Foreign balances were permitted
and encouraged to accumulate in London. But the pound
was not devalued, and no effective ban was placed on
British lending abroad, so that Great Britain drifted into
an increasingly vulnerable position, while her staple export industries continued to stagnate, and unemployment
remained unusually high.

Thus when Great Britain was compelled to leave gold
in September 1931, one school of thought believed that

this was perhaps a blessing in disguise. The pound had been overvalued. It had stood at 4.866 dollars when it should have been at 4.40 or 4.20 or 4.00—exactly where, nobody could say. Now at last British exports would have a chance. They could now compete on more favorable terms with the exports of other countries.

But Great Britain was not the only country to reduce the exchange value of its currency. Australia, New Zealand, and a number of South American countries had already left gold. After September 21, 1931, the rest of the British Empire kept the old relationship with sterling, except for South Africa and British Honduras, both of which remained on gold, Hong-Kong which remained on silver, and Canada, which allowed its currency to fall in value, but less than sterling. A number of countries outside the Empire, including the three Scandinavian countries, Portugal, and Egypt, kept approximately their old parity with sterling. The fall in the values of the currencies of this important group of countries imposed a heavy deflationary pressure on those countries which still remained on gold. Depression increased in the "gold bloc," whose export industries were severely hit. The pressure was increased as time went on and other countries left gold, and it was made particularly severe after the spring of 1933, when the United States did the same—subsequently revaluing the dollar (in January 1934) at slightly below 60 per cent of its former gold parity.

3. THE BAN ON FOREIGN LENDING

For many years Great Britain had made a practice of lending and investing considerable sums overseas. The value of her foreign assets was, in round figures, about £4000 million, yielding some £200 million a year. Much

of this was in the British Empire, but she had also substantial loans and investments in the Argentine and other
foreign countries.

She continued to lend overseas, particularly to Australia,
during the years before the crisis of 1931, although she
was no longer the chief lending nation: during the period
1925 to 1930 the United States lent considerably more
than Great Britain to other countries.

After the crisis of September 1931, all new issues of
capital were subjected to a greater or less degree of government control and a complete "ban" on new issues was
announced simultaneously with the war loan conversion
scheme on June 30, 1932. This "ban" had no legal sanction
whatever. It was merely an expression of the wishes of
the Treasury. Yet the authority of the Treasury and of
the Bank of England, with whom it worked in close collaboration, is so great that its wishes were respected
despite occasional mild protests.

For more than three months the ban was complete. In
October, when the success of the conversion operation was
assured, restrictions on home industrial issues were relaxed and later removed, but issues by municipalities and
Empire governments continued to be carefully regulated
and there was almost complete prohibition upon new
issues for foreign countries.

This prohibition has remained in force ever since. Apparently the only exceptions are loans which will be
spent by the borrowing country entirely on British goods
and services and loans for the purpose of strengthening
the sterling reserves of a foreign central bank. All other
public issues which would result in a transference of
capital, directly or indirectly, to foreign countries have
been banned. It seems that this was intended to be a more

or less permanent policy, for some years ago the government appointed an advisory council to assist the Treasury in carrying out these wholly extra-constitutional functions.

It is interesting to note that the ban did not apply to purchases by British residents of existing foreign securities. Such purchases could have been prevented only by complete exchange control, and the government was not prepared to go to this length. At times, they reached quite large dimensions: for example, the United States Department of Commerce gives the net inflow of funds from the United Kingdom during 1936 in connection with transactions in United States securities at 218 million dollars.

The primary purpose of controlling new issues was to keep interest rates low. It was part of the "cheap money" policy designed to stimulate home industry and promote economic recovery. The ban on foreign issues was also intended to prevent the British balance of payments from becoming too adverse. There would have been some point in this before September 1931, while Great Britain was still on gold. There seems to be no logical argument for it after that date. A free exchange rate automatically prevents an adverse balance of payments. Moreover, the possibility of purchasing existing foreign securities led to foreign investment taking that form instead of the form of new issues.

In so far as the ban had any effect on the exchange value of sterling, it tended to keep it up. Sterling which would otherwise have been acquired by foreign borrowers and offered for sale on the exchange markets was instead invested (or left on deposit at a bank) at home. But it is doubtful whether its effect was at all significant. There was so much uncertainty as to economic prospects in foreign countries and as to the future exchange value of their currencies that it is doubtful whether any very substantial sums would have been subscribed to new issues on foreign account even if they had been permitted.

The ban is important mainly as an indication of the attitude of the government towards economic affairs. The only real hope for the staple British export industries lay in a considerable revival of world trade. Such a revival might have been promoted by British willingness to lend overseas. The loans would have assisted recovery in other countries and would directly or indirectly have stimulated the demand for British exports. The government, however, chose to follow more of an isolationist policy. There was no return to the gold standard and no real attempt at international economic cooperation. Great Britain herself was making a striking economic recovery—other countries must do the best they could. Hence unemployment, mainly in the export districts, remained near 1½ million down to the outbreak of the war.

4. THE EXCHANGE EQUALIZATION ACCOUNT

Early in 1932 capital began to return to London in considerable amounts. The Bank of England appears to have done something to check the consequent rise in the value of sterling. Between the end of February and the end of June it increased its holding of "Other Securities," presumably foreign exchange, by £33 million and in addition bought gold to the value of some £20 million at market prices. But the government soon replaced these makeshift methods of controlling the value of sterling by the Exchange Equalization Account.

The decision to establish the account, more commonly known as fund, was announced by Mr. Chamberlain in his financial statement to the House of Commons on April 19, 1932, although it did not begin operations until June. Its main purpose, he explained, was to smooth out temporary fluctuations in the exchange value of sterling, while permitting "real" causes to affect the long-term trend. Only speculative movements were to be offset.

It soon became clear that the chief speculative movements needing to be offset were those arising from the transfer of "refugee capital." People feared that the dollar might be devalued, and transferred balances from the United States to London. Of course, they were right. The dollar left gold in the spring of 1933 and was officially devalued at the beginning of 1934. It was then feared that the French franc and other "gold bloc" currencies would be devalued; and although France managed to stay on gold until October 1936, there was a fairly continuous inflow of refugee capital into London. For sterling had already depreciated and was unlikely, it was thought, to depreciate much further. Hence London was generally deemed the safest temporary resting place for the liquid funds of capitalists anxious to safeguard themselves against a fall in the exchange value of their money.

In the absence of any control, an influx of refugee capital into Great Britain would have pushed up the exchange value of sterling, thereby hampering British exports. Later, when these refugee funds were transferred to some other center which had come to be deemed safer than London, the exchange value of sterling would have come down with a rush. The fund could prevent such disturbing ups and downs by absorbing the "hot money" as it came in, and subsequently releasing it, without allowing these movements to have any substantial effect on the exchange value of sterling.

The fund began operations with some £165 million of which some £115 million was in the form of Treasury bills, and the rest in foreign exchange or gold.[1] When it intervened in the exchange market to buy foreign currency (absorbing, for example, an influx of foreign capital) it provided the extra sterling required by selling some of its Treasury bills, and it turned the foreign currency which it acquired into gold. Hence part of its assets at any moment consists of sterling, mainly in the form of Treasury bills, and the remainder consists of gold. If it were to try to offset a continued tendency for sterling to fall, it would have to part with gold. When it had parted with all its gold, then—unless it could acquire more gold or foreign exchange, by borrowing from abroad or in some other way —it could do no more. The increased sterling offered for sale could no longer be absorbed by the fund, for it would have nothing to give in exchange, and the exchange value of sterling would therefore fall just as if there were no fund. Conversely, when it had turned all its sterling assets into gold, in order to offset a continued tendency for sterling to rise, it could do no more unless it could acquire more sterling to give in exchange for the foreign currency offered. Mainly for this reason the fund was augmented in April 1933 by a further £200 million of Treasury bills and in June 1937 with yet another £200 million.

There have been times—notably during 1934, when capital was being withdrawn from London after the revaluation of the dollar, and sterling was tending to fall sharply—when the fund has been parting with gold. But on balance it acquired a great deal of gold up to March

[1] See "Twenty Years of the Floating Debt" by F. W. Paish in *Economica*, August 1931. This article gives an excellent account of this whole subject.

1938. At that date the combined gold holding of the Account and of the Bank (to whom the Account had sold some of its gold, valued for bookkeeping purposes at the old price of about 85 shilling an ounce) was at its highest point. It amounted to nearly 120 million ounces, worth at market prices about £840 million. The gold originally held by the Bank, before the fund began operations, was only £121 million, valued at the old price. The long run tendency for the sterling price of gold to rise over this period is partly responsible for the rise in the market value of the gold held. The original £121 million was worth £200 million in March 1938 and there had been an increase or "profit" of between £30 and £40 million on the gold which had been purchased at intervals by the Account. But the bulk of the 120 million ounces had been purchased by the Account. This means that its long-run effect had not been merely to smooth out temporary fluctuations. It had been to keep down the exchange value of sterling.

To some extent, however, this policy was justified by the large influx of refugee capital which had taken place. After March 1938, the trend was reversed. Fears of war led to heavy withdrawals of capital from London. If the fund had not accumulated a large amount of gold, this would have resulted in a very sharp fall in the exchange value of sterling. As it was, the demands were met mainly by the release of gold. It may be mentioned that the sterling acquired in exchange helped to finance rearmament in Great Britain. From March 1938 to the end of 1939 perhaps £400 million of the cost of rearmament and of the war was met, in effect, by sales of gold.

It is also interesting to note that against the "profits" made by the fund up to March 1938 must be set the interest payable on over £300 million of internal long term "funding" loans raised by the British government. As we have seen, some £550 million of Treasury bills were issued, at one time or another, to the fund. It was considered dangerous to allow the total of the floating debt (mainly in the form of Treasury bills) to become too high, and therefore these "funding" loans were raised from time to time. If there had been no fund, they would not have had to be raised, and consequently the interest upon them—averaging slightly over 3 per cent—would not have had to be paid.

It may be that the activities of the fund in acquiring gold, and thus keeping down the value of sterling, in the early months of 1933 may have been partly responsible for the decision of President Roosevelt to let the value of the dollar fall. He may have thought that Great Britain was trying to secure an unfair advantage for her exports, and decided that it was a game at which two could play. In fact, as we have tried to show, the fund was mainly trying to serve as a cushion to prevent disturbing jumps in the value of sterling due to the influx, and efflux at some future date, of refugee capital. Be that as it may, President Roosevelt's action wrecked the World Economic Conference and dealt a blow to international monetary stability comparable only with the departure of Great Britain from gold—and it may well be argued that Great Britain had little choice, whereas the dollar could easily have been maintained at its previous level. The moral is that when one nation adopts economic policies opposed to international cooperation, other nations are very likely to do the same.

Some measure of international cooperation, however, was forced upon both Great Britain and the United States when the French franc was at last devalued in October 1936. Up to that date the exchange funds of both countries had been able to operate upon the franc. They could buy francs and turn them into gold at a fixed price. This was no longer possible. If the British fund, for example, were to buy dollars in order to prevent sterling from rising too high in terms of dollars, it would have to hold the dollars. It could not turn them into francs and turn the francs into gold. The converse applied to the American fund. As neither fund wished to acquire increasing amounts of the other's currency, an agreement was reached and M. Blum —instead of snapping his fingers at Great Britain and the United States, who between them had forced the franc off gold, and letting them solve their own troubles— proved very willing to cooperate. Both the British and the United States Treasury on October 12 issued declarations that they were prepared to sell gold to other Treasuries or central banks, but only upon a day to day basis. Their undertaking could be withdrawn at twenty-four hours notice. The countries previously on gold which had instituted exchange accounts—including France—gave similar undertakings. Thereafter a certain stability was maintained between the pound and the dollar, although the franc had to be devalued again. But although the result was a kind of uneasy gold standard, maintained (so long as the United States kept to its fixed price of 35 dollars an ounce for gold) on a day to day basis, uncertainty did not disappear. It was gradually becoming clear that a substantial reduction of exchange risks and the removal of apprehensions concerning the future value of gold (the stocks and output of which had greatly increased) could be achieved only by some more permanent agreement, when the outbreak of war temporarily put an end to any such hopes.

Chapter VII

IRON AND STEEL

1. The Nature of the Industry

The controversy over protection for the iron and steel industry was particularly fierce. This was largely because iron and steel products are the raw materials of a number of important industries, and much of the British steel output is exported in one form or another. The general rule was not to tax imported raw materials and not to hamper the export trades.

The protectionists won, but in return for restrictions on imports the producers had to agree to reorganize the industry and not to raise prices unduly.

Some account of the main characteristics and problems of the industry is necessary to understand the issues involved in the controversy. We therefore begin with a brief description of the processes of production.

The first stage is the production of pig iron in a blast furnace. Iron ore and coke, with limestone as a flux, are charged into the top of the furnace and hot air is blown in at the bottom. This produces molten iron, which is run out and either allowed to solidify in moulds, before being sent elsewhere, or else poured into huge ladles to be used, in its molten state, for making steel. Other products of the blast furnace are blast-furnace gas and slag, formed from the earthy mineral in the ore and the limestone. It costs a good deal to fire a blast furnace and therefore it is kept going day and night unless it has to be blown out and kept idle for a long period.

Some pig iron is used to make wrought iron products or cast-iron pipes, stoves, ranges, and hardware. But most pig iron is converted into steel. The second stage, therefore, is the production of steel ingots.

Most of the steel produced in the world is made in open-hearth furnaces. The chief alternative process is to use Bessemer converters. France, Belgium, and Luxembourg produce mainly Bessemer steel, and a considerable proportion of the German output also is Bessemer. The process is shorter and requires less fuel than the open-hearth process but the latter yields a more reliable steel. Further, the open-hearth process, unlike the other, permits the use of a high proportion of scrap. In Great Britain, well over 90 per cent of the steel is produced by the open-hearth process and more scrap than pig iron is used.

The ingots are allowed to solidify sufficiently to be handled and then, after re-heating, they are rolled in the cogging mill. This is the third stage. Its products are blooms, billets, and slabs—semi-finished steel products, often called "semis." Some ingots, however, are turned directly into sheet or tinplate bars.

In the last stage, the semis are rolled and re-rolled into all the various shapes and sizes required. Special plants produce plates, tubes, wire, and many other products. Some ingots of high quality steel, however, do not go through the rolling mills but are transformed into tires, wheels, axles, or armament steel in a forging press.

Steel products may end up as parts of buildings, motor-cars, bridges, machines, and so forth. A modern city has been described as a body with a skeleton of iron and steel. The Final Report of the Census of Production[1] shows the consumption of iron and steel in Great Britain in 1935. About half was used in engineering and constructional work; nearly a third was taken by the railways, shipbuild-

[1] Volume II, pp. 36-37.

ing, and the motor industry; and the rest went to produce wire, cars, loops, containers, and so forth.

The fact that iron and steel may pass through so many stages before being embodied in their final form makes it particularly difficult to define the iron and steel industry. Moreover, most of the big steel firms produce engineering products: a few are engaged in shipbuilding; the disposal of by-products links them with the chemical industry; and a number control coal mines, iron mines, and coke ovens.

The Import Duties Advisory Committee presented their *Report on the Present Position and Future Development of the Iron and Steel Industry* in 1937. They give the number of workers engaged in July 1936 as 268,540.[2] They say that complete information as to the capital involved in the industry is not available, but point out that "the published accounts of thirty-seven concerns, estimated to be responsible in 1936 for some 86 per cent of the country's output of steel in that year, show a total capitalization—after very heavy writings off in the preceding decade—of approximately £126.7 million, of which 24 per cent was represented by debentures, 25 per cent by preference shares and 51 per cent by ordinary shares." Clearly the amount of capital per worker is large. This capital is largely in the form of specialized and durable plant and equipment.

Finally we turn to the import and export situation as it was before the tariff. The imports were mainly semis, bars, and the simpler types of structural steel, all coming mainly from the Continent. In 1929, 2,822,000 tons were imported

[2] Made up as follows: pig iron 16,070; steel smelting and rolling 169,960; tinplates 27,410; tubes 31,390; wire, wire netting and wire rope 23,710. These are numbers of insured persons aged 16 to 64 attached to the industry. Around 15 per cent of the total were unemployed.

of which 1,652,000 were consigned from Belgium, 459,000 from Germany, 308,000 from France, and 68,000 from Luxembourg. The consignments from Belgium included a considerable proportion produced in the other three countries. The exports, on the other hand, were mainly more-finished products and went all over the world: about half to British Dominions and Colonies and half to foreign countries. In 1929, 4,380,000 tons were exported to the value of £68 million. The value of the 2,822,000 tons imported was only £24.7 million. Great Britain imported mainly cheap steel and worked it up into more-finished products for home consumption or for export. The industry can very roughly be divided into (a) the "heavy" producers of pig iron, semis, and the simpler rolled products and (b) the re-rollers and finishers, producing more specialized and valuable products. The line of division is by no means clear: many firms produce both. But it was mainly the former who wanted a tariff and the latter who did not. The former were predominant in the industry before 1932 and since then have become still more so.

In 1929 the total output of steel in Great Britain was 9,636,000 tons. Some 40 per cent of this was exported in the form of steel products. In particular, most of the tinplates, galvanized sheets, and tubes, and about half the rails were exported. In addition, a good deal of steel was exported in the form of machinery, motor vehicles, and ships. It has been authoritatively stated that "in normal times the industry as a whole ultimately depends for more than 70 per cent of its production on the export trade in all forms of iron and steel products."[3]

[3] Cmd. 4181 of 1932. *First Report of the National Committee for the Iron and Steel Industry* (made to the I.D.A.C.). During recent years it has been well below 70 per cent, perhaps about 40 per cent or less.

2. THE PROBLEM OF LOCATION

The materials and products of the industry are so heavy in relation to their value that transport costs form a considerable part of total costs. Hence it is of great importance that works should be properly located. We shall discuss mainly the location of blast furnaces. Steel works and rolling mills tend, for reasons explained in the next section, to be near the blast furnaces. But it should be noted that nearness to scrap markets (for example, the Glasgow district) hardly explains the location of some open-hearth steel furnaces.

Coking coal and iron ore are the important materials for a blast furnace. If they are found close together, it pays to erect the blast furnace there and not near the market. For coal loses all its weight in the process of producing pig iron and the iron ore sheds its non-ferrous content. The consequent saving in transport costs may be illustrated as follows. Suppose the iron ore contains 50 per cent iron and that $1\frac{1}{2}$ tons of coal (in the form of coke) are required to smelt a ton of pig iron. If the blast furnace is near the market, $1\frac{1}{2}$ tons of coal and 2 tons of ore must be transported to produce a ton of pig iron; if it is "on" the coal and iron only one ton (of pig iron) need be transported.

But what if the coal deposits are a considerable distance from the iron ore? Transport costs will be saved by producing either on the coal or on the ore. Which of the two depends on the relative amounts of coal and of ore needed to produce a ton of pig iron. If more than two tons of coal are required and there is 50 per cent or more iron in the ore, the transport costs of these materials are minimized if the blast furnaces are on the coal. Until recent years, this was the situation in a number of British districts and, indeed, in most of the steel-producing areas of the world. The iron and steel industry tended to be "based" on coal. A factor which reinforced this tendency was that important markets—including heavy engineering works—were near the coal rather than near the iron ore. In Great Britain, moreover, some of the chief coal deposits are fairly near the coast. Hence iron and steel works near such deposits were also favorably placed for the export trade.

Several influences, however, have combined to make it advantageous to set up blast furnaces in certain districts on the ore deposits instead of elsewhere near coal. For many years the progress of technique has enabled a steady reduction to be made in the amount of coal required to smelt a ton of pig iron. At present, this amount—although it varies between countries and is less for high-grade ore—is in the neighborhood of $1\frac{1}{2}$ tons (in the form of coke). Further, technical progress has made it profitable to exploit low-grade ores which previously were not worth using. Finally, a number of deposits of high-grade ore have given out or have become more difficult to work.

A numerical example will illustrate how transport costs are saved by basing blast furnaces on low-grade ore. Suppose that the ore contains 25 per cent iron. Then if the blast furnaces are on the coal, at least 4 tons of ore must be transported for every ton of pig iron produced. But if they are on the ore, only $1\frac{1}{2}$ tons of coal need be transported, and if the coal is transformed into coke at the collieries, this figure is reduced to 1.1 or 1.2 tons—of coke.

Let us now turn to the situation in Great Britain. The Scottish ore supplies are exhausted. The Scottish blast furnaces now rely almost entirely on ore from abroad.

Similarly, most of the South Wales ore is exhausted. In 1937 the blast furnaces of this district consumed 1,706,000 tons of ore, of which 1,055,000 came from abroad and 604,000 from the Midlands. The rich hematite ore of the North West Coast (from which is produced high quality acid steel) is giving out. Less than 900,000 tons were produced in 1937, as against 1,300,000 tons in 1929, and over two-fifths of the ore consumed in the district now comes from abroad. The important Cleveland ironstone of South Yorkshire, all used in the blast furnaces of the North East Coast, is becoming more expensive to win. Output has fallen from 2,685,000 tons in 1929 to 1,920,000 tons in 1937, and in the latter year the North East Coast consumed also 2,688,000 tons of ore from abroad and 571,000 tons from other parts of England, mainly from the Midlands.

There are, however, vast deposits, estimated at not less than 3,000 million tons, of low-grade ore in the Midlands. The iron content varies from about 22 to 30 per cent. About half the total reserves are in Northamptonshire. In 1937 North Lincolnshire (which for our purpose we may include in the Midlands) produced some 3.3 million tons and South Lincolnshire, Leicestershire, Northamptonshire, and Oxfordshire some 7.4 million tons.

In the light of these facts, we should expect to find that an increasing proportion of the total British output of pig iron is being produced in the Midlands, near the ore. This is so. The proportion has risen from about 16 per cent in 1913 to about 27 per cent in 1929 and about 35 per cent in 1937.

Sea transport is much cheaper than land transport. Hence we should expect works which rely largely on imported ore and have a considerable export trade to be on the seaboard or on tide water or a ship canal. This has indeed long been true of the chief works on the North East and North West Coast and of the Lancashire-Cheshire-North Wales district. In 1929 and 1930 most of the heavy sections of the South Wales industry moved away from the Merthyr district, where the ore deposits had become exhausted, to the coast near Swansea, Cardiff, and Port Talbot. But the big Scottish works remain some distance inland, although the banks of the Clyde would seem a more suitable location.

We have mentioned all the chief iron and steel producing districts with the exception of the Black Country and the Sheffield district, famous for its high-quality steel. The former contains many relatively small specialist firms supplying the engineering, armaments, motor, and other industries which are located there. The Sheffield district produces a wide range of products, from cutlery to heavy forgings, and is the chief center for special steels. Both districts lack ore deposits and produce only a small part of the British output of pig iron.

3. INTEGRATION

For a number of years there has been a growing tendency in all steel-producing countries towards large "integrated" or "composite" works, with blast furnaces, steel works, rolling mills, and perhaps coke ovens all on the same site and close to coal mines or iron ore mines. On the Continent, most of the iron and steel is produced in works of this type, each representing a large investment of capital and numbering its workers in thousands. The Continent has often been held up as a model, in this respect, which the British industry should follow. Integration has certainly come later in Great Britain, and still is less marked than on the Continent, but its extent has increased considerably during recent years.

There are two main advantages of integration. The first is that it economizes fuel. The metal can be passed through its various stages without being allowed to become cold. If, for example, the blast furnace is in one district and the steel works in another, the iron from the blast furnace must be allowed to solidify into cold "pigs": these must be transported to the steel works and there re-heated. Similarly with the "semis"—blooms, billets, slabs, and bars— which are subsequently re-rolled. The second advantage is that the coke-oven gas and the blast-furnace gas can be fully utilized. The former is of high calorific value and can be used for heating open-hearth furnaces. The latter can be used for heating coke ovens, raising steam, heating the stoves for the blast, and can be turned into electricity to work the pumps in the mines or the ore-drying plant or the rolling mills and blowers. No coal need be used except in the coke-ovens.

It is the blast furnaces which consume most of the materials: the iron ore and most or all of the coal, nearly always in form of coke. Hence the location of the whole works tends to be determined by the most suitable site for the blast furnaces.

While an increase in the proportion of integrated works is often a sign of progress, this is not always so. Critics who measure the efficiency of a country's iron and steel industry by the proportion of total output produced in integrated works are taking an oversimplified and possibly a misleading view of a very complex question. There are all sorts of reasons why certain works engaged in only one or two stages of production may be profitable and efficient. For example, a works on the coast may be able to get coal and pig iron or semis cheaply by sea and to work them up into more-finished products, such as sheets or tinplates or wire, using relatively cheap local labor. Open-hearth furnaces may be run largely on scrap from neighboring engineering or ship-building works. Coke ovens may be better situated at the collieries rather than at the steel works if there is a demand for their by-products in the former place rather than in the latter and if transport costs on coal are high. In general, a large integrated works is not very flexible in meeting changes in demand. The more technically efficient the works is, the more likely is it to be planned as a single unit, so that when demand falls off sharply during a trade depression a great deal of idle capacity may have to be maintained. An isolated re-rolling works, for example, may not fare badly for—unlike an integrated works—it is not tied to its blast furnaces, coke ovens, and so forth, but can buy its materials in the cheapest market. Nevertheless there are, as we have seen, considerable technical advantages in integration, and it is probably true that the British iron and steel industry was not sufficiently well organized in this respect until quite recently. Whether considerably more integration is still desirable is much more doubtful. It is relevant to note that in Great Britain coal deposits are far more widely diffused than in the United States or Germany, while engineering, shipbuilding and other centers attract steel works by providing cheap scrap.

4. OTHER TECHNICAL FACTORS

What are the chief other factors, in addition to suitable location and an adequate amount of integration, which make for technical efficiency? One is the best application of up-to-date knowledge in the preparation of raw ma-

terials: "the proper grading of coke, the blending, drying, and sintering of iron ore, and the like."[4] The British
industry is, perhaps, not open to serious criticism on this
score. Others are the sizes and types of various units of
plant and the extent of mechanization.

From a purely technical standpoint, the best size for
blast furnaces, open-hearth furnaces, coke ovens, and indeed most kinds of plant and equipment is larger than
the average size existing in Great Britain.

Consider, for example, a blast furnace. "A large blast
furnace will use less coke, for less heat is lost by radia-
tion; it will cost less to build, for the capacity will vary
with the square of the diameter while the construction
cost varies with the diameter, and the by-products and
process gases will be more easily utilized or disposed of
commercially."[5] It is true that blowing costs tend to increase as the size of the furnace grows. Moreover, the
available fuel may not stand the weight of a very heavy
charge. This was particularly marked with Scottish splint
coal, so that the blast furnaces in Scotland were unusually
small. But the very large modern blast furnaces erected
during recent years in America and the Continent, with an
average weekly output of three or four thousand tons, or
even more, are certainly more efficient than most of the
British. The average weekly output per furnace in Great
Britain is not much over one thousand tons. Much the
same applies to other units of equipment.

Technical efficiency, however, should not be the only

---

[4] "Ingot," *The Socialisation of Iron and Steel*, p. 17. We are considerably
indebted to this admirable work. But while the present volume was going
through the press the authoritative work on the British iron and steel industry has appeared: D. L. Burn, *The Economic History of Steel Making,
1867-1939*, Cambridge University Press.

[5] *Ibid.*, p. 19.

consideration. There is also the question of demand. It is obviously futile to have a very large "capacity" capable of producing on a large scale at a low cost if much of it must remain idle for lack of markets. Moreover, even if a few large furnaces, producing more cheaply, could take the place of a large number of smaller furnaces, it does not follow that the latter should be scrapped. They are already in existence, and it may be cheaper to continue working them than to write them off and build new ones.

Before the world war, most British coke ovens were of the "Beehive" type, producing a high quality coke but no by-products. The modern type of coke oven is considerably larger and yields ammonia, benzol, and tar, and also coke-oven gas. In general, the latter type is better and is now predominant.

The growth of mechanization, which has affected nearly all industries during recent decades, has been particularly marked, in most producing countries, in the iron and steel industry. The use of modern labor-saving devices has made possible a large increase in output per worker. Of course, it involves a larger investment of capital and, particularly if interest rates are high, it can be carried too far. It is certain, for example, that "rationalization" and mechanization were carried too far in Germany. Between 1926 and 1933 the Steel Trust reduced its iron and steel plants from 145 to 66, its blast-furnace systems from 23 to 9, and its rolling mills from 17 to 10. There was an increase of 33 per cent or more in output per worker. Yet the shares of the Trust fell to less than a third of their 1926 value, and most of the big steel firms made losses over a number of years. In Great Britain, on the other hand, interest rates have been relatively low and it seems probable that although there has been a good deal of mechanization there has not been enough.

An outstanding illustration of this is that there was no continuous strip mill in Great Britain until 1938, when the Richard Thomas mill at Ebbw Vale came into operation. This American process, producing tinplates and sheets (mainly for motorcars) requires a high initial capital outlay and does not pay with a capacity of less than 250 thousand tons a year. The I.D.A.C. says: "There are at present 25 sheet works employing some 18,000 operatives, and some 80 tinplate works employing over 22,000 operatives; their whole output of plates and sheets could be replaced by a very few mills of the magnitude of that now in process of erection at Ebbw Vale, with a very large reduction in the numbers employed."[6] Nevertheless, although the process displaces a number of skilled workers, there is little doubt that it is a more efficient and cheaper method of production. Plants employing the process have been installed for some years in most big steel-producing countries.

5. FLUCTUATIONS IN DEMAND

The demand for iron and steel fluctuates a great deal over time. There may be large variations, due to changes in public policy, in the amount of building, or the production of armaments. Such variations may suffice, if they are large enough, to promote recovery from a general trade depression or to hasten a general slump. In any event, general booms and depressions do take place, with or without government intervention, and as most iron and steel products are "investment goods," the demand for them is unusually high during a boom and unusually low during a slump. The iron and steel, in short, is very much

[6] Report, p. 39.

a "trade cycle" industry. When a big fall in demand takes place—owing, usually, to a general trade depression—the difficulties of the industry are aggravated by the fact that most of its plant and equipment is very durable. The industry therefore finds itself with a great deal of "excess capacity" which it cannot easily get rid of. Under free competition, therefore, the prices of iron and steel products tend to come down in a rush to very low levels. Firms continue to work their plant if it earns anything at all above current expenses. Since the costs of closing down and subsequently re-opening, and meanwhile maintaining the works in a reasonable condition, are considerable, some firms may continue operations for a time even if their receipts do not cover their current working costs. The result is a scramble for orders and drastic cuts in prices, so that a number of firms are sooner or later compelled to close down while some of the others may not earn enough to make adequate provision for renewals and repairs, let alone sufficient to pay dividends.

The effects of a large increase in demand tend to be aggravated by the fact that it takes a considerable time to construct and set up new plants on the most efficient modern scale. Thus the I.D.A.C. writes: "A large fully integrated steel works may take as long as four years to complete. The extensions now taking place at Corby and those decided upon at the United Steel Companies' works at Scunthorpe and at Messrs. Colville's works at Clyde-bridge are expected to need from 18 months to two and a half years for completion, though this will be earlier than would be possible for entirely new undertakings."[7] Moreover, investors naturally tend to be cautious about locking up large sums, perhaps running into millions of pounds,

[7] Report, Cmd. 5507 of 1937, p. 33.

in the form of specialized equipment which will last for a long time. New investment on any large scale tends to be made only when it seems clear that a fairly long period of prosperity is ahead, and the new plant comes into production perhaps two or three years after the decision has been taken.

This means that, under free competition, we should expect the prices of iron and steel products to soar during a period of heavy demand, before much new plant had been erected, and to come down with a rush when the demand fell sharply.

This is exactly what happened in Great Britain during and after the world war. For example, the price of pig iron per ton rose from 51s.6d. in June 1914 to 225s. in 1920, only to fall to 100s. in 1921 and 91s. in 1922. Similarly, the price of steel rails per ton rose from £6 in June 1914 to £25.10s. in 1920, only to fall to £9.10s. in 1921 and £9 in 1922.

Whether such a state of affairs is in the best economic interests of the community as a whole is a controversial question on which we shall not give an opinion. On the one hand, it can be argued that the depression weeds out the least efficient firms and methods, that it is desirable at any time to use existing capacity as fully as possible, that low prices for iron and steel during a depression stimulate investment and thereby promote recovery, and that high prices during a boom are the most effective stimulus to new investment. On the other hand, it can be argued that it would be wiser to smooth out large price variations by planned control and to prevent both enormous profits during a boom and sales below cost during a depression.

However this may be, the latter course is certainly the better from the standpoint of the industry, and more or less successful attempts have been made to achieve it in all the main producing countries. The method, of course, is to form cartels to control prices and, if possible, the output of each plant. Cartels stand a better chance of holding together in this industry than in most because the number of firms controlling the great bulk of the output, at any rate in the heavy sections, is usually small.

But national cartels are almost useless if the home market is wide open to a flood of imports at cut prices. And that was precisely the situation in Great Britain from 1930 to 1932, before the tariff was imposed on iron and steel. Continental firms were exporting, mainly semis and the simpler types of basic Bessemer products, at very low prices. For example, sheet bars, which had been £4.17s.6d. per ton in August 1929 had fallen to £2.19s. in August 1931 and to £1.19s.6d. in August 1932. The annual report of the French *Comité des Forges* for 1932 said that at the beginning of that year steel was being exported at 30 to 40 per cent below cost of production. Dr. Reichert, the head of the German Iron and Steel Federation, said in 1932: "Price losses of £2 to £2.10s. per ton were the rule . . . a mania prevailed for maintaining the exports especially with the object of being able to claim as high quotas as possible in connection with future international syndicate negotiations."[8] The British industry declared that high duties were essential to safeguard it from this kind of competition.

6. The Tariff on Iron and Steel

The heavy sections of the industry had been agitating for protection against cheap semis from the Continent for some years before the slump. But the Conservative Govern-

[8] See *First Report of National Committee*, Cmd. 4181 of 1932.

ment of 1924-29, remembering the defeat of Mr. Baldwin at the polls in 1923 on the issue of protection, dared not impose tariffs on such important materials, and the Labor Government which followed was free trade. Further, the finishing sections of the industry, the re-rollers, were opposed to protection because it would raise their costs.

Indeed, there were—and still are—weighty arguments against a tariff on iron and steel, in addition to the general free trade argument that it is against the interests of the ultimate consuming public. In the first place, the consuming industries which use iron and steel products as their raw materials—the engineering and constructional industries, shipbuilding, the railways, the motor industry, and so forth—employed far more workers than the iron and steel industry. It was urged that profits and employment in these industries would suffer if their costs were raised by increased prices for iron and steel. In the second place, a large part of the British output of iron and steel was exported in one form or another—not only as rails, tubes, tinplates, and so on but also as machinery, motorcars, locomotives, as parts of bridges or plants erected (often by British firms) overseas, and in other forms, such as parts of ships. Export industries were notoriously depressed; unemployment was at its greatest in exporting districts; there was general agreement that export industries should be assisted and not hampered. It might conceivably have been possible, despite the great administrative difficulties, to refund the duty paid on imported iron and steel subsequently re-exported in a more finished form. But this would have left such a gateway open in the tariff wall around the iron and steel industry that the value of protection to it would have been greatly reduced. Hence this course was not adopted.

An argument for protection which carried much weight was that an adequate iron and steel industry was vital on grounds of defense. If Great Britain came to rely too much on imported steel, permitting some existing works to close down because they could not make a profit, she would lack the capacity for producing sufficient armaments in case of war and would not be able to set it up with sufficient speed. In particular, the industry relied to a considerable extent on imported ore, pig iron, and semis. Protection was necessary in order to encourage the setting up of plants to utilize more fully the low-grade ore deposits of the Midlands and to produce more semis.

The very low prices of imported steel during 1930-32 caused great depression in the heavier sections of the British industry and even a number of the re-rollers were prepared to consider a tariff, provided that their products also were protected. When the industry was told that it should reorganize itself—whatever that meant—it replied that it would do so if it had a tariff and that otherwise it could not.

In April 1932 the I.D.A.C. accepted these arguments and urged that protection would really benefit the consuming industries also. "We are satisfied that the maintenance of a prosperous iron and steel industry in the highest degree of efficiency is essential to the economic progress of this country, while from the point of view of national security it must still be regarded as vital.

"In arriving at this conclusion we had in mind not only the interests of the heavy iron and steel industry and of the nation generally but also the interests of the users of semi-finished iron and steel products who have been among the largest importers of foreign iron and steel. Although the very low prices at which they have been able to obtain these products have enabled some manufacturers to make very large profits, there can be no doubt that should our native iron and steel industry succumb to foreign competition these secondary industries would be gravely imperilled. In the long run therefore these users of semi-finished products are as vitally interested in the maintenance of a prosperous iron and steel industry in this country as are the producers themselves."[9]

The general 10 per cent duty imposed on March 1, 1932, was raised on April 26 to 33⅓ per cent on pig iron, semis, girders, sheets, and similar products, and to 20 per cent on the "whole range of finished iron and steel goods, from rails and tubes to cutlery and screws. For perhaps the first time in British tariff history a higher duty had been put upon the raw material than on the finished product."[10]

The duties were said to be temporary and were imposed only for three months. Their object was to provide time to enable the industry to evolve a reorganization scheme. The I.D.A.C. said "the grant of protection would not suffice to place the industry in a position to play its proper part in the national economy unless it was accompanied by a considerable measure of reorganization."[11] In fact, the duties were extended for a further three months. The National Committee (representing predominantly the heavy sections) which had been set up to plan a scheme of reorganization, argued that nothing could really be done while the duty was "temporary," and it was accordingly extended for a further two years. The reorganization

[9] Cmd. 4066 and 4181 of 1932.
[10] "Ingot," op. cit., p. 95.
[11] Cmd. 4066 and 4181 of 1932.

scheme was completed, and the time limit on the duties was accordingly removed, in May 1934.

The "reorganization" was described as "a scheme for establishing the machinery whereby a reorganisation might be carried out rather than a scheme of reorganization itself."[12] It contained no definite plans for technical reorganization. The old trade association became the British Iron and Steel Federation. Its objects include the promotion of trade associations, the coordination of their work, the organization of imports and the expansion of exports, but it has no power to compel associations or firms to join it, or to enforce its wishes on its members. It is, however, a body which can represent the industry as a whole in its dealings with the government and the public and with similar organizations in other countries, and which can use its influence to guide and mold the development of the industry as a whole.[13]

We must now say a little about the *Entente Internationale de l'Acier*. This body consists of the steel producers of Germany, France, Belgium, and Luxembourg. It was formed in 1926, and its main object was to limit output in each of the four countries (and the Saar). It broke down, in fact, in the spring of 1930 and the agreement formally lapsed a year later. This was the period when continental producers were scrambling for the British market and prices were so low for their exports.

The *entente*, or cartel, was reconstituted on different lines in April 1933. The object of the new arrangement was to prevent firms in the four Cartel countries from competing with one another, and thus driving down prices,

[12] By the National Committee for the Iron and Steel Industry, appointed June 1932; see Cmd. 4589 of 1934.

[13] See White Paper (63-9999) of 1933: *Iron and Steel Reorganisation Scheme*, and see Cmd. 4589 of 1934 for the B.I.S.F. constitution.

in common export markets. The quantities to be exported
by each country, and by each firm within each country,
were fixed; export prices for each product and each market were fixed; and, to prevent price cutting by secret
rebates, all orders had to go in the first place to a *comptoir*,
which then allotted them among the various firms. There
was a *comptoir* for each of the following six products:
semis, merchant bars, large flats, thick plates, medium
sheets, and joists and girders.

Despite the British tariff of 33⅓ per cent, imports of
cartel products increased from 643,000 tons in 1933 to
912,000 tons in 1934, and the prices received were remunerative. British producers of similar products, however, again complained of "dumping" and wanted the tariff
raised to 50 per cent. The government refused, urging
them to come to an arrangement with the cartel for the
quantitative limitation of imports into Great Britain. The
cartel asked for a quota of 900,000 tons; the British offered 500,000. No compromise could be reached until on
March 26, 1935, the British government, in order "to facilitate negotiation," suddenly raised the duties to considerably higher levels—for example, to £2 per ton on semis
(blooms, billets, slabs, bars, and rods) not over £4 per ton
in value. The cartel had to yield. When Great Britain was
free trade, she had bought double, and more than double,
the quantities to which the cartel was prepared to limit its
exports. When it was asked to restrict them further still, to
a mere 500,000 tons, it had refused. But even that was better than these penal duties. On April 30, a temporary
agreement was made to limit imports to 643,000 tons and
the extra duties were accordingly removed. On July 31, a
more permanent agreement was signed which came into
force on August 8, 1935. Imports of cartel products were

to be limited to 670,000 tons for the first year and to 525,-
000 tons a year thereafter. In return, the duties were reduced to 20 per cent. This is one of the clearest cases on
record of the successful use of the tariff as a bargaining
weapon.

The next step was to develop administrative machinery
for restricting imports of cartel products to the agreed
levels. One possible danger was that imports into Great
Britain from non-cartel countries would increase and bring
down prices in the British market. This was guarded
against, and at the same time the most-favored-nation principle was preserved, by permitting each non-cartel country to send the full amount which it sent in 1934 at the 20
per cent rate of duty. Any amount in excess of that would
pay duty at the high rates imposed, for bargaining purposes, in March 1935. As the total amount of the six "cartel
products" imported into Great Britain from non-cartel
countries in 1934 was less than 10,000 tons, this concession
would have no perceptible effect on prices. The other
danger was that non-cartel firms in the four cartel countries
would increase their sales to Great Britain. 525,000 tons
in all were to come in at 20 per cent; any excess was to be
subject to the high duties. The cartel firms naturally
wanted all, or at least the greater part, of this "tariff quota"
for themselves.

The solution was a system of licensing, legalized by
Clause 6 of the Finance Act of 1936. Quota certificates
were to be issued, up to the permitted amounts, by the
governments of the exporting countries. "These Governments," wrote the President of the Board of Trade,[14] "may
find it convenient to use the Cartel organization as their
agents in this matter but they have agreed to accept re-

[14] Cmd. 5201 of 1936.

sponsibility for any division of certificates that may be necessary between Cartel and non-Cartel members in their own countries."

Arrangements were made whereby the British Iron and Steel Federation was to purchase all the imports coming into Great Britain from the cartel and then in effect to hand them back to the cartel for distribution, by the cartel's own selling agencies in consultation with the Federation. The latter was to arrange that consumers who were not members of an association affiliated to the Federation would receive a fair share of imported steel at the same price as members. The Federation formed the British Iron and Steel Corporation to handle this business. The average charge made to cover its services worked out at 9d. per ton.

The general increase in the demand for steel, due largely to rearmament in a number of countries, led to a shortage of semi-finished products in Great Britain: the cartel countries sent less than their quota. To encourage imports, on March 3, 1937, pig iron was exempted from duty and the duty on licensed imports was reduced to 10 per cent; on July 7, 1937, it was further reduced to a mere 2½ per cent, and the duty on non-licensed imports was reduced to 12½ per cent. Imports from the United States shot up from 18,000 tons in 1936 to 315,000 (mainly pig iron) in 1937. The existing British capacity for producing pig iron and semis was unable to cope with the large and sudden increases of demand in 1937, due mainly to the British rearmament program.

7. British Exports of Iron and Steel

British exports of iron and steel products amounted to over 4 million tons in each of the years 1927, 1928, and

1929. In 1930 they amounted to rather more than 3 million tons; in each of the three following years they were somewhat below 2 million tons; during 1934-36 they were somewhat higher, and in 1937 considerably higher, amounting to 2.6 million tons.

It would be wrong to blame the tariff on pig iron, semis, and similar materials for the marked fall in British exports of iron and steel products, although these are mainly of the more-finished type, such as tinplates, tubes, galvanized sheets, other plates and sheets, and rails. The tariff doubtless raised British costs of production, although not to the full extent of the duties (for part of the burden was borne by the Continental suppliers, who accepted lower prices than they would have demanded under free trade in order to have less "idle capacity" and to retain some hold on the British market). But Great Britain's share in the world exports of her principal iron and steel products was safeguarded by various international agreements. Broadly speaking, the prices fixed gave her an adequate margin of profit, despite any rise in her costs of production; and her markets were reserved.

The reduced level of British exports during 1930-35 was due mainly to the world depression. This greatly curtailed the demand for iron and steel. The world production of steel in 1929 had reached the record figure of 118 million tons. It fell to 50 million tons in 1932, thence rising to 98 million tons in 1935. In 1936, however, it was 122 million tons and in 1937 it was 133 million tons. It remains to be explained why British exports of iron and steel in these years were still far below their 1929 level.

The main reason is that a number of countries had become more self-supporting in iron and steel. The outstanding example is Russia, who increased her output from less than 5 million tons in 1929 to more than 17 million tons in 1937. This, however, is not very relevant to our present question, for Russia took less than 15,000 tons from Great Britain in 1929. Japan is a better example for our purpose. She increased her output of steel from 2.3 million tons in 1929 to 5.7 million tons in 1937, and her imports from Great Britain were only 42,000 tons in 1937 as compared with 158,000 tons in 1929. Again, India between 1929 and 1937 increased her output from 580,000 to 900,000 tons and reduced her imports from Great Britain from 615,000 to 227,000 tons, and during the same years Australia increased her output from 430,000 to 900,000 tons and reduced her imports from Great Britain from 424,000 to 149,-000 tons. The total volume of world trade in iron and steel products (excluding pig iron) was only 9.5 million tons in 1936 as compared with 15 million tons in 1929.[15]

In 1937, it is true, the volume of world trade in iron and steel products increased to 12 million tons, but much of this increase was accounted for by a rise in United States exports from 1.2 million tons to 2.7 million tons. The great increase in the world demand in 1937 is illustrated by the fact that in that year the United States also exported 787,000 tons of pig iron and ferro-alloys, and 4,093,000 tons of scrap. The home demand for steel in Great Britain, as in Germany and France, was too great in 1937 to permit much capacity to be used for increased exports. It will be remembered that the British duty on pig iron was removed in March 1937 and that the tariff on licensed imports was cut down to a mere 2½ per cent in July. Hence the failure of British exports to expand after

[15] *Statistiches Jahrbuch für das Deutsche Reich 1938*, International Section, p. 161.

that date was clearly not due to increased costs arising from the tariff.

Nevertheless the tariff must bear some of the responsibility for the reduced level of British exports as compared with 1927-29, although its effect has been produced in a more roundabout way than by raising British costs of production. The fact that Great Britain had imposed a tariff, and that British producers were pressing for import quotas, made producers in the four cartel countries realize that the British market for their semis would be greatly diminished in the future. They adapted themselves as best they could to this new situation by turning more towards the manufacture of more-finished products. This change was taking place before the world slump, but it was accelerated and carried further after Great Britain turned to protection. In 1929 Belgium had taken 166,000, France 130,000, and Germany 70,000 tons of iron and steel products from Great Britain; in 1937 the corresponding figures were 45,000, 40,000, and 16,000. This in turn resulted, when revised arrangements were made under the agreement of 1935, in Great Britain's obtaining a somewhat smaller share of world exports than she had in 1929.

The various international agreements for the export of different iron and steel products cannot be discussed here in any detail, but a few facts may be given briefly. Great Britain is a member, together with the United States, Germany, France, and Italy, of the International Tinplate Association, under which 65 per cent of total exports are allotted to her. She is a member of the International Rail-Makers Association (I.R.M.A.) together with the cartel countries and the United States. The British Empire, except the Mandated Territories, is reserved to Great Britain. The British quota for the "free" markets is 23.5 per cent.

The Continental producers formed a Tube Cartel in 1936. Great Britain, Canada, and the United States made agreements with one another and came to an understanding with the Continental producers in 1929. The cartel broke down in 1935. It may be mentioned that this led to a temporary rise on August 3, 1935, in the British duty on tubes and pipes: from 20 per cent to £5 a ton. At the end of that year, a price agreement for exports was reached and in April 1938 a new quota agreement was made. This excludes the United States and is much looser than the old cartel.

In January 1934 an International Ship Plate Cartel was formed between the Continental group and Great Britain. Home markets were reserved to national producers. Great Britain was allotted 25 per cent of total exports. This cartel, together with I.R.M.A., was subsequently merged in the International Steel Cartel.

The International Steel Cartel arose from the agreement between the *Entente Internationale de l'Acier* and Great Britain in July 1935. We showed in the last section how the cartel countries were induced to cut down their exports of certain products to Great Britain to 525,000 tons a year. But we did not tell the whole story. The British at first offered an import quota of only 270,000 tons. But the cartel countries were not helpless. They were members, together with Great Britain, of export cartels. Both I.R.M.A. and the Ship Plate Agreement had been prolonged provisionally only to the end of April 1935. The Continental producers could and did threaten not to renew these agreements unless Great Britain was more reasonable. A period of unrestricted competition in common export markets would have been bad for Continental producers but probably still worse for British. As we have seen, an agreement was reached upon imports of "cartel" products into Great Britain. The agreement also covered exports to common markets. Sectional agreements had to be made—in so far as they were not already concluded—to regulate the export of the four cartel countries and Great Britain, together with any other countries who were already members of existing agreements or might become parties to new ones, of the following products:

(1) I.R.M.A. materials,
(2) Semis (ingots, blooms, billets, slabs, sheet bars, tinplate bars);
(3) Joists, channels and broad-flanged beams;
(4) Merchant bars and sections;
(5) Thick plates ($\frac{3}{16}$ in. and up);
(6) Medium plates ($\frac{1}{8}$ in. and less than $\frac{3}{16}$ in.);
(7) Large flats or universals (6 in. and up);
(8) Hoops and strips;
(9) Tube strips;
(10) Wire rods, Iweco and other wire products;
(11) Tinplates;
(12) Sheets less than $\frac{1}{8}$ in., black and galvanized.

Negotiations about these sectional export agreements took some time. Item (12) proved the most troublesome but in the summer of 1936 a Thin Plate Syndicate was formed. Great Britain received a quota of 33.24 per cent for black plates (or sheets) and of 53.05 per cent for galvanized plates (or sheets). The formation of this syndicate completed the negotiations.

All this means that most exporters of most iron and steel products throughout the world are parties to a number of cartels or agreements intended to prevent competition leading to price cutting in export markets. It may be that the fear of paying "monopoly prices" has been a factor in inducing a number of consuming countries to expand their own iron and steel production, thereby keeping down the total volume of world trade in iron and steel products. But certainly British exporters of iron and steel have gained by these arrangements. Certain markets for certain products are reserved to them, and the prices obtained have been relatively high. The average value per ton of British exports of iron and steel products was nearly £19 in 1937 as compared with some £15.10s. in 1929, and this increase was due to higher prices rather than to an increased proportion of the more valuable products.

8. THE PROGRESS OF THE INDUSTRY UNDER PROTECTION

There can be no doubt that the industry was very depressed during 1931 and 1932. There was much idle capacity. Most firms earned little or nothing on their ordinary capital and some were working at a loss. Equally there can be no doubt that since 1932 the position of the industry has progressively improved. In 1935 the index of profits,[16] shown in the table on page 192, was higher than it had been for eleven years, and since 1935 it has nearly doubled.

To what extent was this revival of prosperity due to protection? We discuss the consequences of the general policy of protection in our final chapter. Our present question concerns the effect of duties upon imported iron and steel on the fortunes of the industry. It is a question on which different opinions may be held, for it is impossible to be

[16] The index of profits is taken from an article entitled "Steel Shares in War-Time" in the *Economist* of November 4, 1939. The writer says that it is "based on the *Economist's* annual computation of representative company earnings (after debenture interest)." It relates to iron, steel, *and coal* companies but "its chief constituents are, in fact, the heavy steel producers of Great Britain."

Years	Imports	Exports	Production of steel, ingots, and castings (million tons)	Index of profits (1914 = 100)
	Of iron and steel (million tons)			
1924.......	2.4	3.9	8.2	66
1925.......	2.7	3.8	7.4	27
1926.......	3.8	3.0	3.6	18
1927.......	4.4	4.2	9.1	32
1928.......	2.9	4.3	8.5	35
1929.......	2.8	4.4	9.6	51
1930.......	2.9	3.2	7.3	42
1931.......	2.8	2.0	5.2	22
1932.......	1.6	1.9	5.3	15
1933.......	1.0	1.9	7.0	28
1934.......	1.4	2.3	8.9	52
1935.......	1.2	2.4	9.9	67
1936.......	1.5	2.2	11.8	90
1937.......	2.0	2.6	13.0	119
1938.......	1.3	1.9	10.4	125

sure of what would have happened had there been no duties or quotas.

The fundamental factor in the revival of prosperity has been the great increase in the British demand for iron and steel. As the table indicates, the consumption of steel in Great Britain increased rapidly over the period 1933 to 1937. In 1938 it fell back somewhat (owing largely to the slowing-down in building and construction) but even so it was nearly twice as great as it had been at the bottom of the slump. During January-June 1939 steel output was 6,406,000 tons, and after that it was considerably higher. (War broke out in September.)

This great increase in demand, which led to a level of output during and after 1936 higher than any previously attained, was associated with the general revival of economic activity in Great Britain and in particular with the large and progressive increase in building during 1933-37 and with the rearmament program of the last two or three years. The latter resulted both in direct orders from the government and also in increases of plant and equipment by manufacturers expecting to increase their sales owing to the rearmament program. It can plausibly be argued that none of these sources of increased demand had anything to do with the tariff on iron and steel. Indeed, it can be urged that the tariff, in so far as it raised prices, prevented the demand from increasing as much or as quickly as it would otherwise have done. It can also be pointed out that when the industry was really flourishing, during and after 1936, the tariff had already been in existence for some years, and the demand for steel was so great that the agreed quotas were increased and the duties practically abolished.

But it would certainly be misleading to conclude that the prosperity of the industry owed nothing to the tariff. The heavy sections obtained immediate relief from the duties against the cheap pig iron and semis from the Continent, and they were further safeguarded by the quota arrangements, which in turn were made possible by the use of the tariff as a bargaining weapon. Under free trade, the British demand might have increased even more, but a larger proportion of it would have been met by imports. Further, it must be remembered that protection provided some guarantee of remunerative sales in the home market and thereby stimulated investment in the industry. Over £30 million have been invested in new plant and equipment since the tariff was imposed. Much of this would doubtless have taken place sooner or later under free trade, but it would probably have been later rather than sooner. The tariff gave a direct and immediate stimulus to new investments such as the integrated works costing well over £3 million erected by Stewarts and Lloyds at Corby to produce basic Bessemer products. Hence increased capacity was available to meet the very large demand of the last two or three years—although, even so, it could not fully cope with the big increase in 1937. Under free trade, it is at least possible that a considerable part of this new capacity would simply not have been brought into being by 1937.[17] Finally, it seems probable that protection has enabled prices to be raised to more remunerative levels. We discuss this point towards the close of this section.

It will be remembered that the industry made a tacit bargain with the public that in return for protection it would reorganize itself. The I.D.A.C. explicitly insisted on reorganization and made the continuance of import duties conditional upon it. How much reorganization has in fact been achieved?

We must distinguish between administrative reorganization and technical reorganization. The former has been achieved fairly fully and successfully, although the process took some time. We had better quote the I.D.A.C. "In 1933 the industry decided to adapt and improve the existing machinery, consisting of trade associations and the National Federation of Iron and Steel Manufacturers, by grouping the associations into a smaller number of effective instruments for the control of production in the several main divisions of the industry, and by giving to a new central organisation power to support and co-ordinate

---

[17] On the other hand, the tariff probably caused some rather hasty and ill-considered expansion to snatch quick profits. The fact, for example, that Barrow made an arrangement with Colville's in 1938-39 not to produce any more heavy steel suggests that the installation of heavy steel capacity at Barrow had been a mistake.

the activities of the associations and to give effect to the will of the industry in matters of general policy extending beyond the sphere of any one association. Accordingly the British Iron and Steel Federation was set up in April, 1935, with a constitution . . . giving it the necessary powers to carry out this policy. . . . There were at 1st December, 1936, twenty-seven affiliated associations; . . . the most important of the branches not yet affiliated are Foundry Pig Iron and the Tube Industry."[18]

The I.D.A.C. terms the federation "a real instrument of progress" which "is making its authority and guiding influence felt" in various ways. The federation does indeed have a good deal of influence. The affiliated associations have undertaken not to increase prices without first consulting the federation and the council of the federation resolved in December 1936 "that all proposals in regard to the expansion of plant should be submitted to a Committee of the Federation." It has been proposed that a central fund, amounting to the first instance to £1 million, should be raised by a levy on the tonnage of steel ingots produced. This would be used for some or all of the following purposes:

(i) to assist and expand export trade in steel products and the export trade of manufacturers using steel products as their raw materials;

(ii) to maintain a reasonable price-level, by making grants to meet the position of certain high-cost plants whose output is essential in busy periods but whose costs are too high by which to determine the price-level;

(iii) to make provision for elimination of redundant or inefficient plants, thereby bringing efficient producing capacity into relationship with market demand;

(iv) to maintain on a "care and maintenance" basis in less

[18] Cmd. 8507 of 1937, p. 16 *et seq.*

busy periods plants which might well be necessary to meet the peak demands of busy periods;

(v) to establish greater equality of delivery charges to the consumer, in connexion with schedule prices;

(vi) to assist associations in the development of new uses for steel and market research;

(vii) these and any other purpose which the Council may approve in conjunction with the associations concerned as being to the benefit of the industry and in the public interest.[19]

We shall not criticize these purposes, for the scheme has not been adopted. As yet, the Federation has very little power to compel firms to comply with its wishes. The I.D.A.C. points out that independent firms may undermine an organization, particularly in times of depression, by reducing prices in order to work nearer to full capacity. It realizes that the industry as a whole will be more prosperous if all firms belong to the relevant associations for regulating output and prices. But it will not go so far as to suggest compelling firms to join. Independent producers must still be allowed to exist, although the I.D.A.C. obviously hopes that there will be few of them. It looks forward to the voluntary enrollment of nearly all firms in associations under the aegis of the Federation. This, in fact, has largely been achieved.

On the technical side, there have been considerable improvements, although some critics claim that Great Britain still lags behind her chief rivals. We have already mentioned changes in location. A growing proportion of pig iron and steel is produced on or near the ore of the Midlands, and the heavy sections in South Wales have moved to the coast. Further changes, however, would seem desirable, notably in Scotland. Moreover, the Richard Thomas

[19] Report, p. 19.

works at Ebbw Vale would be able to produce considerably more cheaply on the site originally chosen—at Redbourn in Lincolnshire, near the ore and near the sea. The company yielded to the protests of the workers and went instead to Ebbw Vale, where, although transport costs are higher, there were large numbers of unemployed.

The industry has become more mechanized during recent years. This has led to a marked increase in output per worker. The number attached to steel furnaces, rolling mills, etc., in 1937 was about the same as in 1929 (some 180,000) and the number attached to blast furnaces was appreciably less (17,000 as against 22,000), but the output of steel was over 30 per cent greater, and that of pig iron over 10 per cent greater, in 1937. Part of this increase was due to fuller employment, both of the workers and of the plant, but much of it was due to increased mechanization and efficiency.

A growing proportion of the total output is produced in integrated works, and considerable progress has been made in fuel economy. The amount of coke used per ton of basic pig iron produced has fallen from 26.76 cwts. in 1930 to 22.73 cwts. in 1937, and the amount of coal used (apart from blast furnace consumption) per ton of steel has fallen from 0.925 tons to 0.688 tons.[20] The average size of blast furnaces has increased. Output per furnace was 47.9 thousand tons in 1929 and 68.5 thousand tons in 1937. The average size of open-hearth furnaces has increased. The proportion of total capacity represented by furnaces large enough to produce more than 75 tons per heat has risen from a quarter to a half. The average size of coke ovens has increased, a larger proportion are modern by-

[20] From an article on "Iron and Steel Re-organisation," in the *Economist* of December 17, 1938.

product ovens, and the cost of producing metallurgical coke has fallen.

A critic can still find plenty of room for improvement.[21] The blast furnaces in some districts, notably Scotland and the Black Country, are still far too small. In general, the size of blast furnaces and steel furnaces and coke ovens is considerably smaller than in the United States or Germany, and fuel consumption is greater. Out of a total coking capacity of over 22 million tons per annum, 4.3 million tons consist of "entirely obsolete waste heat ovens."[22] The continuous strip-rolling process was introduced (by Richard Thomas) only after it had already been adopted for years by other countries.

Such criticisms may or may not be well founded. To decide what the British iron and steel industry should be like—where a plant should be located, how large the furnaces should be, what type of coke ovens should be used, and so forth—if one were starting with a clean sheet, and creating an entirely new industry, is one matter. From this standpoint, the criticisms are abundantly justified. But to decide how far it is wise to scrap or abandon plant and equipment in good technical condition, but not up-to-date or not situated in the most suitable place, is quite another matter. The history of the German Steel Trust surely serves as a warning that scrapping and modernization can be proceeded with too rapidly and on too large a scale. As it happens, it was just as well that the sweeping proposals put forward in 1933 for scrapping "obsolete" plant and equipment, in order to concentrate output in more modern and integrated works, were not carried out. For most of the

[21] These criticisms are set out more fully in the article mentioned above.
[22] Quoted from the same article.

plants which would have been scrapped were needed to meet the increased demand of recent years.

Probably some of the criticism is justified. Nevertheless it cannot be denied that very considerable technical progress has been made. The point we wish to emphasize is that this progress has not been due, to more than a very small extent, to any central planning or compulsion from above. It has taken place on the initiative of the firms themselves.

In other words, the "re-organisation" which the I.D.A.C. accepted in fulfillment of the pledge given by the industry was mainly administrative: a reorganization, so to speak, on paper. The incentive of a tariff was used to induce the industry to make its trade associations (or, we might say, cartels) stronger and more comprehensive, and to set up a body (the Federation) to represent the industry as a whole. This means that the industry is now in a more monopolistic position, and therefore better able to cope with the problems arising from fluctuations in demand, to which we drew attention in Section 5, and to negotiate with monopolistic organizations in other countries. But it is a monopoly based on the consent of the member firms. No firm is compelled by law to join; and the proposals for a Central Fund, mentioned above, have not yet been put into effect.

The chief possible danger of a monopolistic organization is that it may raise prices unduly, especially if it is protected by restrictions on imports.[23] The I.D.A.C. observe: "In our view, and that of the Federation also, it is essential that the regulation of prices thus exercised should be

[23] A minor danger is that it may discriminate among its members. Thus in 1937 the Federation stabilized the home price of scrap and kept down the price of imported scrap, making a levy on ingot steel produced to cover the costs of this operation. It was alleged that it thereby benefited districts, such as the Scottish district, using a high proportion of scrap.

supervised by some body outside the industry and responsible only for seeing that the public interest is properly and adequately considered."[24] In fact, there is no compulsory control over prices, but apparently most price changes have received the approval of the I.D.A.C., and the various trade associations have regarded the prices fixed as standard prices not to be exceeded. The general principle has been, it is stated, to change prices only in accordance with changes in cost of production, although these are admittedly difficult to measure and vary between firms.

Nevertheless there have been complaints from consumers, such as Lord Nuffield, that prices had been fixed too high. It is pointed out that the federation practically promised not to raise prices above the levels of 1934-35. For example, the I.D.A.C. reported[25] that on March 14, 1935, "the Federation categorically renewed the assurance . . . that it is not their intention to raise prices as a result of increased protection." Perhaps the best single measure of iron and steel prices is the Board of Trade index-numbers. These are shown in the following tables, together with the Board of Trade index for wholesale prices in general.

Year	Iron and steel	All commodities
1930	100	100
1931	92.8	87.8
1932	91.5	85.6
1933	94.3	85.7
1934	98.7	88.1
1935	100.5	89.0
1936	106.6	94.4
1937	129.6	108.7
1938	139.1	101.4
July 1939	129.3	101.7

[24] Report, p. 53.
[25] Cmd. 5201 of 1936.

On November 1, 1939, after the war had caused a great increase in the demand for iron and steel, prices were raised, but only by 10 per cent.

The I.D.A.C. have stated the problem, as they conceive it, of reorganizing the industry. It is "to secure the systematic planning of the industry as a whole and the maintenance and development of internal co-ordination and co-operation, with the aid of a tariff so far as necessary and with the continuance of international agreements, whilst at the same time avoiding the evils of monopoly, safeguarding the public interest and fostering efficiency."[26] It will indeed be a remarkable feat if all these objects are achieved.

[26] Report, p. 77.

Chapter VIII

AGRICULTURE

1. Why Agriculture Was Depressed

British agriculture was undoubtedly hard hit by the great depression. British farmers had to meet the competition of imported foodstuffs selling at prices far below the levels ruling two or three years before: for some commodities the fall in price was 50 per cent or more.

A general trade depression usually forces down the prices of agricultural products more than those of manufactured goods. For manufacturing employs mainly wage labor; very drastic cuts in wages are often difficult or impossible; and a fall in demand leads to unemployment and a reduction in output rather than to a heavy fall in prices. Agriculture, employing largely family labor, is in the opposite position. Farmers continue to work and to produce, for there are no alternative occupations to which they can easily turn; the volume of output remains much the same but prices, and therefore farmers' incomes, fall heavily.

Moreover, there were aggravating circumstances which forced down the prices of some agricultural products still further. Take wheat, as the leading example. During the twenties the world wheat acreage was greatly increased[1] and after 1926 stocks began to pile up. Action taken by government agencies—such as the Federal Farm Board in the United States—to prevent the price of wheat from sagging, resulted only in a stimulus to further increases in the acreage sown, and in the end the great accumulation

[1] See P. de Hevesy, *World Wheat Planning*, p. 706.

of stocks, which could no longer be held off the market, brought prices down with a rush.

Again, the very severe agrarian protection adopted by most countries of western Europe, to save their own farmers, increased and prolonged the fall in the world prices of most foodstuffs. Grain, meat, butter, and similar products were allowed to enter important markets such as France, Germany, and Italy, in only small quantities or not at all; overseas farmers had to sell for what they could get; and in consequence the prices at which such goods were sold to Great Britain fell to very low levels indeed.

The facts we have just cited are, of course, relevant. They help to explain why the troubles of British farmers were so sharply aggravated after about 1929. But they do not go to the root of the matter. They do not show why British agriculture was depressed even before 1929 or why most countries of western Europe had to impose penal tariffs, or quotas, or outright prohibitions, to keep out overseas produce. The fundamental explanation is that the twenties saw a particularly rapid advance in technical progress in most branches of agriculture—an advance which favored overseas producers more than European producers and thus increased the comparative advantages of the former.

Perhaps the most striking aspect of technical progress during the twenties was the more widespread use of agricultural machinery, including many new and improved types. This considerably reduced the costs of production per unit of product. But full advantage could be taken of mechanization only on the vast prairies and plains of the New World, where land was plentiful and cheap and labor relatively scarce. In western Europe the nature of the land or the large number of relatively small farms into which it was carved up imposed obstacles, so that the factory-farms of the new world increased their competitive advantage.

Other kinds of technical progress tended, on balance, to have the same effect of reducing costs overseas more than in Europe. For example, a new and prolific type of sugar cane was discovered, which of course benefited tropical producers as against European growers of beet sugar; and improvements in dry-soil farming could be applied mainly in Canada.

Yet even overseas farmers reaped little benefit from the technical progress of the twenties. The stagnation of American agriculture, when American industry was booming, was merely a striking instance of a practically worldwide phenomenon. Particular groups—for example, Danish pig-farmers—were fairly prosperous, and of course the most efficient farmers made money, but broadly speaking agriculture throughout the world was less profitable than most branches of production.

Overseas farmers blamed partly the tariffs and subsidies by which a number of European countries tried to help their own agriculture, although in fact these did not become very severe until after 1929. European farmers partly blamed the fiercer competition from overseas. But the true explanation lies in the consumption habits, and the recent tendency towards a stationary population, of the western world.

Technical progress in, let us say, the production of shoes may lead to a fall in the price of shoes and a large increase in their consumption. Profits and employment in the shoe industry may increase, because the demand for shoes expands considerably in response to a fall in price.

This does not apply to wheat. An exceptionally large harvest of wheat probably gives wheat-farmers as a whole less money than a poor harvest.

The same holds good when the incomes of consumers increase, prices remaining more or less the same, which is very much what happened during the later twenties. A person whose income has increased spends more on goods and services which he previously regarded as luxuries or semi-luxuries. He is unlikely to spend much, if any, more upon the simpler foodstuffs such as bread and potatoes.

For a long time the tendency has been for the general standard of living in western countries to rise, and for the *per capita* consumption of wheat flour to fall. For example, in Great Britain it has fallen from 252 lbs. a year in 1861-65 to 212 in 1936. Until recent times the fall in *per capita* consumption was considerably more than offset by the rapid growth of population, but this has now greatly slackened or actually ceased in a number of wheat-consuming countries.

Of course the demand for all foodstuffs does not resemble the demand for wheat. The demand for butter, for example, is fairly elastic—the *per capita* consumption of butter in Great Britain has increased by nearly 50 per cent over the last fifteen years; and much the same probably applies to most dairy produce, fruit, and fresh vegetables other than potatoes. But most of the cheaper foodstuffs are somewhat like wheat in this respect. When people become better off they increase their consumption of such foodstuffs relatively little. In the United States, where the standard of living has long been higher than in most countries, even the *per capita* consumption of meat has tended to diminish during recent years.

Hence increased productivity in agriculture, or rather

in those branches producing the cheaper foodstuffs, coupled with an upward trend in the general standard of living, has meant that agriculture has been, to say the least, less flourishing than most branches of economic activity. Profits, and chances of remunerative employment, have been greater in expanding occupations, engaged in satisfying growing demands, than in agriculture. Farmers have tended—of course with numerous exceptions—to make relatively small profits, or even losses, and to be unable to pay good wages.

If this has been true of world agriculture in general, how much more has it applied to Great Britain! Ever since the early seventies of the last century the British farmer has been fighting a losing battle against the competition of imported foodstuffs coming from overseas where land is abundant and cheap. The opening up of new countries by rail and road, improvements which cheapened sea transport, the discovery and perfection of devices, such as refrigeration, for preserving foodstuffs, progress in the invention of agriculture machinery, have all increased the competitive advantage of the overseas farmers. The twenties, as we have seen, saw a quickening of this tempo, and the collapse of most agricultural prices during the great depression gave the British farmer a final terrific blow. He appealed to the government for aid in order that he might continue to exist.

2. How Agriculture Was Assisted

From a strictly economic standpoint there was not much to be said in favor of state assistance to agriculture—apart, possibly, from grants to tide farmers over a particularly bad period. It is true that during the previous fifty years the numbers engaged in agriculture had fallen by 300,000, although the total working population had increased by two-thirds. It is true that in 1931 the area under wheat was the lowest ever recorded, 1¼ million acres, and that hundreds of thousands of acres which had grown crops some years ago were in danger of being abandoned to weeds. But what did this mean? It meant that British labor and capital in the export industries could obtain much more food, imported in exchange for their manufactures, than if they had been diverted towards producing food directly at home. Although minimum wages were fixed for agricultural workers these were still well below the wages paid in most occupations; most landlords received a very small percentage return from their property; and farming was a depressed occupation. If some branch of activity was going to be encouraged, then on purely economic grounds agriculture would have seemed about the last to choose.

Various non-economic arguments were also put forward in favor of helping agriculture, but these too were rather weak. It was said that Great Britain would need to grow more food in time of war. But clearly Great Britain would also need many things, such as petroleum and cotton, which would have to come from overseas. The wisest course seemed to be to spend on the Navy, to keep communications open. It would be necessary in time of war to economize labor, and it would still pay best to import most of the food from overseas. When the war came, it would be time enough to decide to what extent it was worth while to put more land under the plow. The war argument was really an argument for storing large quantities of such foodstuffs as wheat and sugar, and for maintaining British supremacy of the seas, rather than an argument for immediately promoting agriculture. Some people, usually those living in towns, declared that it was desirable to maintain a large population living on the soil. This was largely pure mysticism. Statistics lend little support to the view that countryfolk are healthier than townfolk, and the chief desire of most farm laborers is to escape to the comforts and amusements of the towns. Anyway, the best way to get a larger population in the country would probably have been to encourage the setting-up of factories in country districts—an object which the development of cheap electric power and road transport was already assisting—rather than to subsidize farming.

Nevertheless agriculture was assisted in a number of ways, which we shall describe very briefly.

To begin with, since 1929 agricultural land had been completely exempt from local rates. In so far as the rates were used for such purposes as poor relief, this was reasonable, but in so far as they were spent in ways which directly benefited agricultural land—for example, in making local roads or providing for sewage disposal—it meant that farmers were getting something for nothing. Only a relatively small part of the rates, however, are in fact spent in such ways.

Another very valuable concession was that farmers were given the privilege, denied to persons following other occupations, of choosing each year on which of three bases they should be assessed for income tax.[2] They could be assessed either on their previous years' profits or on their present year's profits, or on the rent which they paid to their landlord. This system of options had been in force for many years.

Some of the schemes for helping growers of particular

[2] See R. S. Edwards, "Farmers and Income Tax" in *Economica*, May 1937.

products were discussed in Chapter III, and little more need be said about them. The subsidy on beet sugar, it will be remembered, dates from 1924, whereas nearly all the other products which now receive assistance obtained it only after Great Britain adopted protection. The beet sugar scheme has proved very expensive—it has been calculated that it would be cheaper to pension off all the workers producing beet sugar at their present wages and to import cane sugar instead—but at least the subsidy is a charge on the Exchequer, so that the public can see how much they are paying. The same cannot be said of the wheat subsidy, which comes, as we have explained, from a "processing tax" which is outside the budget. The raising of the limit in 1937 to 36 million cwts. virtually meant a guaranteed minimum price for wheat, since this figure is most unlikely to be exceeded in peacetime. From the standpoint of consumers, this type of subsidy is better than a tariff. A tariff, which applied also to Dominion wheat, would raise the price of all wheat in Great Britain above the world price by the full amount of the tariff. As it is, consumers pay only about a quarter of what they would pay under a tariff which raised the price to 10s. per cwt., since only about a quarter of the wheat consumed is produced at home. The Agriculture Act of 1937 fixed guaranteed prices for barley and oats. For barley, an average yeld of 6 cwts. per acre was assumed with a standard price of 8s. per cwt. If the market price was lower, each barley grower would receive per acre six times the amount by which the market price fell short of 8s. per cwt. Similar provisions applied to oats. As the market prices ruling at the time were considerably above the standard prices, these provisions were intended to insure growers against a substantial fall in price rather than to guarantee them, as the wheat scheme did, a profitable return.

Potato growers were assisted, in addition to the licencing of imports, by restrictions on home production. Every registered grower was given an acreage quota, which he could exceed only on payment of £5 for each extra acre to the Potato Marketing Board. Similarly, any newcomer had to pay £5 per acre per year in order to become registered and to be permitted to sell to the market. This was intended to stabilize the acreage. The danger of a fall in the price owing to a particularly good crop was guarded against by the use of riddles. Potatoes of less than a certain diameter could not be sold for human consumption, and the Board prescribed each year the size of the diameter—of the holes in the riddle—making them larger when the crop was heavy.

The home production of hops has similarly been restricted since 1931 by means of quotas. For some years the price has been stabilized at about £9 per cwt., which is considerably above the price ruling before the great depression. All sales must be made through the Board, which may destroy any surplus. The scheme virtually gives existing growers a monopoly and keeps up prices, as is shown by the fact that quotas—giving their possessor the right to grow hops in future years—are bought and sold at about £12 per cwt. All that can be said in defense of the scheme is the classic excuse that it is only a little one: there are only some 18,000 acres under hops.

The prices of fat cattle fell by some 15 per cent between 1932 and 1934. In the latter year they were nearly 30 per cent below pre-slump levels and from September 1934 subsidy payments were made on heifers, steers and cowheifers (but not on cows or bulls). £11.4 million were paid in subsidy between September 1, 1934, and August 31, 1937. The scheme was then revised; an amount not exceeding £5 million is to be voted each year by Parliament for the subsidy and for the expenses of the Livestock Commission. This body fixes the rates of subsidy per cwt. It fixes them in such a way as to encourage the production of high quality fat cattle in Great Britain. Quality standard animals receive a higher subsidy than ordinary standard animals, and home-bred ones receive a higher subsidy than those imported for fattening.

Milk and milk products form nearly one-third in value of the output of British agriculture. Milk producers have been helped since 1933 by the establishment of Milk Marketing Boards. We shall consider, but only in barest outline, the scheme for England and Wales. The other schemes are similar in their effects.

Some two-thirds of British milk is sold to be consumed liquid; the rest is sold to "manufacturers" of butter, cheese, chocolate, and other products. For brevity, we shall speak of "liquid" milk and "manufacturing" milk.

A statutory minimum price is fixed for "liquid" milk. Nobody may sell "liquid" milk below this price. The price has been fixed relatively high: during recent years it has been over 15d. per gallon wholesale. (Minimum retail prices are also fixed. They vary between districts, averaging some 26d. or 27d. per gallon.)

The prices of butter, cheese, and other "manufactured" milk products are kept down by the low prices at which imports come in. Hence English milk sold for "manufacturing" purposes fetches only a low price—during recent years somewhere near 5d. a gallon wholesale.

Clearly all the milk produced could not be sold "liquid" at the price fixed. The problem was to restrict the quantity sold "liquid," in order to maintain the price, and yet to give all farmers the same return (after allowing for transport costs, and similar expenses) for their milk.

This was achieved through the Milk Marketing Board. All payments between farmers and distributors are made through the Board and the Board pays the farmer a "pool price." This is what he actually receives, whatever the buyer has paid and whatever the use to which his milk is put. In effect, producers of milk which happens to be sold "liquid" subsidize producers of milk which happens to be sold for "manufacturing" purposes. This involves a payment from eastern regions (where the bulk of the milk is sold "liquid") to western regions (where much of the milk is sold for "manufacturing").

The scheme therefore rests on a foundation of discriminating monopoly enforced by the state. Exactly the same milk commands a much higher price if sold "liquid" than if sold for "manufacturing" purposes. Under free competition, this could not continue; milk would be diverted towards the "liquid" market, bringing down prices there, until the net price in both markets was the same. The "manfacturing" price cannot be raised much owing to the competition of imported butter, cheese, and so forth, but fresh liquid milk enjoys a "natural protection" and imports are small unless its price is very high. Hence the receipts of milk producers are increased by maintaining a high price for milk sold "liquid," restricting the quantity thus sold to the amount which the market will take at that price, selling the rest to "manufacturers" for what it will fetch, and pooling the receipts among all producers.[3]

[3] This is obviously a very brief summary. For a fuller account and indeed on the whole subject of this chapter, see *British Agriculture* (published 1938), a Report of an Enquiry Organised by Viscount Astor and B. Seebohm Rowntree.

The scheme helps milk producers at the expense of consumers of "liquid" milk. The government itself contributes relatively little. When the market price of "manufacturing" milk is below a certain minimum, it makes up the difference; and it subsidizes a scheme by which children attending elementary schools can get one-third of a pint per day, either free or at half-price.

It may be doubted whether the scheme for pigs and bacon did much to help the producers. What really helped them was the quantitative restriction of imports. About two-thirds of the English output is sold as pork; the rest is cured and sold as bacon and ham. The government arranged for pig farmers to make contracts, if they chose, to sell pigs to the curers at prices varying mainly with the cost of feeding-stuffs. In the first years of this system, the curers did not obtain enough pigs and had to buy more pigs in the open market at prices higher than those which they were paying under their contracts. This caused discontent; farmers became reluctant to make contracts; and in 1937 the scheme broke down. The real trouble was that the pork market was uncontrolled, many pigs could be sold either for pork or for bacon,[4] and the price of pork was tending to rise under the stimulus of increased demand.

In addition to the subsidies and schemes we have mentioned, farmers were of course protected by tariffs and by the quantitative regulation of certain imports. They complained, however, that this was of much less benefit to them than might be thought, for their chief competitors were the Dominions, whose products came in free.

[4] A pig is usually killed for pork when about five months old and for bacon when about eight or nine months old. Hence it is quite possible for a farmer to decide to kill pigs now for pork instead of keeping them another three or four months to be sold as baconers. Moreover, pigs of certain weights can be sold either as heavy porkers or as light baconers.

Some farmers nevertheless were considerably helped by protection: notably pig producers and growers of certain vegetables and fruits.[5]

3. AGRICULTURE DURING RECENT YEARS

The various measures of assistance which we have briefly described soon succeeded in restoring a fair measure of prosperity and security to most branches of agriculture. The gross volume of output in 1937 was about one-sixth greater than in 1931, and the prices received by British farmers for nearly all products were considerably higher.

It is true that the net volume of output probably increased relatively little over this period. The total quantity of feeding-stuffs imported rose from 6.8 million tons to 8.1 million tons.[6] On the other hand, the downward trend in the number of workers continued. In 1931 the total number of employed workers[7] was 829,000 (as compared with 925,000 in 1925); in 1939 it was only 708,000. Hence there must have been a considerable increase in net output per worker.

It will be noted that protection did not succeed in maintaining, let alone in increasing, the number of agricultural workers. There can be no doubt, however, that the number would have fallen still more had no assistance been given. In 1924 the wages of farm workers were brought under the control of county committees and local minimum wages

---

[5] C. S. Orwin in *Britain in Recovery*, p. 173, gives the Cornish broccoli growers as an illustration, stating that they "have a protection equivalent to some £25 an acre."

[6] See *British Agriculture*, pp. 53-4.

[7] *Statistical Abstract for the United Kingdom* (published 1938), page 295. The figures cover workers employed on agricultural holdings of more than one acre in Great Britain in June. They exclude occupiers, occupiers' wives, and domestic servants, but include members of occupiers' families working on the holdings.

were fixed from time to time. These were low relatively to wages in most occupations, but they were higher than they had been in the past, and of course they had to be paid however low the prices of farm products might fall. Hence farmers have been doing all they can to economize labor. They have considerably increased the use made of agricultural machinery of all kinds. In particular, the number of tractors has gone up from under 17,000 in 1925 to some 50,000 in 1939. Crops which require a good deal of labor, such as mangolds and turnips, are grown much less than twenty years ago, and greater use is made of fertilizers. But part of the increased volume of output per worker is due to greater efficiency, for example, to the more scientific feeding of stock, better breeding of both plants and animals, and greater control of diseases.

The main changes in the nature of the agricultural output over the last ten years have been a marked increase in the pig population (which rose from below 3 million in 1930 to 4½ million in 1935) and an increase of some 50 per cent (since 1931) in the acreage under wheat. The acreages under oats and under barley have both continued to decline. The number of fowls has increased by 50 per cent. There has been some increase in the number of dairy cattle, and some change in their geographical distribution, the milk schemes having stimulated milk production in areas such as the West of England which formerly had to sell most of their milk at somewhere near the "manufacturing" price.

The policy of protecting and assisting agriculture has met with no really strong opposition. This is perhaps partly because it was introduced when food prices were falling. The retail price of food remained well below the pre-slump level until August 1939. During the next four months it rose by more than 10 per cent, owing mainly to the war, but even so it did not quite reach the 1929 level.

We cannot discuss the changes which must be made owing to the war. A good deal more land will be put under the plow, and the use of labor-saving machinery, especially tractors, will have to be considerably increased in order to do this and to economize labor-power.

Some critics allege that the steps taken to aid agriculture have diverted it from its most natural and desirable lines of development. Crops such as sugar beet and wheat, in which British farmers are at a marked disadvantage compared with overseas producers, have been encouraged. The output of other products, in which they have an advantage owing to their nearness to the market, has not been stimulated enough. By far the most important of such products is milk.

Liquid milk, we may repeat, enjoys a high degree of "natural protection." The *per capita* consumption of milk in Great Britain is well below that of most countries with a comparable standard of living. Most of the unemployed consume little or no fresh milk, and in poor families the consumption per head is lower the greater the number of children. Experts on diet consider that the consumption of milk, especially by children, should be increased. And the demand for milk would respond considerably to reductions in price and to suitable propaganda. Yet the whole point of milk schemes is that they keep up the price of liquid milk, thereby restricting its consumption, whilst protection, subsidies, and so on, encourage farmers to produce other products rather than milk.

It is claimed that the costs of producing milk could be considerably reduced by prolonging the life of the dairy cow, and by making use of new discoveries in connection with the growing and drying of grasses. Further, it is claimed that the most useful form of government subsidy would be one which enabled poor people and children to increase considerably their consumption of certain foodstuffs, including milk.

The present writer is not qualified to express an opinion on this subject. He does feel, however, that the price paid for a little more agriculture—mainly in the form of pigs and sugar beet and wheat—than we should have in the absence of any state assistance is a high one, and that if agriculture is to be helped it seems hardly fair that much of the burden should be borne by consumers of milk, bread, and meat.

Chapter IX

ECONOMIC RECOVERY

1. The Main Features of the Recovery

THE RECOVERY of Great Britain has been one of the most striking features of the economic world during recent years. Before the great depression, Great Britain was lagging behind her rivals. After the great depression, the position was almost reversed. Great Britain forged ahead while some other important countries seemed to be stuck in the economic quagmire. Thus the volume of industrial production was well below the pre-slump level almost throughout the thirties in both the United States and France. In the United States it was regained for a brief period in 1937 only to be followed by a sharp relapse. In France there was nothing like a real recovery until the economic program of M. Paul Reynaud began to take effect early in 1939.

The British recovery began in 1933 and proceeded, at first slowly and then with gathering momentum, until 1937. Towards the close of 1937 there was some falling-off, largely reflecting the recession in the United States, but industry and trade revived under the stimulus of large government expenditure on armaments and in 1939 British economic indices stood higher than ever. If we compare 1937 with 1929, the peak pre-slump year, we find that the volume of industrial output was over 20 per cent greater, the number of insured persons employed (excluding agricultural workers) had increased from 10.2 million to 11.5 million, industrial profits were at least 10 per cent higher, and money wages, despite a 5 per cent fall in the cost of living, were some 7 per cent higher.

All the existing indices of British industrial output are for one reason or another somewhat unsatisfactory,[1] but all agree in showing a considerable increase during the thirties. For many years the trend has been for output per person engaged to become greater. Mr. Colin Clark estimates[2] that whereas in 1911 some 8.6 million persons engaged in industry produced only 39.3 per cent of the national income, in 1934 some 7.9 million persons engaged in industry produced 49.3 per cent of the national income. This tendency was undoubtedly accelerated in the thirties, when output per person engaged in manufacturing may have increased by as much as 25 per cent.[3]

In so far as this increase was due to the stimulus to efficiency provided by the slump it must be set down as one of the effects of the trade cycle which are not to be deplored. For the most part, however, it was probably the result of technical progress and of increased investment which often took the form of greater mechanization. For many decades the state of technical knowledge has tended to improve and the volume of investment to increase. Can it be shown that the tariff was responsible for a quickening of the tempo?

It can perhaps be argued that the tariff may have stimulated inventions and improvements in manufacturing, owing to the expansion of the home market which it made possible, but there is no evidence that this was quantitatively of much importance.[4] It can be urged, more

---

[1] For a good critical account of them see "Indices of Industrial Output" by Richard and Winifred Stone in the *Economic Journal*, September 1939.

[2] *National Income and Outlay*, p. 238.

[3] See *Output, Employment, and Wages in the United Kingdom, 1924, 1930, 1935*, by G. L. Schwartz and E. C. Rhodes, London and Cambridge Economic Service Memorandum No. 75; and Richard and Winifred Stone, *op. cit.*

[4] The total number of patents applied for reached a peak of 39,898 in 1929 and was somewhat lower during the following years.

plausibly, that the tariff did tempt money from idle balances into investment in protected industries. We have seen that it stimulated investment in iron and steel, and the same is probably true of some other protected industries. The results of the inquiry by the Import Duties Advisory Committee into employment in protected industries may be summarized as follows:

PERSONS EMPLOYED

	1930	1933	1934
	(thousands)		
Iron and steel............	494	445	498
Engineering...............	685	541	606
Textiles..................	1,045	1,009	1,025
Others...................	1,038	1,020	1,079
All covered by the Inquiry..	3,262	3,015	3,208
Industries not covered (Mainly motor and cycle)	245	—	249

As the total number of insured workers in employment (excluding agriculture) increased from 9,797,000 in 1930 to 10,139,000 in 1934 the results of this Inquiry do not support the claim that the tariff directly increased *employment*, but it is probable that it encouraged *investment* which largely (as in iron and steel) took the form of labor-saving devices and thereby helped to increase output per worker.

Nevertheless it can hardly be claimed that the tariff played a major part in the British recovery. For its effect on the export trades, accounting for perhaps a quarter of all manufacturing output, was adverse rather than favorable, while the growth of employment took place, as we have seen, mainly in the non-protected occupations. It is beyond dispute that the chief symptom of recovery was the building boom. This is discussed in the following section, but clearly its connection with protection was extremely slight. After 1936, government expenditure on rearmament provided an important stimulus.[5] This again had little to do with protection; indeed as we have seen, it led to the temporary removal of the duties on iron and steel.

Between 1929 and 1939 striking changes took place in the numbers engaged (whether employed or unemployed) in various occupations. The number of agricultural workers decreased from 888,000 to 708,000. The numbers engaged in coal-mining fell from 1,075,000 to 839,000, and in the cotton industry from 555,000 to 378,000. The numbers engaged in "manufacturing" as a whole increased by 12.5 per cent to 6,705,000, as compared with an increase of 16.6 per cent in the total number of insured persons.[6] Among the industries showing particularly great expansion were motors, cycles, and aircraft (245,000 to 459,000), electric cables, apparatus, lamps (94,000 to 185,000), and electrical engineering (84,000 to 123,000). Government service, public utilities, road transport, and most occupations providing "services" showed increases well above the average. In particular, the numbers engaged in building and contracting expanded by 42 per cent to 1,405,000.

The trend to the South continued. Over these ten years the number of insured workers in the London area increased by 27.5 per cent, in the South-East area by 35.9 per cent, in the South-West area by 29.7 per cent, and in

---

[5] Defense expenditure increased from £157 million in 1935-36 and £186 million in 1936-37 to £262 million in 1937-38 and £383 million in 1938-39. The 1939-40 estimates show an increase of over 50 per cent on the previous year.

[6] See "A decade of industrial change" in the *Economist*, January 6, 1940.

the Midlands by 21.0 per cent. Other administrative divisions (and notably the North-West and Wales) showed increases well below the average. Early in 1939 the Royal Commission on the Location of Industry reported that some members were in favor of taking steps to control the establishment of new factories in and around London.

Only the staple export industries, with the exception of those benefiting from rearmament, failed to share in the general recovery. Throughout the thirties (with the exception of 1937, when the corresponding figure was around 20 per cent) the volume of British exports was at least 25 to 30 per cent below the 1929 level.[7] The large decreases in the numbers engaged in coal-mining and in the cotton industry have been cited; there was also some decrease in the numbers engaged in shipbuilding and in the woolen and worsted industries.

The continued depression in the export industries, and consequently in the exporting districts, was mainly responsible for the continued high level of unemployment. The total number of insured workers unemployed was as follows:

	(Thousands)
July 1929	1,178
" 1930	2,070
" 1931	2,806
" 1932	2,921
" 1933	2,508
" 1934	2,162
" 1935	1,992
" 1936	1,660
" 1937	1,321
" 1938	1,773
" 1939	1,256

The depreciation of sterling and the adoption of protection left the volume of British exports much lower, and

[7] See Statistical Appendix.

the amount of unemployment appreciably higher, than before the great depression.

2. THE BUILDING BOOM

The great increase in building activity was the most out-standing feature of the British recovery. At first, this took the form of an increase in the number of houses built. The output of factories and other non-residential build-ings remained well below the pre-slump level until about 1935; thereafter it also showed a considerable increase, and during the last two or three years it has helped to compensate for the slowing-down of the housing boom.

House building was not seriously affected by the slump. The annual number of houses built in England and Wales remained near the 200,000 mark during the years of depression. The number rose to 267,000 in 1934, 329,000 in 1935, 325,000 in 1936, and 346,000 in 1937. The rate of house building during these years was far above any level previously attained in this country.

After the war of 1914-18 there was a marked shortage of houses, and various subsidies were given by the state. From 1920 to 1930 inclusive about 1.5 million houses were built in England and Wales, and of these little more than a third were built without state assistance. More than this number were built during the five years 1934 to 1938, and over three-quarters of them were built by private enterprise without any state assistance. The great majority of them were *not* in the very cheapest class (although "wage earners" formed a considerable and increasing percentage of the purchasers) and only a small proportion of them were built to be let. In other words, the housing boom was characterized largely by increased purchases of houses (for the most part on some instalment payments plan) by people of moderate means.

The housing boom played a very important part in the economic recovery. It came early. Speculative builders were getting ready to increase their output towards the close of 1932, when the value of plans for dwelling houses (approved by local authorities) shot upwards by one-third. Their plans resulted in increased employment from the following summer onwards and in increased housing output from 1934 onwards. Indeed, the number of houses built without state assistance increased considerably throughout the depression. Housing was the main channel for investment which was both reasonably safe and fairly profitable. Moreover, the increase in house building gave employment to workers in many industries. These included industries making materials, such as bricks and tubes and stoves, and industries engaged in supplying gas, water, electricity, furniture, and other amenities to the new houses, together with industries such as the manufacture of electric cables and apparatus. It has been estimated that perhaps a third of the increased employment during the recovery was more or less directly due to the housing boom.

The number of workers classified as attached to "building," increased from 857,000 in 1932 to 1,035,000 in 1937, and the percentage unemployed was only 11.2 in July 1937 as compared with 27.6 in July 1932. There is no close correlation between the output of houses and the number of workers employed in building, for the latter are largely engaged in repair work and non-residential building.

It is interesting to consider the causes or conditions which produced this increase of activity in building and consequently in the wide circle of allied trades. During recent years, there has been considerable activity in the construction of factories, aerodromes, and other buildings as a result of actual and expected expenditure on rearmament by the government, but we shall examine only the housing boom.

Sir Harold Bellman, who should know, declares[8] that "it derived its ultimate motive force from an intensive public demand for improved standards of accommodation." Certainly there was a considerable need for more housing. The census of 1931 showed that in England and Wales there were 9,123,000 "houses"—a term which throughout this discussion means a structurally separate dwelling—of which 660,000 were occupied by two families, 122,000 by three families, and 57,000 by four or more families. Out of every 100 families, only eighty-one had a separate dwelling each. Moreover some of the "families" must have wanted to break up, thus creating additional "families," and in particular the considerable migration to the South was constantly increasing the need for housing. In 1931, 12 per cent of the population in private families were living at a density of two or more persons per room.

To some extent the housing boom was due to a fall in costs. Building materials fell a little in price after 1930, but this was quite a minor factor. The fall in the rate of interest was much more important.

We have already pointed out that during the depression, with foreign lending risky and the prospects of home industry not attractive, the obvious outlet for investment was housing. But the capital required by builders is relatively small. If houses costing £200 million are built in the course of a year and a house takes, on the average, three months

[8] "The Building Trades" in *Britain in Recovery*, p. 435.

to build, and is sold as soon as it is finished, the average amount of capital required at any moment does not much exceed £25 million. In fact, builders obtained their working capital largely from their banks or from their suppliers of materials. Most of the capital required in connection with the housing boom was required by *purchasers* of houses who wanted to borrow the purchase price on mortgage and to repay it with interest over a period of years. Hence there was a great increase in loans for this purpose. The balance due on mortgages to building societies increased from £268 million in 1929 and £388 million in 1932 to £587 million in 1936.

The effect of the fall in interest rates upon borrowers (needing loans to purchase houses) was to reduce considerably the weekly interest cost of house purchase. The rate charged on mortgages by the large building societies fell from 6 per cent in the middle of 1932 to 4½ per cent in the middle of 1934, a fall of 25 per cent. Moreover, the building societies extended their periods of repayment to meet the needs of borrowers with small means. The monthly amount to be repaid over sixteen years per £100 borrowed at 6 per cent is 16s.6d.; per £100 borrowed at 4½ per cent over twenty-five years it is only 11s.3d.

This reduction in the cost of house purchase undoubtedly stimulated building, but the main influence was a great increase in the effective demand. We have shown the need for more housing. The great increase in the purchasing power of the mass of the people made it possible for them to satisfy this need. Between 1929 and 1933 the cost of living fell by no less than 25 per cent while average rates of wages fell by only 6 per cent. It has been estimated that between 1924-27 and 1932 the expenditure of the public on food, clothes, liquor, and tobacco fell by over

£300 million a year from £2,116 million to £1,797 million per year. Much of this "saving" was utilized to purchase new homes on the instalment system. The average inhabitant of Great Britain, provided that he was not unemployed or on short time, had a greater "real income" after 1930 than he had ever enjoyed before. He spent this partly on better housing. It is noteworthy also that the number of private motorcars in use increased from less than a million in 1930 to more than a million and a half in 1936. This too was clearly due to the general increase in purchasing power. And this in turn, as we shall see, was largely the result of cheap imported food.

3. "Cheap Money"

The "cheap money" policy, of deliberately keeping rates of interest at a low level, probably played some part in promoting recovery. Whether that part was of major or minor importance is a controversial question.

During a depression interest rates are usually low. So long as business prospects remain poor there are relatively few opportunities for investment in industry and trade which seem both fairly safe and likely to yield a good return. Many people prefer, therefore, to hold a large part of their assets in a fairly liquid form, and to keep their money in the bank or in government securities, especially short-term securities, rather than to gamble on a trade revival. Hence short-term rates are forced down to low levels and long-term rates also fall, although to a less extent. Only "safe" borrowers, however, can benefit from these low rates. The government, provided that it follows what is believed to be a "sound" financial policy, can borrow cheaply. So can borrowers who can give good security for their loans. But the "risk premium" demanded for loans to other borrowers may be very high.

As time goes on, some investors will become less contented with the low yields on safe securities and will try to increase their incomes by taking greater risks. The mere lapse of time will make some people feel that a trade revival may be close at hand. Borrowers who can offer good security will become more willing to borrow, for they can do so at low rates and if trade does improve they will make good profits. Other borrowers may find that the growth of optimism enables them to raise money at a lower risk premium than was demanded before. Hence investment may increase and recovery follow; and this may appear due largely to the stimulus of cheap money.

If cheap money does stimulate investment and recovery, why not shorten the depression by deliberately forcing down interest rates to levels lower than they would otherwise reach? This is the argument for a cheap-money policy.

This policy was tried in Great Britain in 1930. The collapse on Wall Street had led to a flow of funds back to London. This induced the Bank of England to bring down the bank rate to 3 per cent, and in the spring of 1931 it was again reduced, to 2½ per cent. But the attempt was a complete failure. Other conditions were adverse, and the crisis, culminating in the departure from gold, brought it to an abrupt end.

In 1932, however, cheap money came again and stayed. The contrast between the level of interest rates before 1932 and after 1932 is very striking. From 1925 to 1929 the average level of Bank Rate was nearly 5 per cent. From the summer of 1932 until the summer of 1939 Bank Rate remained unchanged at 2 per cent; and even so it was far above the market rate. From 1925 to 1930 the yield on

War Loan hardly moved from 5 per cent. From 1933 to 1939 it averaged less than 3½ per cent. It fell to around 3 per cent in 1935 and 1936, thereafter showing an upward trend to some 3¾ per cent in 1939.

The main features of the cheap-money policy were the War Loan conversion, the expansion of the "cash" of the joint-stock banks, and the control of new capital issues.

The War Loan, amounting to over £2000 million, was converted from a 5 to a 3½ per cent basis in the summer of 1932. This great mass of securities, forming one-third of the total internal public debt, was redeemable at par during the period 1929 to 1947. It had therefore dominated the gilt-edged market. It is not correct to argue, as some writers do, that because one could get 5 per cent on War Loan with the certainty of repayment at par before 1948, the minimum rate on first-class long-term investments was inevitably around 5 per cent. But it is true that, so long as industry and trade were not too depressed, the existence of this enormous block of 5 per cent securities did give rise to the belief that 5 per cent was a reasonable minimum return to expect. By the summer of 1932 industry and trade were very depressed and the yield on other long-term government securities had fallen to around 4 per cent. It was generally expected that War Loan would be converted on a 4 per cent basis. When the rate of 3½ per cent was announced at the end of June 1932 it came as rather a shock. But the market, with some help from the government,[9] soon adjusted itself to the new situation and the loan did not fall to a discount. The government had taken a bold step; it had led the market instead of

[9] The Accounts show £25.9 million, mainly for the payment of commissions, for expenses in connection with the conversion. See U. K. Hicks, "The Finance of British Government 1920-1936," p. 363.

following it; but "the very size of the Loan to be converted and the obvious impossibility to re-invest on better
terms gave assurance of success."[10]

From 1932 onwards the monetary authorities took
strong and persistent action to expand the "cash" basis of
the banking system. The Exchange Equalisation Account
acquired gold, some of which it sold to the Bank of England. This enabled the Bank to increase its total note
issue without exceeding the limit of £260 million for the
"fiduciary" issue (not backed by gold). Further, the Bank,
by purchasing bills and securities on the open market, increased the deposits with it of the clearing banks—the
latter, of course, regard these deposits as "cash." The banks
were thus enabled to increase very considerably their investments and, provided that they could find borrowers,
their loans and overdrafts. In order to induce more people to borrow from them, and to borrow larger sums, they
reduced their rates of interest. Before the depression, a
borrower with first-class security usually had to pay at least
5 per cent. This was reduced to 4 per cent or even less.

The most important part of the control of new issues
was the unofficial ban on the raising of public loans in
London by foreign governments or companies. This tended
to increase the supply of loan money available to British
borrowers and to keep down interest rates in Great Britain.
There was some control over other public issues also.
For more than three months after the war loan conversion
scheme was announced on June 30, 1930, the Treasury
"ban" on all new issues was complete. In October 1932,
when it was clear that the conversion operation had been

[10] "Reflections on the Cheap-Money Policy Particularly in England" by
Frederic George Conolly, p. 5. Supplement to Svenska Handelsbanken's
Index, October 1939. This article gives an excellent account and criticism
of the cheap-money policy.

successful, restrictions on home industrial issues were relaxed. They were subsequently removed, but new issues by
municipalities and Empire governments continued to be
subject to careful control. Would-be borrowers were said
to take their place in a "queue" and if the loan market
seemed to show signs of "indigestion" new corporate issues
were apparently forbidden until the authorities believed
that the market had recovered.

The primary object of the cheap-money policy was to
assist the Treasury in its task of converting the government debt to lower rates of interest. In this, as we have seen,
it succeeded. The government could borrow on long term
at 3½ per cent or less until about 1937. It could borrow on
short term, by means of Treasury bills, at little more than
½ per cent. But it did not wish the floating debt to
become too large, as it would have weakened control of
monetary policy by the Treasury and the Bank to have
too large a volume of bills falling due for repayment each
week. Hence temporary increases, through the issue of
Treasury bills to the Exchange Equalisation Account,
were followed by "funding" loans of nearly the same
magnitude.

The secondary object of the policy, however, was to
make available an abundant supply of cheap money to
promote trade revival. How far was this successful?

On the surface, its success was very slight. Despite lower
rates on loans and overdrafts, the banks did not greatly
increase their advances, which remained lower than in the
late twenties until 1937, and which went more to private
persons and less to industry than in the past. Despite the
very low short-term rates, commercial bills outstanding
declined from over £500 million in the twenties to little
over £250 million in the thirties. Over 80 per cent of all

conversion and refunding loans issued on the London market from 1932 to 1938 inclusive were for the British government and over half the rest were for Empire governments, notably Australia. Similarly with issues for new money. The government took advantage of low interest rates but private industrial issues were lower than in the twenties.

Nevertheless this does not mean that business obtained no benefit from the cheap-money policy. The reduction of £90 million a year in the budget charge for debt interest and management made taxation lower than it would otherwise have been. Lower interest rates raised share prices as well as the prices of fixed-interest securities and this gave a considerable "psychological" stimulus. The banks, finding themselves with more "cash," and unable to expand their advances very much, were constrained to purchase more bills and securities, thus greatly increasing their "investments." This caused a large increase in customers' deposits. The total deposits of the London clearing banks rose from £1775 million in the third quarter of 1929 to £2075 million in the spring of 1936. This in turn helped many firms and industries to become sufficiently liquid to finance a considerable expansion of production without recourse to the banks. Finally, as we have already noted, the reduction in mortgage and similar charges gave relief to many persons and played some part in bringing about the building boom.

The controversy as to how far the cheap-money policy was responsible for the recovery falls outside the scope of this book. The present writer, however, may perhaps be allowed to express his opinion. He believes that it played a minor rather than a major part, for it must be remembered that in any event interest rates would have been fairly low during the depression. Moreover, he agrees with Mr. Conolly[11] that a cheap-money policy, artificially prolonged, as it was in Great Britain owing to political pressure, after recovery has begun, "has many and real disadvantages and dangers." In particular, artificially low long-term rates redistribute income at the expense of working-class and middle-class savings and, by causing expected profits to be capitalized at too high a figure, may lead to unhealthy boom conditions. But however this may be, it clearly has very little to do with the tariff. The tariff can hardly claim a share in whatever praise or blame may be attached to the cheap-money policy and to its part in promoting revival.

4. Budget Policy

The report of the May Committee on National Expenditure thoroughly alarmed the country. When Mr. Snowden, who remained Chancellor of the Exchequer after the National Government had fallen, presented his supplementary budget on September 10, 1931, he announced that he was going "to face up to the position." If no changes were made, a deficit of £75 million was to be expected for the financial year ending March 31, 1932, and a deficit of £170 million for the following financial year. Mr. Snowden proposed properly to balance the budget, avoiding any deficit whatever, by increases in taxation and reductions in expenditure. Borrowing for the Unemployment Fund (which had been taking place at the rate of about £1 million a week) and for the Road Fund was to cease: unemployment relief and road work were to be paid for out of current revenue.

The standard rate of income tax was raised from 4s.6d.

[11] *Op. cit.*

to 5s. and considerable reductions were made in "allowances"—these brought a large number of persons with small incomes within the range of income tax for the first time. These changes in income tax were expected to yield an extra £51 million in 1932-33. Surtax was increased by 10 per cent. This was expected to yield an additional £6 million in 1932-33. Higher duties were imposed on beer, tobacco, petrol, and entertainments. These increases were expected to yield £24 million in 1932-33.

Contributions of employers and employed towards unemployment insurance were to be increased by £10 million in 1932-33, rates of unemployment benefit were to be reduced by about 10 per cent (saving £13 million in 1932-33) and further restrictions on benefit, including a "means test," were expected to save £13 million in 1932-33. The other main items on which savings were to be effected were education (£10.4 million), road fund (£7.9 million), and defense services (£5.6 million, including £3.6 million reduction in pay and pensions).

In one respect alone can Mr. Snowden possibly be held to have deviated, in this grim budget, from the strictest financial orthodoxy. In the depths of the depression, with nearly 3 million unemployed, he permitted himself to depart from the previous practice of setting aside some £60 to £70 million towards debt redemption. Only some £32 million, required to meet specific sinking funds, was earmarked for this purpose.

Expenditure by local authorities also was considerably cut down. The exchequer was reluctant to make grants towards the completion of public works which had already been begun by local authorities and discouraged the commencement of new ones unless they were of the most urgent nature.

As time went on, various factors made the task of successive chancellors easier, and enabled them to grant concessions. Economic recovery increased the yields of taxes and reduced the amount required for unemployment relief. Nothing was paid on the War Debt owed to the United States after the token payment made in December 1933. This default relieved the exchequer of an interest charge which had exceeded £27 million a year. The conversion of the War Loan, together with a number of smaller operations, reduced the interest charge on the long and medium term internal debt by some £40 million. Low short-term rates of interest reduced the interest on Treasury bills, which in the late twenties had exceeded £25 million, to a mere £3 or £4 million. And the new protective duties brought in around £30 million a year.

Thus it was easy for the next few years to keep the British budget balanced. It is true that there was some increase in the national debt—from £7,413 million in 1931 to £7,800 million in 1935. But this was negligible when compared, for example, with the rate of increase of the national debt in the United States; it was due mainly to the Exchange Equalization Fund (for which Treasury bills were issued, funding loans subsequently being raised in order to keep down the total of Treasury bills) and was largely offset by the gold acquired by the Fund; and the interest charge on the Debt was, as we have seen, very substantially reduced.

The facts recorded in this section are surely very interesting in view of the reams which have been written advocating public works and budget deficits in order to promote recovery from a depression. Doubtless it can be argued that Great Britain recovered in spite of her budget policy, just as it can be argued that budget deficits in the

United States and France tended to relieve the depression but were outweighed by other factors. Our own view is that the success or failure of public works and budget deficits during a depression will depend largely on whether the public in general, and investors in particular, approve of these policies. There can be no doubt that the stern measures enforced by Mr. Snowden, whether or not they were unnecessarily severe, did meet with general approval and did succeed in restoring confidence remarkably quickly. Instead of a flight from sterling, London became a kind of safe-deposit for foreign funds; the British government was enabled to borrow very cheaply; and after a time private investment in Great Britain began to revive. Further, these years of "sound finance" meant that no apprehension was felt when it was announced that part of the £1,500 million rearmament program was to be covered by loans and not by taxation.

5. THE TERMS OF TRADE

The total consuming power of the mass of the British people—those with small and moderate incomes—probably *increased* a little during the years of depression, 1930 to 1932. It increased considerably, perhaps by 10 per cent, in 1933, and thereafter continued to rise, although more slowly than in 1933.[12] This increase in consuming power was perhaps the chief single factor in promoting recovery. It provided a margin, above current living expenses, out of which purchases were made of goods such as motorcars, wireless sets, furniture, household appliances, and, above all, houses.

[12] The statistical difficulties of measuring this increase are so great that we prefer not to be more precise. A good discussion of the question, with references to original sources, will be found in G. D. A. MacDougall's "General Survey" in *Britain in Recovery*, Pitman, 1938.

It may be thought that we are "reasoning in a circle." The growth in output and employment certainly increased consuming power, but it is precisely this growth in output and employment which constituted the recovery and which, therefore, we have to explain.

Once recovery really gets under way it may continue, so to speak, by its own momentum. Increased investment in one field means taking on more workers and buying more materials. The newly-engaged workers spend their wages; the suppliers of materials probably increase their labor force and perhaps order new equipment and, later, invest or spend their profits; and thus recovery spreads to other fields. Increased purchases of consumers' goods may lead firms providing such goods to expand their plant, equipment, and stocks; this increases activity and employment in the industries supplying the plant, equipment, and stocks; the workers newly engaged by these industries spend their wages, thus increasing still further total purchases of consumers' goods; and so recovery goes on, unemployed labor and resources being absorbed into employment at every stage. But whence comes the initial impulse which gets the recovery started?

In Great Britain it certainly did *not* come from increased expenditure by the government. To some extent, the depreciation of sterling and the tariff doubtless stimulated investment in home industries, notably iron and steel. But against this must be set the great fall in world trade in general, and in British exports in particular, which was due in part to the movement of Great Britain towards economic isolation. The main impulse came from outside the British economy, so that our reasoning was not circular. It came from the striking fall in the prices which she had to pay for her imports.

Great Britain imports much of her food and all or most of some important raw materials—for example, timber, cotton, and wool. Nearly half her imports are classed under "food, drink, and tobacco," and over a quarter under "raw materials." Before the slump, the value of her imports came to more than a quarter of her national income. Hence she benefits considerably by a substantial fall in their prices.

During the years 1931 to 1935 the *volume* of imports (retained for home consumption) into Great Britain was about the same as in the pre-slump years, but their *money cost* averaged only some £700 million a year as compared with over £1,100 million a year before the slump. In particular, most foodstuffs fell heavily in price. It was mainly as a result of this that the cost of living fell considerably. In 1931 it was 10 per cent and in 1933 (when it was at its lowest) 15 per cent below the 1929 level.

This meant that the great majority of wage and salary earners, who kept their jobs with only small reductions, if any, in their pay, were better off than they had ever been before. All who received more or less fixed incomes—and continued to get them—gained by the fall in the cost of living. They now had a margin to spend upon housing and semi-luxury goods. We have already argued that this expenditure was a powerful factor in promoting recovery. It was due mainly to the fall in import prices. Later, import prices rose somewhat, but by that time recovery was under way, with more employment and less short time, and hence the upward trend continued.

We have implied that the fall in import prices was all clear gain to Great Britain. In fact, the situation was much more complicated.

In the first place, it is clear that a nation as a whole

does not gain by cheaper imports if she receives correspondingly less per unit for what she gives in exchange. Great Britain pays for her imports partly by exports of commodities. The prices of her commodity exports did fall, but considerably less than the prices of her imports. Over the period 1931 to 1935 a representative "unit" of her commodity exports purchased a volume of imports some 20 per cent greater than before the slump.[13] The "terms of trade," had swung heavily in her favor. This conclusion is not substantially altered when we take account of the prices per unit received for her other "exports." Her net income from overseas investments fell from £250 million in 1929 to a low point of £150 million in 1932, and her net receipts from shipping services fell from £130 million in 1929 to a low point of £65 million in 1933, and her net receipts from short interest and commissions fell from £65 million in 1929 to a low point of £25 million in 1932.[14] But these heavy reductions were partly due to a fall in the volume of these "exports"—for example, British ships carried fewer goods and passengers and the City of London did much less business on international account than before the slump. Prices "per unit"—for example, freight rates—fell, on the average, less than the prices of imported commodities, so that even when we take account of these so-called "invisible exports" our conclusion that the terms of trade swung heavily in favor of Great Britain remains valid. But it is worth mentioning that whereas before the slump these "invisible exports" had more than covered the surplus of commodity imports over commodity exports, during and after the slump they failed to cover it. Before the slump,

[13] See Statistical Appendix.
[14] See Statistical Appendix.

Great Britain lent substantial sums abroad every year. Since the slump she has lent comparatively little, but has received substantial sums from overseas in repayment of loans previously made.[15] In other words, she has been drawing to some extent upon her foreign assets. The fact that she has maintained her pre-slump volume of imports while her volume of exports has remained well below the pre-slump level is to be explained mainly by her more favorable terms of trade but partly by the fact just mentioned.

In the second place, a favorable swing in the terms of trade may be of little real benefit if it merely means that a smaller volume of exports purchases the same volume of imports while labor and equipment are thrown out of employment and remain idle and stranded in the export industries. This did happen to some extent in Great Britain, but as time went on there was some movement out of the depressed export industries into expanding home industries.

In the third place the slump brought about a redistribution of the national income. There were more unemployed, and those thrown out of work or on very short-time were worse off than before. Many of those who retained their jobs suffered from the fear of being thrown out of work. But in terms of actual purchasing-power received, the workers as a whole gained. The unemployed were assisted to a considerable extent at the expense of the richer members of the community—the taxpayers and the employers. Those who remained in work, on full time, received nearly the same money wages as before—the lowest point reached by the index of wage rates, in 1933, was only 5 per cent below the 1929 level—and benefited

[15] See Statistical Appendix.

from the fall in the cost of living. The material losses of the slump fell mainly upon receivers of profits, landowners, and the unemployed. And this redistribution of the national income resulted, we may repeat once more, in an increased demand for housing and other consumers' goods of a durable nature.

We may conclude this section by considering how far the favorable change in the terms of trade—or, to revert to our previous simplification, which is not really misleading in this context, the fall in import prices—was due to the adoption of protection. It is an accepted economic doctrine that a country may turn the terms of trade in its favor by means of tariffs and similar devices. Her success will depend largely on her importance as a market and on the difficulty experienced by her suppliers in switching over to the production of other commodities for their home market or for other foreign markets. It may seem, therefore, that Great Britain was in a position to turn the terms of trade perceptibly in her favor. It is true, as we have seen, that she did use her bargaining power to promote certain exports to Scandinavia and other countries, and presumably the prices obtained for them were as high as possible. But it is a curious fact that apparently the British Government did not want to force down the prices of imports. Its avowed aim, during the depression and the early stages of recovery, was to raise wholesale prices. And on the whole the quantitative restrictions imposed on imports were so administered as to permit "the foreigner" to charge more per unit for a smaller quantity.

In fact, the big fall in the world prices of foodstuffs and raw materials had already taken place before Great Britain imposed a general tariff. The fall in food prices was doubtless intensified and prolonged by protection—but by protection in other countries rather than in Great Britain. The fierce restrictions on food imports imposed by such countries as France, Germany, and Italy constrained overseas farmers to sell for what they could get to Great Britain. Moreover, British import duties were imposed mainly on manufactures. Hence, although British tariffs and quotas did exert a downward pressure on the prices of some imports, they tended to raise the prices of others (for example, bacon) and on the balance they probably did relatively little to improve the terms of trade.

CHAPTER X

CONCLUSIONS

WE NOW give a brief summary of our main conclusions. Great Britain adopted free trade about the middle of the nineteenth century. Cobden and Bright won their campaign against the corn laws mainly on the slogan of "cheap bread," but they believed that free trade would lead to prosperity and peace among nations.

Until the great war of 1914 Great Britain enjoyed a period of rapid economic progress. This was due largely to the growth of technical knowledge and of investment, but her policy of free trade was undoubtedly a contributing factor. From 1860 onwards she negotiated a number of trade treaties embodying a most-favored-nation clause: in 1914 she had eighty such treaties in force.

During the twenties, however, Great Britain was lagging behind her economic rivals. She had over a million unemployed, and towards the close of this decade her large adverse balance of trade was causing some concern. Much of her trouble was due to depression in her staple export industries. Other countries were producing more cotton cloth for themselves, subsidizing their shipbuilding, and producing coal from seams more easy to work than most of those remaining in Great Britain. These were obstacles, as subsequent events showed, which neither a tariff nor a depreciation of the pound sterling could really remedy.

The great depression brought a rise in the number of unemployed to nearly three million, a heavy fall in the volume of exports, and considerable distress in a number of industries, including agriculture. Towards the close of

1931 Great Britain left gold and imposed emergency tariffs.

Protection was adopted mainly because free trade seemed to have failed to maintain prosperity, while the competition of cheap imports was hitting a number of industries hard. It was hoped that tariffs would increase employment. Some economists had previously suggested a general revenue tariff as an alternative to devaluation, in order to reduce the adverse balance of trade and to enable Great Britain to stay on gold. Once she had left the gold standard, this "balance of trade" argument no longer applied, but it continued to be put forward in Parliament and in the Press.

The following generalizations can be made about the British tariff, which rests mainly on the Import Duties Act of February 1932. The great bulk of the customs receipts —about £214 million out of £264 million in 1938—still comes from "revenue" duties; most imports from the Empire are free; most imports of raw materials are free; nearly all other imports are subject to duty; but most rates of duty are relatively moderate. Changes in the tariff are made mainly by the Import Duties Advisory Committee, and Parliament has little effective control.

The tariff is not the only form of protection. By the spring of 1938, the Exchange Equalization Fund had purchased over 100 million ounces of gold. Much of this was made necessary by the influx of refugee capital, but the effect was to keep the value of sterling down, thus affording further protection to home industries. The British government gave assistance, by subsidies and in other ways, to various industries and notably to agriculture. Quantitative limitations were imposed upon imports of certain commodities, notably bacon and meat, from non-

Empire countries. The quantity of bacon taken from Denmark was reduced from around 7 million cwts. to about half that amount, the gap being filled mainly by increased home production, but as the restriction was administered by export licenses granted in Denmark the Danes obtained most of the benefit from the rise in the British price of their bacon. The country mainly hit by the meat restrictions was the Argentine.

For many years most Dominions had given some preference, by imposing lower rates of duty, on British goods. When Great Britain turned to protection she could and did reciprocate by admitting most Empire products free. At the Ottawa Conference of August 1932 she made agreements with most of her Dominions arranging for mutual preferences. The proportion of British imports coming from the Empire rose from 29 per cent in 1930 to 40 per cent in 1938 and the corresponding percentage for her exports rose from 43.5 to 50. But imperial preference has been getting less popular in recent years. British farmers do not like it, for the Dominions are their main competitors. It has been less help to the Dominions than it was expected to be. The British Empire as a whole has an "export surplus" of a number of products, including wheat, so that the British preference on such products is not of much use. Some other products receiving preference, for example, sugar and butter, are subsidized by the Dominions which export them. And the British market is not likely to expand at all fast. The agreements reached between the United States, Great Britain, and Canada towards the close of 1938 represented an important move away from imperial preference and towards greater freedom of trade.

Great Britain attempted to promote her exports by

means of trade treaties during and after 1933. She succeeded with most Scandinavian and Baltic countries, to whom the British market was of vital importance, and also with the Argentine. But it may be doubted whether the resulting net increase in her total exports was very large. For example, she secured for herself a predominant position in the Scandinavian and Baltic markets for coal, but the competition of Germany and Poland was diverted to other markets and total exports of British coal actually fell.

There was considerable controversy as to whether iron and steel should be subject to duties. Iron and steel products are the materials of other industries, which together employ far more workers than the iron and steel industry. Moreover, a substantial proportion of the British iron and steel output is exported in one form or another. Protection was given, but only on condition that the industry reorganize itself. The reorganization which took place consisted mainly of the formation or strengthening of price-fixing associations grouped under the British Iron and Steel Federation. But it was perhaps just as well that no grandiose schemes for scrapping plant were put into effect. When rearmament came, all available plant was needed.

An outstanding example of the successful use of a tariff as a bargaining weapon took place in 1935, when the threat of penal tariffs induced the Continental Steel Cartel to come to terms with the British Iron and Steel Federation.

The recovery of Great Britain from the depression began in 1933 and continued with gathering momentum until 1937. By 1937 output, employment, profits, and real wages were all substantially higher than in 1929, the peak preslump year. Towards the close of 1937 there was some falling off but in 1939, owing largely to the stimulus of rearmament, British economic indices stood higher than ever.

The main cause of the recovery was perhaps the low prices of imported foodstuffs, which increased the purchasing power available for other expenditure, especially on houses. A contributory cause was the "cheap money" policy of keeping interest rates low. Moreover, there was a considerable increase in most fields, due mainly to technical progress, in the volume of output per worker.

Employment in protected industries was probably greater than it would have been under free trade. But the only inquiry made into this question (by the I.D.A.C.) showed that between 1930 and 1934 employment in protected industries fell by about 50,000. Over the same period, employment in other industries increased by some 400,000. The numbers employed in agriculture (which is not included in the above figures) continued to fall despite protection and state assistance of various kinds. Considerably more use was made of labor-saving equipment and methods in a number of industries, including iron and steel and agriculture.

It is probable that tariffs did assist recovery by stimulating investment in iron and steel and other protected industries. Moreover the threat to increase tariffs or to impose new or heavier quantitative restrictions on imports served as a bargaining weapon which enabled Great Britain to obtain advantages for her exports in certain markets, notably Scandinavia and the Argentine.

It can hardly be claimed that the tariff was a very significant factor in promoting recovery. The building boom and, later, rearmament were the two outstanding features of recovery and neither obtained much help from protection.

Throughout the thirties (with the exception of 1937, when the corresponding figure was around 20 per cent) the volume of British exports was at least 25 to 30 per cent below the 1929 level. The continued depression in the exporting industries and districts was mainly responsible for the high level of unemployment, which was above that prevailing in the twenties.

During the thirties the volume of world industrial production increased considerably more than the volume of world trade, which remained nearly all the time below the 1929 level. This was due largely to the exchange restrictions practised by a number of countries and to the high agrarian protection of most countries in western Europe. But British trade policy was a contributory factor. Great Britain, by insisting on her most-favored-nation rights, scotched projects for forming low tariff customs unions between neighboring countries such as Holland and Belgium or the Danubian States. The Ottawa agreements virtually prevented Great Britain and most of her Dominions from reducing their tariffs to foreign countries on important categories of goods. The fall in the value of the pound imposed considerable hardships on the exporting industries of competing countries, as of course did the contraction of the British market for non-Empire goods.

In the short run, British trade policy and exchange policy doubtless succeeded in obtaining a competitive advantage for British exports. But this grew less as time went on. First the dollar and then the franc and other currencies were devalued, until the exchange value of the pound stood as high as before the slump or even higher; and the growth of bi-lateral trade agreements among other countries reduced the openings for British goods. In fact, as we have seen, there was a substantial fall in the volume of British exports.

The prosperity of Great Britain depends on her international trade. In the long run she is bound to lose by a greater movement towards greater self-sufficiency on the part of other countries. Yet her own economic policy during recent years has inevitably fostered such a movement. The British market is so large and so important to most of her suppliers that when it is restricted they must perforce reduce their own purchases from other countries, including Great Britain. It is true that during recent years Great Britain has maintained and increased her total volume of imports. But she has done so by buying much more from the Empire and much less from foreign countries; she has lent little abroad; and she has covered part of her adverse balance of payments by reducing her overseas assets.

With the signature of the Anglo-American trade treaty in November 1938 it seemed possible that Great Britain was preparing to adopt a more liberal trade policy, and was coming to realize that her true interests lay in a general revival of world trade. But the outbreak of war temporarily put an end to all such hopes.

STATISTICAL APPENDIX

I

UNITED KINGDOM—BALANCE OF PAYMENTS ON INCOME ACCOUNT, 1932–1938

	1932	1933	1934	1935	1936	1937	1938
			Credits £ Millions				
Exports of British produce	365	368	396	426	441	521	471
Exports of silver coin and bullion	6	5	13	55	18	10	29
Exports of gold coin and bullion	134	60	129	174	87	216	302
Estimated net national shipping income	70	65	70	70	85	130	100
Estimated net income from overseas investments	150	160	170	185	200	210	200
Estimated net income from short interest and commissions	25	30	30	30	35	40	35
Estimated net receipts from other sources	15	10	10	10	10	10	—
Net excess of government receipts	—	—	7	—	—	—	—
TOTAL	765	698	825	950	876	1,137	1,137
			Debits £ Millions				
Retained imports of merchandise	651	626	680	701	787	953	859
Imports of silver coin and bullion	8	10	22	41	17	20	18
Imports of gold coin and bullion	152	252	262	244	314	295	240
Net excess of government payments	24	2	—	2	3	4	13
TOTAL	835	890	964	988	1,121	1,272	1,130
CREDIT (+) or DEBIT (–) on above items	–70	–192	–139	–38	–245	–135	+7

Sources:

The actual figures for exports and imports are from *Statistical Abstract of the United Kingdom* for each of the fifteen years 1913 and 1924 to 1937, 1939; merchandise, p. 372, and bullion and coin, p. 431.

The estimates for the years 1932 to 1935 inclusive are also from *Statistical Abstract of the United Kingdom*, p. 438. The estimates for the years 1936 to 1938 inclusive are from the *Board of Trade Journal*, 23 February, 1939, p. 288.

II

NEW OVERSEA ISSUES AND REPAYMENTS

(£'000,000)

	British subscription to new issues	Repayments to the U. K.	Difference
1929	96	49	+47
1930	98	39	+59
1931	41	27	+14
1932	37	48	−11
1933	83	67	+16
1934	63	42	+21
1935	51	81	−30
1936	61	107	−46
1937	60	61	− 1
1938	29	39	−10

Source: "British Overseas Investments, 1938" by Sir Robert Kindersley, *Economic Journal'* December 1939.

III

VARIATIONS IN VOLUME AND AVERAGE VALUE OF THE IMPORT AND EXPORT TRADE OF THE UNITED KINGDOM

I. Based on Average Values in 1924

Year	Imports Retained				Exports of U. K. Produce			
	Declared value £'000	Value on basis of average values in 1924 £'000	Index numbers (1924 = 100)		Declared value £'000	Value on basis of average values in 1924 £'000	Index numbers (1924 = 100)	
			Average values	Vol- ume			Average values	Vol- ume
1924	1,137,469	1,137,469	100.0	100.0	800,967	800,967	100.0	100.0
1925	1,166,678	1,181,436	98.8	103.9	773,381	795,136	97.3	99.3
1926	1,115,866	1,234,797	90.4	108.6	653,047	711,841	91.7	88.9
1927	1,095,388	1,265,076	86.6	111.2	709,081	819,382	86.5	102.3
1928	1,075,315	1,225,835	87.7	107.8	723,579	838,348	86.3	104.7
1929	1,111,063	1,296,919	85.7	114.0	729,349	867,575	84.1	108.3
1930	957,140	1,266,516	75.6	111.3	570,755	710,719	80.3	88.7

II. Based on Average Values in 1930

Year	Imports Retained				Exports of U. K. Produce			
	Declared value £'000	Value on basis of average values in 1930 £'000	Index numbers (1930 = 100)		Declared value £'000	Value on basis of average values in 1924 £'000	Index numbers (1930 = 100)	
			Average values	Volume			Average values	Volume
1924	1,137,469	869,930	130.8	90.9	800,967	662,263	120.9	116.0
1930	957,140	957,140	100.0	100.0	570,755	570,755	100.0	100.0
1931	797,385	984,390	81.0	102.8	390,622	436,763	89.4	76.5
1932	650,649	864,499	75.3	90.3	365,024	438,363	83.3	76.8
1933	625,935	877,653	71.3	91.7	367,909	449,464	81.9	78.7
1934	680,171	927,696	73.3	96.9	395,986	481,690	82.2	84.4
1935	700,738	940,613	74.5	98.3	425,834	518,383	82.1	90.8
1936	786,982	1,005,506	78.3	105.1	440,605	531,286	82.9	93.1

III. Based on Average Values in 1935

Year	Imports Retained				Exports of U. K. Produce			
	Declared value £'000	Value on basis of average values in 1935 £'000	Index numbers (1935 = 100)		Declared value £'000	Value on basis of average values in 1935 £'000	Index numbers (1935 = 100)	
			Average values	Volume			Average values	Volume
1930	957,140	745,193	128.4	106.3	570,755	489,641	116.6	115.0
1935	700,738	700,738	100.0	100.0	425,834	425,834	100.0	100.0
1936	786,982	749,722	105.0	107.0	440,605	432,263	101.9	101.5
1937	952,690	797,399	119.5	113.8	521,391	473,140	110.2	111.1
1938	858,830	761,811	112.7	108.7	470,883	419,973	112.1	98.6
1939*	419,784	388,675	108.1	110.9	236,319	217,057	108.9	101.9

* January to June only.
Source: *Board of Trade Journal.*

IV

BRITISH TRADE WITH EMPIRE AND WITH FOREIGN COUNTRIES

A. IMPORTS

Imports from:	1913	1921	1925	1927	1929	1930	1931	1932	1933	1934	1935	1936	1937	1938
VALUES—£'000,000														
Canada	30.5	62.0	70.6	55.2	46.4	38.1	32.8	43.0	46.2	50.4	56.0	75.1	88.8	78.7
Australia	38.1	68.1	72.6	52.7	55.6	46.4	45.7	46.0	48.6	49.9	54.3	61.4	71.7	71.8
New Zealand	20.3	48.7	51.3	46.5	47.7	44.9	37.8	37.0	37.2	40.4	38.1	43.6	49.9	46.9
South Africa	12.3	18.7	25.1	21.3	24.3	20.2	13.1	15.4	14.4	11.9	13.7	13.6	17.9	14.6
Irish Free State	—	—	43.4	43.2	45.1	43.0	36.5	26.5	17.8	17.2	18.8	20.4	21.1	23.0
India	48.4	44.3	80.1	65.8	62.8	51.0	36.7	32.3	37.4	37.4	41.2	51.9	64.7	55.9
Rest of Empire	41.9	89.0	86.0	82.0	76.9	60.4	44.8	47.9	47.5	59.4	62.5	66.4	91.1	80.6
Total Empire	191.5	330.8	429.1	366.7	358.8	304.0	247.4	248.1	249.1	271.3	284.6	332.4	405.2	371.5
Total, excluding I.F.S.	191.5	330.8	385.7	323.5	313.7	261.0	210.9	221.6	231.3	254.1	265.8	312.0	384.1	348.5
Total, Foreign Countries	577.2	754.7	891.6	851.7	861.9	739.9	613.8	453.5	425.9	460.1	471.5	515.4	622.6	548.0
Total, World	768.7	1,085.5	1,320.7	1,218.3	1,220.8	1,044.0	861.3	701.7	675.0	731.4	756.0	847.8	1,027.8	919.5
PROPORTIONATE DISTRIBUTION—PERCENTAGES														
Canada	4.0	5.7	5.3	4.5	3.8	3.6	3.8	6.1	6.8	6.9	7.4	8.9	8.7	8.6
Australia	5.0	6.3	5.5	4.3	4.6	4.4	5.3	6.6	7.2	6.8	7.2	7.2	7.0	7.8
New Zealand	2.6	4.5	3.8	3.8	3.9	4.4	4.4	5.3	5.5	5.5	5.0	5.1	4.9	5.1
South Africa	1.6	1.7	1.9	1.7	2.0	1.9	1.5	2.2	2.1	1.6	1.8	1.6	1.7	1.6
Irish Free State	—	—	3.3	3.5	3.7	4.1	4.2	3.8	2.6	2.4	2.5	2.4	2.1	2.5
India	6.3	4.1	6.1	5.4	5.1	4.9	4.3	4.6	5.5	5.8	5.4	6.1	6.3	6.1
Rest of Empire	5.4	8.2	6.5	6.7	6.3	5.9	5.2	6.8	7.2	8.1	8.3	7.9	8.7	8.7
Total Empire	24.9	30.5	32.5	30.1	29.4	29.1	28.7	35.4	36.9	37.1	37.6	39.2	39.4	40.4
Total, excluding I.F.S.	24.9	30.5	29.2	26.6	25.7	25.0	24.5	31.6	34.3	34.7	35.1	36.8	37.3	37.9
Total, Foreign Countries	75.1	69.5	67.5	69.9	70.6	70.9	71.3	64.6	63.1	62.9	62.4	60.8	60.6	59.6
Total, World	100.0	100.0	100.0	100.0	100.0	100.0	100.0	100.0	100.0	100.0	100.0	100.0	100.0	100.0

BRITISH TRADE WITH EMPIRE AND WITH FOREIGN COUNTRIES (Continued)

B. Exports

Values—£'000,000

Exports to:	1913	1921	1925	1927	1929	1930	1931	1932	1933	1934	1935	1936	1937	1938
Canada	23.8	19.5	27.6	29.3	35.0	29.1	20.6	16.4	17.4	19.7	21.4	23.2	27.6	22.5
Australia	34.5	45.6	60.2	61.2	54.2	31.7	14.5	20.0	21.3	26.2	29.3	32.3	37.5	38.1
New Zealand	10.8	14.9	23.1	19.6	21.4	17.9	11.2	10.4	9.5	11.4	13.4	17.3	20.3	19.2
South Africa	22.2	29.8	30.6	30.3	32.5	26.5	21.9	18.1	23.4	30.2	33.6	37.5	41.4	30.5
Irish Free State	—	—	40.2	36.2	36.1	34.5	30.5	25.8	19.0	19.5	20.2	21.1	21.6	20.3
India	70.3	108.9	86.0	85.0	78.2	52.9	32.3	34.1	33.4	36.7	37.8	34.1	39.1	36.4
Rest of Empire	33.7	79.9	67.4	65.1	67.1	55.7	39.7	40.7	39.5	41.9	48.6	51.4	64.4	58.7
Total Empire	195.3	208.6	335.1	326.7	324.5	248.3	170.7	165.5	163.5	185.6	204.3	216.9	251.9	234.7
Total, excluding I.F.S.	195.3	208.6	294.9	290.5	288.4	213.8	140.2	139.7	144.5	166.1	184.1	195.8	230.3	214.4
Total, Foreign Countries	329.9	404.8	438.3	382.4	404.9	322.4	219.9	199.5	204.4	210.4	221.5	223.7	269.5	236.0
Total, World	525.2	703.4	773.4	709.1	729.3	570.8	390.6	365.0	367.9	396.0	425.8	440.6	521.4	470.8

Proportionate Distribution—percentages

Exports to:	1913	1921	1925	1927	1929	1930	1931	1932	1933	1934	1935	1936	1937	1938
Canada	4.5	2.8	3.6	4.1	4.8	5.1	5.3	4.5	4.7	5.0	5.0	5.3	5.3	4.8
Australia	6.6	6.5	7.8	8.6	7.4	5.6	3.7	5.5	5.8	6.6	6.9	7.3	7.2	8.1
New Zealand	2.1	2.1	3.0	2.8	2.9	3.1	2.9	5.0	2.6	2.9	3.1	3.9	3.9	4.1
South Africa	4.2	4.2	4.0	4.3	4.5	4.6	5.6	5.0	6.4	7.6	7.9	8.5	7.9	8.4
Irish Free State	—	—	5.2	5.1	4.9	6.0	7.8	7.1	5.2	4.9	4.7	4.8	4.1	4.3
India	13.4	15.5	11.1	12.0	10.7	9.3	8.3	9.3	9.1	9.3	8.9	7.7	7.5	7.7
Rest of Empire	6.4	11.4	8.6	9.2	9.3	9.8	10.1	11.1	10.6	10.6	11.5	11.7	12.4	12.5
Total Empire	37.2	42.5	43.3	46.1	44.5	43.5	43.7	45.3	44.4	46.9	48.0	49.2	48.3	49.9
Total, excluding I.F.S.	37.2	42.5	38.1	41.0	39.6	37.5	35.9	38.2	39.2	42.0	43.3	44.4	44.2	45.6
Total, Foreign Countries	62.8	57.5	56.7	53.9	55.5	56.5	56.3	54.7	55.6	53.1	52.0	50.8	51.7	50.1
Total, World	100.0	100.0	100.0	100.0	100.0	100.0	100.0	100.0	100.0	100.0	100.0	100.0	100.0	100.0

Source: *Statistical Abstract for the British Empire*, 1938.

V

QUANTITIES AND VALUE OF SOME SELECTED ARTICLES OF IMPORTED MERCHANDISE RETAINED IN THE UNITED KINGDOM

		1931	1932	1933	1934	1935	1936	1937	1938
I. Food, drink and tobacco	£	396,487,556	357,737,370	327,756,705	333,934,497	342,567,644	369,891,022	417,912,542	417,817,327
Grain and flour	Tons	10,696,133	9,497,172	10,122,676	10,029,851	9,957,212	10,578,291	10,201,750	9,869,195
	£	54,796,985	56,872,089	54,257,908	53,427,255	55,951,719	68,736,134	89,497,438	72,911,869
Feeding-stuffs for animals	Tons	1,115,323	1,264,148	1,326,487	1,651,120	1,603,154	1,722,175	1,806,416	1,895,828
	£	5,213,794	6,431,355	5,892,658	7,346,462	7,652,341	8,420,326	11,298,234	11,351,305
Meat	Tons	1,698,058	1,663,295	1,555,491	1,522,344	1,465,111	1,448,090	1,530,643	1,539,470
	£	91,078,832	79,485,459	76,745,060	80,771,549	76,945,840	78,136,382	86,435,791	90,121,137
Butter	Tons	385,431	492,947	437,301	479,809	474,030	483,467	465,175	471,943
	£	44,335,307	39,486,502	33,979,473	32,908,326	38,748,450	44,017,345	46,740,002	50,403,857
Eggs in shell	Th. Doz.	258,729	199,332	183,536	187,031	197,186	244,622	246,407	276,474
	£	13,748,377	9,030,422	7,295,387	7,036,410	7,746,234	9,823,556	10,402,184	12,349,532
Fresh fruit and vegetables	Tons	—	—	—	1,965,470	2,116,384	2,094,124	2,131,776	2,058,082
	£	47,773,682	40,970,397	35,588,313	33,935,553	37,853,093	35,038,607	35,144,506	36,332,976
Tea	Tons	198,851	217,733	188,832	196,665	180,592	183,433	186,521	205,634
	£	23,675,513	20,915,017	20,487,099	23,597,575	21,358,418	21,921,585	24,823,739	26,173,945
Fish	Tons	211,765	196,440	175,342	179,702	185,796	173,482	174,361	178,483
	£	9,779,204	8,276,795	6,908,055	8,930,703	8,649,448	8,856,265	9,514,203	9,648,004
Sugar, unrefined	Tons	1,776,761	2,350,190	2,007,670	1,911,625	1,911,944	2,211,569	2,214,504	2,368,336
	£	14,293,474*	17,990,934	14,960,497	13,205,666	12,218,166	14,815,469	19,980,571	18,866,662
Tobacco, manufactured and unmanufactured	Tons	83,513	74,521	90,249	99,040	107,818	116,251	117,238	149,783
	£	10,769,181*	9,500,946	11,095,004	15,739,570	16,716,708	17,600,845	17,518,331	22,503,641

258

II. Raw materials and articles mainly unmanufactured	£	147,327,841‡	141,234,310	155,164,705	182,170,113	183,149,222	215,005,776	278,360,346	217,673,058
Wood and timber	Th. Tons	6,384	6,272	7,472	8,877	8,439	9,292	10,160	7,462
	£	28,851,943	25,430,840	29,671,165	39,274,982	35,234,291	43,259,539	61,456,910	42,562,809
Raw cotton (excl. linters)	Tons	468,699	537,718	662,878	534,889	534,654	662,950	714,500	518,324
	£	25,099,353	28,806,697	34,168,380	32,855,998	33,639,174	42,305,617	44,852,966	27,163,947
Raw wool: sheep's and lamb's wool	Tons	260,699	267,934	268,281	236,021	270,099	289,711	251,087	278,842
	£	21,761,707	20,570,342	22,161,974	24,537,272	24,150,234	30,818,333	35,302,835	28,494,266
Seeds and nuts for oil	Tons	1,354,554	1,367,491	1,286,531	1,399,783	1,572,374	1,472,436	1,621,563	1,628,567
	£	11,213,213	11,864,523	10,664,614	8,863,225	12,799,523	14,122,356	17,489,974	14,674,372
Wood pulp	Tons	1,463,664	1,835,049	1,933,565	2,240,494	2,217,021	2,374,081	1,788,144	1,612,078
	£	8,401,772	8,373,867	7,891,942	9,599,801	9,115,772	10,048,291	13,649,351	14,182,961
III. Articles wholly or mainly manufactured	£	244,398,925‡	145,652,225	139,425,112	160,399,546	171,182,156	196,844,791	250,458,481	215,534,217
Iron and steel, and manufactures	Tons	2,837,743	1,589,736	968,657	1,363,209	1,148,739	1,475,626	2,026,022	1,310,501
	£	19,461,911‡	8,579,225	6,067,104	9,103,768	8,634,669	11,474,282	19,666,823	14,291,569
Refined petroleum	Th. Gals.	1,790,948	1,808,231	2,001,450	2,216,442	2,255,611	2,354,994	2,481,951	2,666,421
	£	24,821,124*	26,447,307	25,659,874	26,514,911	28,028,596	31,302,140	41,054,373	49,002,169
Paper, cardboard, etc.	Tons	1,001,704	892,984	945,946	1,054,452	1,067,743	1,166,949	1,304,865	1,069,521
	£	16,238,688	12,970,337	11,987,366	13,080,299	13,383,817	14,420,631	17,123,890	14,772,751
TOTAL VALUE OF IMPORTED MERCHANDISE RETAINED IN UNITED KINGDOM	£	797,385,089	650,648,805	625,935,392	680,170,436	700,737,918	786,983,007	953,690,757	857,984,287

Sources: *Annual Statement of the Trade of the United Kingdom with British Countries and Foreign Countries*, Vol. I.

* These articles in 1931 were liable to duty on importation prior to the first operation of the Abnormal Importations (Customs Duties) Act, 1931, on November 25, 1931.

‡ These groups of articles for 1931 do not compare strictly with those given for later years.

VI

QUANTITIES AND VALUE OF SOME SELECTED ARTICLES, THE PRODUCE AND MANUFACTURE OF THE UNITED KINGDOM, EXPORTED FROM THE UNITED KINGDOM

Articles		1931	1932	1933	1934
I. Food, drink and tobacco	£	34,775,152	31,506,547	27,766,197	30,454,729
Spirits, home-made	Tons	33,126	30,672	27,549	35,769
	£	5,974,100	4,726,002	4,830,670	7,587,195
Fish	Tons	272,209	258,092	198,843	211,132
	£	5,102,553	4,556,838	3,738,960	3,593,141
Tobacco manufactured or unmanufactured	Tons	15,438	13,638	16,192	17,363
	£	5,216,377	4,199,877	4,094,530	4,366,063
II. Raw materials and articles mainly unmanufactured	£	47,039,396	43,633,204	46,014,459	48,292,252
Coal	Tons	42,749,740	38,898,801	39,067,926	39,659,880
	£	34,653,774	31,633,354	31,426,236	31,854,490
Wool, raw and waste and woolen rags	Tons	35,048	37,304	61,351	56,373
	£	3,270,996	3,454,701	5,315,970	5,977,857
III. Articles wholly or mainly manufactured	£	292,775,779	276,342,439	281,667,254	304,805,612
Coke and manufactured fuel	Tons	3,158,830	2,992,199	3,079,956	2,922,136
	£	2,960,349	2,638,129	2,658,672	2,748,103
Iron and steel and manufactures	Tons	1,978,958	1,870,556	1,903,866	2,224,413
	£	30,375,155	27,666,963	29,498,227	34,526,113
Machinery	Tons	329,368	303,773	279,218	338,279
	£	33,095,736	30,285,670	27,872,121	33,593,132
Cotton yarns	Tons	59,605	63,153	60,318	58,226
	£	10,895,216	10,419,740	10,075,995	10,236,061
Cotton piece goods	Tons	149,396	191,336	174,985	174,193
	£	37,327,672	43,614,893	40,234,252	39,820,026
Woolen and worsted yarns	Tons	20,262	21,205	24,025	23,228
	£	5,410,103	5,707,688	6,267,354	6,821,752
Woolen and worsted manufactured tissues	Tons	22,547	21,635	24,534	27,268
	£	15,810,371	13,375,837	13,900,623	15,875,080
Motor cars, new*	Number	19,419	28,968	36,050	37,216
	£	3,436,419	3,964,900	4,919,755	5,506,287
Paper, cardboard, etc.	Tons	162,105	193,256	187,763	180,303
	£	6,324,269	6,506,459	6,129,136	6,276,112
TOTAL EXPORTS	£	390,621,598	365,024,008	367,909,052	395,985,521

* Second-hand motorcars are included in the years 1931, 1932 and 1933.

QUANTITIES AND VALUE OF SOME SELECTED ARTICLES,
THE PRODUCE AND MANUFACTURE OF THE
UNITED KINGDOM, EXPORTED FROM
THE UNITED KINGDOM (*continued*)

Articles		1935	1936	1937	1938
I. Food, drink and tobacco	£	31,579,170	35,585,462	38,774,840	35,894,023
Spirits, home-made	Tons	36,341	48,437	54,219	51,828
	£	7,633,943	10,928,435	12,727,129	11,362,386
Fish	Tons	229,403	227,247	200,944	219,079
	£	3,750,926	3,954,803	3,735,198	3,870,262
Tobacco, manufactured	Tons	16,873	16,395	19,080	18,063
or unmanufactured	£	4,214,761	4,504,696	5,038,385	4,914,904
II. Raw materials and articles mainly unmanufactured	£	52,835,911	51,306,707	64,629,164	56,920,431
Coal	Tons	38,714,104	34,519,384	40,338,030	35,856,227
	£	31,558,678	29,299,239	37,653,529	37,406,306
Wool, raw and waste and	Tons	74,656	66,484	62,802	54,301
woolen rags	£	8,170,592	7,868,410	9,069,350	6,262,842
III. Articles wholly or mainly manufactured	£	328,817,163	340,777,991	404,655,940	365,244,030
Coke and manufactured	Tons	3,155,961	2,828,660	3,124,917	2,326,966
fuel	£	3,019,143	2,992,322	4,234,918	3,291,723
Iron and steel and man-	Tons	2,312,359	2,203,061	2,574,079	1,915,202
ufactures	£	35,958,498	35,966,688	48,370,349	41,555,579
Machinery	Tons	383,833	380,495	438,052	459,263
	£	39,352,247	41,179,280	49,740,963	57,867,565
Cotton yarns	Tons	63,248	67,377	70,995	54,888
	£	11,161,702	11,849,446	13,694,406	9,674,911
Cotton piece goods	Tons	173,241	178,201	179,041	129,462
	£	39,531,954	40,318,839	44,768,650	31,961,174
Woolen and worsted	Tons	22,620	20,844	18,473	15,482
yarns	£	6,494,465	6,509,375	6,712,133	5,329,370
Woolen and worsted	Tons	28,838	30,827	32,110	23,961
manufactured tissues	£	16,453,217	18,028,060	20,436,406	15,535,120
Motor cars, new	Number	46,167	54,543	57,395	47,507
	£	6,269,560	6,779,256	7,472,659	7,126,125
Paper, cardboard, etc.	Tons	195,062	207,950	219,504	176,441
	£	6,579,899	6,746,629	8,095,878	6,930,313
TOTAL EXPORTS	£	425,834,428	440,604,879	521,391,494	470,755,320

VII

TRADE OF EMPIRE WITH GREAT BRITAIN[1]

I. Percentage of Total Imports Coming from the United Kingdom

Country	1930	1931	1932	1933	1934	1935	1936	1937	1938
Canada.........	16.1	17.4	20.7	24.4	22.1	21.2	19.4	18.2	17.6
Australia........	39.6	40.6	42.5	43.4	43.6	41.5	43.6	42.1	42.5
New Zealand....	47.4	49.0	49.8	51.3	50.4	50.3	49.4	49.6	47.9
South Africa.....	46.9	45.5	46.3	50.3	48.8	48.7	46.3	42.4	43.6
Irish Free State...	80.0	80.8	76.6	69.9	66.7	72.4	53.2	50.0	50.5
India..........	39.2	36.7	37.6	41.8	41.1	39.3	39.0	31.5	31.4

II. Percentage of Total Exports Going to the United Kingdom

Country	1930	1931	1932	1933	1934	1935	1936	1937	1938
Canada.........	26.7	28.5	36.4	39.9	41.5	42.1	42.1	40.2	40.6
Australia........	44.9	50.3	47.6	47.7	52.8	49.9	50.0	46.1	51.2
New Zealand....	82.1	89.7	90.2	87.3	82.3	84.5	80.6	76.0	83.8
South Africa.....	47.9	43.4	42.1	37.9	41.1	42.5	40.9	41.1	40.7
Irish Free State...	92.1	96.3	96.1	93.9	93.4	91.7	91.5	90.7	92.6
India..........	23.4	27.4	27.8	32.0	31.6	31.4	32.4	32.4	33.7

[1] *Statistical Abstract for the British Empire*, 1938.

INDICES OF COST OF LIVING, RATES OF WAGES, WHOLESALE PRICES, AND INDUSTRIAL PRODUCTION

	1924	1925	1926	1927	1928	1929	1930	1931	1932	1933	1934	1935	1936	1937	1938	1939
Cost of Living Index																
July, 1914 = 100*	175	176	172	167½	166	164	158	147½	144	140	141	143	147	154	156	158
July, 1914 = 100†	170	171	164	160	157	154	145	131	126	120	122	125	130	139	140½	141
Mean 1924 = 100*	100	100	98½	96	95	94	90	84	82	80	81	82	84	88	89	91
Rates of Wages, Index Numbers																
Mean 1924 = 100	100	101½	101	101	99	99	98	96½	95	94	94	95½	98	102	106	107
Wholesale Price Index, All Articles																
Mean 1913 = 100	166.2	159.1	148.1	141.6	140.3	136.5	119.5	104.2	101.6	100.9	104.1					
Mean 1924 = 100	100.0	95.8	89.1	85.2	84.4	82.2	72.0	62.7								
Mean 1930 = 100							100.0	87.8	85.6	85.7	88.1	89.0	94.4	108.7	101.5	102.6
Industrial Production, Index Numbers, All Industries																
1924 = 100	100.0	—	—	106.8	105.5	111.8	103.2	93.7	93.3	98.6	106.1	113.6	124.6	132.8	124.1	132.2††
1930 = 100							100.0				110.8					

* All items.
† Food only.
†† For 1939 data for only the first two quarters are available.

Sources: *Statistical Abstract for the United Kingdom for Each of the Fifteen Years 1913 and 1924 to 1937.* For 1938 and 1939, *Ministry of Labour Gazette* and *Board of Trade Journal,* which give quarterly figures from which the yearly averages are derived.

INDEX

Abnormal Importations Act, 21, 32

Agriculture, depression, in British, 10, 202-203, 206; in American, 204; Ministry of, power to levy duties, 21, 32, 39; power of Ministry to restrict imports, 50; government aid to, 49, 206-214, 216-217; livestock and, 66; technical progress and increased efficiency in, 203-204, 215, 216, 247; subsidies in, 204, 209, 211, 216; increased productivity in, 205-206; competition with imports, 206; Act of 1937, 209; restrictions on home production, 210; restrictions on imports, 213, 214; Milk Marketing Board, 212-213; Astor-Rowntree Report on, 212 n.; changes in, 215-216, 247; war's effect on, 216, 243; *passim*

Argentine, exchange control adopted by, 135; agreement of Great Britain with, 137; financial arrangements with Great Britain, 146; imports from, 146; Great Britain's investment in, 155; meat restriction, 245; British exports to, 247

Ashley, Sir Percy, 38

Australia, protection and Ottawa agreement, 95-96, 98-99; exports to Great Britain, 107-108; trade dispute with Japan, 121; shipments of meat, 138, 146; abandonment of gold standard, 154; British loans to, 155, 232; *passim*

Bacon (Import Regulation) Order, 63

Balance of trade, 11, 14, 17; argument for a tariff, 24; unfavorable, 120, 122; between United Kingdom and Estonia, 129

Baldwin, Stanley, quoted, 31, 91; compromise by, 88-89; on Ottawa agreements, 91

Bargaining position, of consuming country, 120; of Great Britain with other countries, 122; of France, 132; of Denmark, 140

Beaverbrook, Lord, advocate of free trade, 77, 78; on Argentine agreement, 136

Beet sugar industry, subsidy on, 53-55, 209

Bellman, Sir Harold, 225

Bentham, Jeremy, 5

Blum, Léon, 162

British Iron and Steel Corporation, 185

British Iron and Steel Federation, 69, 182, 185, 195-196, 246

British Shipping (Assistance) Act, 58

Budget, unbalanced, 11; deficit, 20, 235; framing of, 36; policy, 233-235

Building, Derating Act, 46; taxation on buildings, 220; and economic recovery, 220; housing, 223-225; boom, 224-227; employment figures, 224; stimulus to other industries, 224; and rearmament, 225; capital investment, 225-226; reduced costs, 226-227

Canada, first to grant imperial preference, 86; protection and preference, 94-95; pact with Great Britain, 99-100; trade agreement with U.S., 101, 107; trade with Great Britain, 106, 109; *passim*

Cartels, International Steel, 69, 246; in iron and steel industry, 182-185, 188; Tube, 189; products, 190; Continental Steel, 246